ROADS TO THE TOP

Roads to the Top

Career decisions and development
of 18 business leaders

Ruth Tait

First published 1995 by
MACMILLAN PRESS LTD
Houndmills, Basingstoke, Hampshire RG21 2XS
and London
Companies and representatives
throughout the world

ISBN 0–333–63108–0

A catalogue record for this book is available
from the British Library.

10   9   8   7   6   5   4   3   2   1
04   03   02   01   00   99   98   97   96   95

Copy-edited and typeset by Povey–Edmondson
Okehampton and Rochdale, England

Printed and bound in Great Britain by
Biddles Ltd, Guildford and King's Lynn

For Andrew, Alexander and Nicholas
and for
Jack, Eleanor, Pam, John, Jim and David

Contents

Acknowledgements

My grateful thanks must go first to each of the contributors to this book for their extraordinary generosity in sharing their experience and thoughts. To say that the book is essentially theirs is a truism, although as interpreter, I take full responsibility for any error or omission contained herein.

I would also like to thank all my colleagues at Korn/Ferry Carré/ Orban International for their helpful comments in reading each of the chapters, and most particularly, Ed Kelley, Head of Europe, Buzz Schulte, current Managing Partner and Paul Buchanan-Barrow, former Head of the London office, for providing me unquestioningly with all the support I needed to complete the book. Vitally important were the contributions of Catherine Littlewood, the Head of the Word Processing Department at Korn/Ferry Carré/Orban in London, my Personal Assistant in the early stages of the book, Sharon Perks and my current PA, Fiona Birkmire and I thank them for their professionalism and assistance.

In the course of writing the book, I also spoke to many academics, management consultants and senior managers, both in human resources and in line management, including other chief executives and chairmen of large public companies. Without naming each person, I am deeply grateful for their contribution.

Lastly and critically, I would like to thank my husband, Andrew Doman, first to read each word and first to offer insightful comments and generous encouragement.

RUTH TAIT

1

Introduction

Many books have been written about the way business leaders manage their corporations, but little is known about how they have managed their own careers. How have they made career decisions and what has been instrumental to their success and development as leaders?

Head-hunters and career counsellors almost invariably advise people to adopt a rational approach to their careers – to analyse carefully their strengths and interests, develop clear career goals and systematically explore opportunities. The emphasis is on taking control of one's career, based on self-knowledge: there is often an assumption that unless you are single-minded and focused, you are unlikely to be successful.

However, I have been intrigued by an apparent contradiction that confronts me so often when I interview managers for senior positions. Most senior managers attribute their career choices to external forces beyond themselves – to chance, luck, the influence or intervention of others (including parents, teachers, mentors, partners). Successful professional managers usually have clear goals or a vision for their businesses but rarely have, or say they have, clear objectives or a plan for their own careers.

I asked myself whether chief executives of major public companies are more likely than less successful colleagues to be strategic and purposeful in the way they have chosen and planned their working lives? What characterises the career decision-making of business leaders? What has fundamentally motivated them? Can one plan a career to the top and, if so, what are the necessary and desirable elements of such a career?

Are there common key success factors for business leaders, whether of background, experience, personality, style, approach or values? Will the requirements change in the next ten to twenty years? Are the qualities, career paths and approaches to their careers similar enough to learn from and can others develop the qualities required, plan to acquire the experience and practice the approaches?

I have therefore interviewed 18 business leaders to examine influences on their early lives, their motivation and belief systems,

1

how they have made career decisions, what has been important to them developmentally (including how they have overcome obstacles and mistakes), how they have balanced their professional and personal lives and their views on what is important to leadership and how to succeed professionally.

What advice do business leaders offer both about decision-making and about the elements of a successful business career? This book seeks to provide insight not only into the way they have made choices and conducted their careers, but also their advice about what is important in equipping oneself for the top.

THE BUSINESS LEADERS

The 18 business leaders were chosen to fall into two groups: The first group of nine were in their mid-fifties or older with reputations among their peers and the public as outstanding managers/leaders. These individuals were either no longer actively managing companies:

Sir Graham Day – ex-Chairman, Cadbury Schweppes, British Aerospace and PowerGen
Baroness Jean Denton – ex-Managing Director, Herondrive and Parliamentary Under-Secretary of State for Northern Ireland
Richard Giordano – Chairman, BOC; Chairman, British Gas
Sir John Harvey-Jones – ex-Chairman, ICI
Sir Christopher Hogg – Chairman, Courtaulds and Reuters
Steve Shirley – Founder Director, FI Group

Or had been in the Chief Executive role for over ten years:

Sir John Egan – Chief Executive, BAA
Sir Neil Shaw – Executive Chairman, Tate & Lyle
Lord Sheppard – Chairman, Grand Metropolitan

This group has already been the subject of a great deal of press and also books exploring their careers and achievements, but none to my knowledge has examined early life, motivation, decision-making, views about leadership now and in the future, and career advice.

The second group were newer and as a group, younger chief executives, who had been five years or less in the role . It is noted that two of the new chief executives are in their mid-fifties (Neville Bain, Charles Mackay) and less than a year separates them from John Egan, who has been a chief executive for over fifteen years. The new chief executives have been chosen because they have had outstandingly successful track records, appear to be particularly promising and for one reason or another have careers of particular interest:

Penny Hughes – President, Coca-Cola Great Britain and Ireland
Archie Norman – Chief Executive, Asda
Martin Taylor – Chief Executive, Barclays
Bill Castell – Chief Executive, Amersham
Gerry Robinson – Chief Executive, Granada
Ann Iverson – former Chief Executive, Mothercare; Chief Executive, Kay-Bee Toys
Liam Strong – Chief Executive, Sears
Neville Bain – Chief Executive, Coats Viyella
Charles Mackay – Chief Executive, Inchcape

In examining experience and motivation, views, attitudes and values, I was interested in possible cross-generational differences that might be illuminated by interviewing chief executives at the beginning of their experience in this role and another group at or toward the end of their experience as chief executives. For this reason, I have ordered the interviews by age.

As international experience, the ability to manage across borders and to work with people of different backgrounds and cultures are becoming increasingly important, I also consciously sought business leaders in the UK who were not British: Richard Giordano (American), Ann Iverson (American), Neil Shaw (Canadian), Graham Day (Canadian) and Neville Bain (New Zealander).

Although there are few women chief executives of major public companies in the UK, it was important to include women business leaders in the sample, not just to provide role models for women readers, but also because the nature of women's careers and decision-making is often different. Each of the women business leaders represents a different set of circumstances personally and professionally, something of interest to women trying to understand how to balance their working and personal lives and to be successful professionally.

Not only are women business leaders few in number but many of those approached showed a marked reluctance to speak about their careers and their views. A far higher proportion of the men I approached agreed to be interviewed (80 per cent) than women (less than 40 per cent). Women declined formally because of lack of time and because of frequent requests for such interviews. One modestly deferred until 'my achievements catch up with my reputation'. Privately, two confided that they would be happy to speak to me about their business, but not about themselves as they could not be both truthful and positive. Discrimination had featured prominently in their careers and they were unwilling, at least at this stage, to be critical and revealing.

I am therefore especially grateful to the women who agreed. All have led businesses, though only two have been chief executives, one of a business she founded (Steve Shirley, Founder Director, FI Group) and one of a large public company (Ann Iverson, former Chief Executive, Mothercare and Chief Executive, Kay-Bee Toys). Two others have led divisions of a large multinational (Penny Hughes, President, Coca-Cola, Great Britain and Ireland) and a large conglomerate (Baroness Jean Denton, ex-Managing Director, Heron Drive). Baroness Denton is also now Parliamentary Under-secretary of State for Northern Ireland where she leads as Minister in the areas of Economic Development, Agriculture and Women's Issues. As with the male business leaders, the women are at different career stages: Steve Shirley and Baroness Denton have retired from active business management and Ann Iverson and Penny Hughes are in relatively new positions of leadership.

Although I will analyse their experience in the concluding chapters, trying to draw out common themes, conclusions and 'principles of success' as guidance, each business leader's 'story' is told, largely from their own perspective, in a separate chapter. The lessons implicitly fall out of their experience, their views and their advice. The following issues/questions were covered at interview:

- What were the important influences in your early life?
- Have you ever had a goal or objective or plan for your career?
- How was each career decision made and what were the most important developmental experiences in each role?
- What failures/setbacks/obstacles have you experienced and how have you dealt with them?
- Have you had a mentor or role model? What has been their influence/impact?
- What have been the highest and lowest moments of your career?
- What do you consider to be the qualities of leadership and do you think that they will be the same in the next ten years?
- How have you balanced your personal and professional lives?

- What advice would you give to (a) your children about how to make career decisions? (b) a twenty-five-year-old interested in business about how to get to the top?
- Do you have a belief system underpinning your life?'

Although these were the core questions, interviews necessarily evolved with the greatest amount of time devoted to those issues important to each individual. Therefore, the thrust of each 'case study' chapter is slightly different. In the concluding five chapters I have not resisted drawing conclusions based on the experience and views of this small and biased sample, at times also referring to other research to illuminate these findings.

2
Penny Hughes
President, Coca-Cola
Great Britain and Ireland

Date of birth:	31 July 1959
Place of birth:	West Kirby, Wirral, UK
Nationality:	British
Marital status:	Married
Family:	One child
Languages:	Some French

Education:	Birkenhead High School, 'A' levels in Maths, Physics and Chemistry, General Studies
1977–1980	Sheffield University, BSc with 1st class honours, Chemistry
1994	Honorary LL D

Career:	
1980–1982	Procter & Gamble
	Graduate trainee
1982–1984	Milk Marketing Board
	Brand Manager, Milk
1984–1987	CC Soft Drinks
	Senior Brand Manager
	Marketing Manager
	Marketing Controller
1987–1992	Coca-Cola and Schweppes Beverages Limited
1987–1989	Marketing Director
1989–1992	Commercial Director
1992 to October 1995	Coca-Cola Company
	President, Great Britain and Ireland
	Coca-Cola International
	Vice President, Non-executive Director

Outside appointments:	The Body Shop, Non-executive Director
	Institute of Grocery Distribution, Member of Council
	Business in the Environment, Board Member
	Producer Responsibility Group, Member
	Ronald McDonald Children's Charities, Trustee Judge
	Institute of Management Studies, Cambridge University, Board Member

Interests:	Golf, tennis, skiing, food and wine

INTRODUCTION

In her mid-thirties, Penny Hughes as President of Coca-Cola Great Britain and Ireland occupies a role that has never before been filled by a woman, a 'Brit' or anyone under forty. Her position as a young woman business leader is almost as unique in British industry as it is at Coca-Cola.

She is the youngest of three daughters of a stable middle-class family in Merseyside and leadership came early as head girl of Birkenhead High School and captain of most sports teams. A scientist by training, her career has been a linear progression through product development and blue-chip marketing initially with Procter & Gamble, then the Milk Marketing Board and Coca-Cola and Schweppes Beverages, gaining breadth in commercial operations and early general management. She has been strongly influenced by excellent advice, and by at least two powerful mentors. As yet, she has experienced no major professional setbacks or failures. Other than working for an American company and cross-border travel, she has had no significant international experience and recognises this as her next professional challenge.

Extremely self-confident, with an excellent strategic and analytical brain, informal style and strong interpersonal skills, Penny Hughes is natural, irrepressibly positive and impressively well-balanced. She made it clear to The Coca-Cola Company when she joined that she wanted to have children while continuing her career. Having had success so young, however, she is very flexible about her options should her own objectives of combining a stimulating career with a full personal life be at risk. Indeed, expecting her first child in February 1995, she let The Coca-Cola Company know that she would be leaving in October 1995, following maternity leave and a handover period to new management.

What has 'made' Penny Hughes as she is, how has she chosen academic and professional paths and developed along them, and how would she advise others?

EARLY INFLUENCES

As with many successful women, Penny Hughes had a very stable, supportive and aspirational family. Her father was an insurance broker, and her mother the bedrock that provided a happy and very secure home life. Penny Hughes followed her two older sisters to the same school, Birkenhead High School, from the age of four to 18. 'So it was an incredibly stable and predictable start to life and I think that security actually helped a great deal. I was extraordinarily fond of school and still go back.'

She excelled at school, was head girl and 'led games, tennis, lacrosse, the lot'. There was an unspoken, unpressured expectation from school and from family that she would do 'A' levels and go to university.

Her decision to study chemistry at Sheffield is described as 'not very well thought out'. Having done maths, physics and chemistry at 'A' level, she found maths 'increasingly dry' and did not want to become an accountant, thought physics would be incredibly hard and so chose chemistry 'the subject I was roughly best at and the one I enjoyed'. Science in hindsight was the right choice, providing her with the training and discipline that her friends in arts subjects missed, because of the rigour of laboratory work and lectures. 'A lot of my friends who did arts subjects were so much on their own to learn and over the three years, their interest in academics just faded.'

Both her sisters had gone to university, one in London and one in Nottingham and she chose Sheffield because it was 'more Yorkshire'. Oxbridge had no appeal.

> I had quite a 'reject' feel about Cambridge or Oxford. I never thought about Oxbridge seriously although I probably had the ability to do it. I am terribly informal anyway and even at school the people who were going to stay and do their Oxbridge were all the people I did not associate with. I was more interested in the social environment and university was where I finally grew up.

After two years at university, and observing her sister as a qualified pharmacist rarely being asked to perform to her full potential, she lost her interest in chemistry which, though obviously different from pharmacy, seemed to carry the same professional risks. With a growing interest in business and commercial management, she approached the university to take economics as a subsidiary in her third year. Although no chemist had ever asked to do economics, the curriculum was changed for her. She thoroughly enjoyed it and 'that was the first stage of beginning to think about what I was best for'.

CAREER DECISION-MAKING AND DEVELOPMENT

As with the majority of the older generation and several of the 'new generation' of chief executives, Penny Hughes has never had a career goal or plan: 'You will find me quite unusual because I have never really planned my career. Things have always happened more quickly than I was thinking of moving on!'

Her first career decision was serendipitously influenced by her career adviser at university, Dr Bernard Kingston.

> He gave me a really excellent piece of advice which I always go back to as one of those nuggets. He could see that I was going to get impatient with the technical side of life, but I was clearly very capable. I had a first class honours degree in chemistry without trying that hard, so one side of the university was desperate for me to stay on and do research. But Bernard Kingston knew that that wasn't what I wanted to do and suggested the job he had done twenty years before at Procter & Gamble as Product Development Manager. 'You can't go wrong because they are a brilliant company, they provide good training and the job is half-way between a bench chemist and marketeer,' and sure enough, it was.

Penny Hughes set her heart on joining Procter & Gamble and was immediately impressed at interview. As predicted, product development manager proved to be an ideal first job for a chemist interested in business. Procter & Gamble have two or three technical centres of excellence around the world from which local product development managers draw technology as required to meet local market needs. She sat alongside local brand managers, gaining an understanding of consumer requirements, for instance, for the perfume or colour speckles for Bold 3 and then accessed the necessary technology from the research centres. 'I was like a switchboard, I could communicate well with the technical community at the same time as learning about marketing and research.'

After eighteen months Penny Hughes was given another lucky break, being made responsible for the product development of Bold 3, 'the first detergent that cleaned, softened and freshened'. Procter & Gamble had decided to do a test market in the Channel Islands to see whether the technology was working and giving the consumers what they want. Penny Hughes was made the Project Manager, responsible for both the product development and marketing. For eight weeks, she worked out of a hotel room, pretending to be a researcher and walked around the Channel Islands talking to consumers. 'I was the Brand Manager, Bold 3, Channel Islands. It was fabulous because I felt I had my own little business and it was an amazing success and went national.'

She then had another unusual and valuable opportunity. Procter & Gamble had recently launched Pampers Disposable Nappies but had no one selling to chemists and little knowledge of the customer base. 'So I got a car and a warehouse full of disposable nappies in deepest darkest Manchester and off I went for ten weeks, literally cold selling, which was a wonderful experience.'

On her return she was made Product Development Manager for the personal care side of the business which included Crest toothpaste and Pampers. Procter & Gamble were looking beyond detergents and washing products to further development of Head & Shoulders shampoo, other shampoos and soaps. She was devoted to working on these developments, spending 20 per cent of her time on technology and 80 per cent on commercial work.

At this stage, Penny Hughes took the initiative by asking to become 'a proper Brand Manager, not just doing the work and not called one'. Procter & Gamble, notorious for its rigid professional development programme, required her to start at the beginning and go through the conventional process, albeit at an accelerated rate. When she pointed out that she had the necessary experience, they still refused. Only when she determined to leave did they seriously discuss the position of Brand Manager. It was too late. Although P&G was 'absolutely brilliant', she could already see that it would be stifling, 'going through a funnel', having to spend the required number of years at each level. 'So at the ripe old age of 23, I said, "I'm off".'

As so often with women and less frequently with men (or at least expressed less often) her next decision was influenced by her personal life. Her boyfriend was working in London and, tired of commuting at weekends, Hughes took a job as Brand Manager, Milk at the Milk Marketing Board. Although her decision was not particularly well-informed, and offered a limited future, the Board, in fact, gave her invaluable experience.

In its favour was the role itself of Brand Manager and a strong advertising budget which she had never had before. It was also highly political and uncommercial in its approach and she brought needed discipline, planning and structure to the marketing function. The need for her services was clear. The Milk Marketing Board was desperate to sell the milk which by law it was obliged to buy and for which demand was falling. Her task was to develop and promote other milk-based products, whether flavoured milk or yoghurt drinks, milk for cats, cereal cream, whatever would sell. She had worked on about twelve development projects including joint ventures with major companies such as Unigate and Walls and her development budget of two to three million pounds was enormous by commercial standards.

Although Penny Hughes is characteristically positive about the experience, after eighteen months she understood that there was no career path for her and indeed that the Board's role would inevitably change and milk supply become regulated legislatively. She had been working on milk in cans and had fortuitously undertaken research into soft drinks and carbonated milk. When she saw a Senior Brand Manager job at Coca-Cola advertised, she naturally applied for the job.

As a franchise company, The Coca-Cola Company owns the trade mark and the brand and franchises the brand to companies to physically take the product to market. In 1984, Great Britain was divided into three franchises, two owned by Beechams but run as separate companies and one by Grand Met. At this time, the ludicrous situation prevailed of three salesmen approaching retailers such as Sainsburys to sell Coke with three different price lists. Although Penny Hughes was initially hired by Grand Met, four weeks later the franchise was bought back by The Coca-Cola Company. 'Again, it was a bit of good luck, because being honest, I doubt that Grand Met could have been as committed to marketing Coca-Cola as TCCC itself – so that opened up new opportunities for me.'

Penny Hughes progressed from senior brand manager to marketing manager and then marketing controller in three years. For the last nine months, she worked for Harry Teasley 'the best and biggest coach one could ever have had, an absolutely brilliant man who is probably my management guru'.

She describes Teasley as much, much bigger than the job, and clearly in the UK for the sole purpose of restructuring the industry. He had previously run Coca-Cola's wine business, Wine Spectrum, which was sold to Seagram and also Coca-Cola Foods, which was the juice and juice drinks business. He currently runs the joint venture business, Nestea, that Coca-Cola has with Nestlé.

By 1 January 1987, Coca-Cola and Schweppes Beverages was formed, a joint venture between Cadbury Schweppes and Coke which purchased the franchises back from Beecham and put together both brand portfolios, forming for the first time a national company for selling soft drinks.

Having contractually set up the Coca-Cola and Schweppes Beverages structure, nine months remained before it actually took place. Teasley said to her, 'I know that I'm not coming into this business with you and I'm not going to influence who goes into the new company because that is the responsibility for the new management team so all that I can do to make sure that (1) you get a job and (2) you get the job you want, is to coach and train you'.

> He chose six people who he thought were high-flyers and would do a good job for The Coca-Cola Company, and spent two or three hours a week on a one-to-one basis tossing out scenarios, hypotheses, seeing how we would react. 'If Pepsi halve their prices tomorrow, what would you do?'. He has an extraordinary brain and that really was my management training and far more practical than any formal training.

In 1986, Penny Hughes had considered another path to gain management training when Coopers & Lybrand offered her a job as a management consultant. She in fact had resigned and Harry Teasley persuaded her not to go – she also realised that her professional needs were best met in a large organisation.

In practice, Penny Hughes has relied exclusively on experience and mentors to develop herself professionally.

> I have never been on training sessions or read management books because I am so practical I get really fed up sitting in a conference room for a few hours, even for internal issues. In the nicest way, I am just itching to get back to action. I am not a workaholic!

Nor have obstacles or failures figured prominently in her development. In spite of being thrown in the deep end several times at an early age, Penny Hughes has not yet had any significant setbacks – 'I'm sure one's coming!'

She tributes Harry Teasley with setting her up to become Marketing Director of Coca-Cola and Schweppes Beverages when it was created on 1 January 1987 'which was probably the most frightening appointment anyone could have given me'. This is a good example of 'trial by fire', the experience of being thrown in the deep-end that so many chief executives have faced.

> I was twenty-seven. It was a joint venture between two totally different cultures, British Cadbury Schweppes and American Coca-Cola, with a massive portfolio of brands which needed to be rationalised and put into a complementary form. I had been working for this little company which covered one third of the country and all of a sudden I was responsible for all of Great Britain. I went from managing seven to managing fifty-eight people, which I then had to reduce to thirty-five in the first four weeks. My marketing budget went from £10 million to £60 million.

By September 1989, in less than two years, they had doubled the business and increased profits from £15 to £45 million. At 30, she was given her boss's job as Commercial Director on the Board of Coca-Cola and Schweppes Beverages.

For the first time, with a team of 1300–1400 people and a turnover of £650 million, she had to learn to be less hands-on.

> I really had to stop doing and begin coaching and influencing, creating the environment and the organisational structure to make the thing work. It was quite tough because I love actually seeing the results of things I do and I love 'playing' in the game, being on the pitch so that was a huge learning curve.

She was helped enormously in this role by her second mentor and boss, Derek Williams, Managing Director of Coca-Cola Schweppes and Board Director of Cadbury Schweppes. Williams's background had unusually been in personnel and manufacturing, and together they had complementary and well-rounded skills.

> He taught me all the things about management I did not know and I taught him sales and marketing, so we got on brilliantly as a twosome. He would toss me ridiculous marketing ideas, which with my classic marketing background I would never have thought of and I would think 'Hey, that's a good idea'.

Penny Hughes is rare among successful women in having had two mentors, Harry Teasley and Derek Williams, both outstanding in their generosity.

Both of them had rationalised they had probably plateaued, and they saw in me someone who should be encouraged to 'get to the top'. They have gone out of their way to coax and encourage me and I have been so lucky – it has been absolutely wonderful.

As Commercial Director, she participated as a task force member in the building of Europe's largest soft drinks plant at Wakefield, responsible for foreseeing the brands and packages to be sold both at the time of opening and into the future. As an example of the challenge, multipacks of Coke in sixes and twelves now represent 40 per cent of the can business but in 1987 did not exist!

I had the opportunity to influence some really fabulous and unique circumstances, and contribute to brand share, profits and volume. It's been a phenomenal success story, written up by analysts as the success story of the late eighties and contributed very significantly to the financial growth of Cadbury Schweppes in the last four years. Certainly it has been a highlight of the company.

Her learning curve was further steepened when the venture's success led to a monopolies and mergers enquiry.

We next went through a monopoly and mergers commission enquiry which of course is part of the success, raising the question 'Are you doing *too* well, are you being bullyish?' We concluded that very well, with a tiny amount of 'parking fines', really tidbits which were symptoms of the merger. When you put that many people together, some of the trading practices round the edges get a bit ragged but there was nothing structurally wrong with the industry or company. Being asked about every corner of the business was extraordinarily stretching and many individuals who have been through this process acknowledge that it is the best way to learn more about your company. I now know everything there is to know about competition law! It was a whole new learning curve which was fun.

Although Coca-Cola and Schweppes Beverages' performance was impressive, Coca-Cola itself was not exploiting the operating company's strength. As an insightful critic of Coca-Cola, Penny Hughes was logically next offered the job as President, Great Britain and Ireland.

To be candid, The Coca-Cola Company's representation in this country was below standard – they were just throwing in some American advertising, thinking that was good enough and it wasn't. I was one of the biggest critics of The Coca-Cola Company so when they moved out my predecessor they came after me. I thought, 'Oh, God, you've opened your mouth once too often'. I had to think really long and hard before I accepted, because it was strategic, not operational, with 120 or 130 staff as opposed to 1200 or 1300.

I finally agreed because I had done everything I possibly could do at CCSB. I had been there five or six years. The volume and profits had increased several times over. You get to the point where you really believe that your way is the only way and I realised that I was quite happy to pass on to someone else and go and learn something new. I hadn't worked that one out until Coca-Cola came after me. There were opportunities for me to keep on progressing within Cadbury Schweppes, consistent with starting a family and so they said 'look', you can stay with us, you're so much on top of the job, you can have children as well, and then lead a business unit. What more do you need?'

I remember thinking 'Help, now they're trying to plan my family life as well!'

Penny Hughes is fundamentally motivated 'by challenge and applying my skills to achieve demonstrable results'. Her decision to join Coca-Cola was clearly motivated by intrinsic interest in the job, the challenge, the ability to learn and to contribute something fresh. A safer, equally statusful course would have been to remain at Cadbury Schweppes. Coca-Cola sought industry knowledge and a change, and that is what Penny Hughes has delivered.

When I went to The Coca-Cola Company they told me 'First this job has never been done by a woman, it has never been done by anyone British before or anyone under forty.' I thought, 'Oh, OK. I'll have a crack!' I told them that if they wanted the job done the way it had been done in the past and in much of the under-developed world, I was the wrong person. The Coca-Cola Company had a very parent/child attitude, providing a set of operating rules for its bottlers and distributors, which was appropriate when they were family businesses but not with partners like Cadbury Schweppes, with huge competence inside the business.

Coca-Cola's real responsibility was to add strategic value to the business, not to give prescriptions on how to do things and I told them I would come if they wanted to experiment on how to run a franchised business into the future.

As Coca-Cola understood, Penny Hughes was unusually well-placed to establish an appropriate role for the company, eliminating the wasteful duplication and providing strategic direction.

We're very clear on who does what – whether The Coca-Cola Company or the franchisee – and how it is achieved. As a result, the business has found new acceleration so it has been very, very satisfying. If I'm honest, it was one of those opportunities where I was almost the only person who could have done the job because at CCSB I had been vocal about what The Coca-Cola Company should do and what CCSB could achieve. So I was the perfect antidote!

Penny Hughes developed a mission and strategic goals for the region that for the first time was separate from Head Office and introduced individual performance appraisal and personal development plans. She also reviewed the performance of service agencies, including advertisers McCann Erickson, forcing them to change their team, and to respond to her strategic objective of making Coca-Cola relevant to British youth.

The McCann team has great experience of advertising round the world but are now providing some excellent material for us. We've done lots of local advertising and have launched new 'contour' packaging – a fresh new way of doing business relevant to British youth.

In America, Coca-Cola is the number one icon – here it is number seventeen. So what do I have to do to get it to number one? I have to make it British. I have to make it passionate for the Brits – it doesn't mean we have to shed all the American stuff but we have to find the American icons that work in Britain. A little bit of Americana goes a long way in Britain but not too much and we must get it back into the social context of British life. This is why we use football, about which we Brits are passionate. We're refocusing to make our brands relevant.

As of November, 1993 Penny Hughes had achieved her objective with Coca-Cola for the first time becoming Britain's biggest selling grocery brand. Hughes recognises that the one major gap in her experience is an international assignment, although her role on the European Board gives her a broader European perspective on the business.

> I have done pretty much every job within the system so it has obviously given me the competence, capability and experience to do this job on a local basis . It comes naturally to me because I come from a British society. Would I spot the right opportunities as easily if I were operating in a foreign country and in a different language?

Continuing as she began, she has only loose goals and plans for her career but there are clear parameters for a next step. She needs to be part of a large but not necessarily global organisation, from which she derives a sense of the importance of her contribution – not for her the increasingly common step for women senior managers of starting her own business. She would also like to remain in the UK. She has just started a family but intends to continue her career development.

Following maternity leave and a period of transitioning the Coca-Cola business to new management, Penny Hughes has chosen to leave The Coca-Cola Company in October 1995. She has taken on non-executive Board Director responsibilities at The Body Shop and has a number of other commitments under consideration.

> I want to balance bringing up a family and continuing to gain satisfaction from my contribution to commercial life. For now, that balance can best be achieved staying in the UK and not committing myself to international moves with The Coca-Cola Company in the near term. The Body Shop was an important start to making me realise life beyond Coke could be fun, could be important!

FAMILY AND PERSONAL LIFE

Part of Penny Hughes's conviction that she can effectively balance career and family stems from her already balanced life. Career does not come first. 'Life comes first but business is a fundamental part of life, and if there were an imbalance either way, I would correct it.'

She works reasonable hours, from 8.30 or 9.00 in the morning until 6.00 or 6.30 in the evening, never takes work home or works on weekends.

> Those are my rules. If ever I have a job that takes more time, I'll probably pack it in. It is so important to enjoy life. In fact, I believe that it is this confidence and stability that allows you to do your job. I get up every morning and look forward to work. If I was tired, or making too many compromises, I wouldn't. My job involves a lot of entertaining but most of that is with my husband and we go to nice places and meet nice people, so I don't treat that as work. I warned Coca-Cola up front that I wanted to have children, because they had probably never had a woman at this level before. They gulped and said 'OK, carry on!' Also if anyone doesn't like the way I operate, just let me know. Feedback is critical. Achieving success so young has made me personally very secure.

Sports including golf, tennis, skiing continue to be important to her and she does not take physical fitness for granted.

In understanding her own good fortune she also tries to give something back to the community involving herself in charity work and giving time to various educational initiatives including a recent appointment to the Judge Institute's Board.

LEADERSHIP AND SUCCESS FACTORS

Penny Hughes does not underestimate how important circumstance has been to her early success. 'One of the reasons I have progressed so quickly is that the companies I have worked in have either merged or changed, providing me with more opportunity faster.' On the other hand, she acknowledges that she has always delivered very good financial results and increased shareholder value.

She believes that her success also derives from clear analytic and strategic thinking and a relaxed management style that brings out the best in people.

> I have an uncanny feel for business which I find very hard to share with or teach other people. It probably goes back to my training as a chemist and my maths. Without a calculator, or bit of paper I can

work out the value of any decision almost to the last pound which really makes decision making easy. I think I have got a clear strategic brain and one that reaches the bottom line very quickly. Also, I'm very informal and I don't show stress. My practice is to walk the floor and people come up and talk to me. I create an environment where people want to do their best.

She is not uncritical about her management practice, however, acknowledging that she can be pretty unforgiving: 'I sometimes forget that I have learned quickly and been very fortunate in my experience, and I am not always as patient with others as I could be.'

A close colleague independently confirms that Penny Hughes's approach to people, as well as her intellect, judgement, self-confidence and multidisciplinary background have been critical to her success as a business leader.

Penny is really excellent at establishing rapport with people and encouraging them to be more open, more challenging. To an unusual and refreshing degree she genuinely values people and is totally fair with them. She often walks around the office, sits on the back of a chair and shares a joke with us. There is always lots of laughter! Within a framework of clear objectives, established annually and revisited monthly, she leaves her managers to run their own show.

Penny is also very bright and has a strong vision of what she is trying to achieve, which can be disarming. She has extraordinary self-confidence, is very achievement driven and highly focused.

Penny is also quite a private person. She keeps her personal life separate from her business life. If you were to meet her in a wine bar, you would find her vivacious, fun-loving, bright and completely without pretensions and would never guess how senior she is.

Unlike many senior women ten or fifteen years older, Penny Hughes has never felt any discrimination as a woman. 'I believe that women are their own worst enemies – they expect to be treated differently and therefore discern a difference. In my experience, organisations value performance.'

In selecting high flyers, she looks for intelligence and good interpersonal skills. 'As the world grows smaller and the relationships with preferred suppliers and customers stronger, it is critically important to know how to influence and encourage relationships across the business.' As an eternal optimist herself she also looks for a positive approach to life and business. In response to a question about the importance of political astuteness, Hughes notes: 'Tact and awareness are important, but the world is moving quickly enough for performance to be far more important than politics'. Hughes believes that business leaders in the future will need to be more service-oriented, fast-moving and adaptive. They will have to create the environment for performance, rather than exercise direct control. Organisations are changing and already more people work part-time at Coca-Cola, including merchandisers who add enormous value working four or five hour days. She subscribes to Charles Handy's and Rosabeth Moss Kanter's view that employability, flexibility and the ability to learn will be key for employees in the future, and that the best organisations will provide an environment that develops these strengths.

> We are introducing learning contracts in our business so that our people are equipped with the functional and managerial skills to succeed, not only in their current position and within The Coca-Cola Company but also to position them for future jobs – perhaps in a different function, perhaps also for a lateral move rather than a move up the hierarchy, which will become more and more common with flatter organisations. Both companies and individuals must make sure they get the most from their work, not only in the short but in the long term.

She recently heard the Chief Executive of General Motors speak at a four-day conference, and recognised that over ten years he had created the kind of organisation that she is trying to create at The Coca-Cola Company in Great Britain and Ireland; one in which everyone is motivated by a job well done. He achieved this by setting the direction regarding the three or four things that are critical to the business, getting the right people on board and then ensuring that everyone uses their skills and makes a contribution.

Although most senior managers at her level in Coca-Cola are over 50, there is a younger minority who she describes as 'discernibly more challenging and questioning about the way the company is run'.

Penny Hughes believes that young people ambitious to reach the top should be very clear about their performance objectives in each job, clear about the direction of the company and how they might contribute to it. In choosing a company, they should look for an environment where individual accountability, as well as team accountability operates.

She also believes that education was critically important in equipping her for business leadership, although she points out with irony that three of her most admired business leaders – John Harvey-Jones, Anita Roddick and Richard Branson – all did not go to university.

I admire them because they have achieved against the odds, and they all run exciting businesses or have done exciting things with their capabilities. Anita Roddick and Richard Branson are entrepreneurs, and have created something where there was nothing before. John Harvey-Jones was a corporate manager when he ran ICI, but then he shared his ideas and experience in his books and on television, which was incredibly generous. All of them clearly lead balanced lives, and are very much in control in a total life sense.

3

Archie Norman
Chief Executive, Asda Group Plc

Date of birth: 5 January 1954
Place of birth: Westminster, London, UK
Nationality: British
Marital status: Married
Family: One daughter

Education:	Charterhouse, 'A' Levels, Economics, French, Maths
1971–1972	University of Minnesota, Minneapolis, USA
1972–1975	Emmanuel College, Cambridge University, BA/MA Economics, Exhibition Award
1977–1979	Harvard Business School, Cambridge, Mass., USA MBA

Career:	
1975–1977	Citibank NA, Account Officer
1979–1986	McKinsey & Company Inc
	Associate
	Engagement Manager
	Partner
1986–1991	Kingfisher Plc, Group Finance Director
	Chartwell Land Plc, Chairman
1991 to date	Asda Group Plc, Chief Executive

Outside appointments:	Railtrak Plc, Non-executive Director, 1994–
	British Rail Plc, Non-executive Director, 1993–94
	Geest Plc, Non-executive Director, 1989–91

Interests:	Practising member, Church of England; sports; opera; farming in Scotland

INTRODUCTION

Archie Norman became Chief Executive of Asda at age 38 and his path to the top through two years of banking, two years at Harvard Business School, eight years at McKinsey and six years as Finance Director of Kingfisher is highly unusual. Not many senior consultants or partners of consulting firms in the UK have been able to make the transition to a Board position of a major public company, let alone go on in their thirties to become Chief Executive. Norman himself sees the profile of Chief Executive and that of effective consultant as fundamentally different.

Although he had an early career objective to head up an organisation and consciously sought a fast track into business life, Archie Norman attributes most career choices to chance and to luck. He certainly had early senior functional responsibility, becoming Finance Director at 32, and also breadth of understanding not only of different functions, but of different companies and industries, all viewed from a senior and strategic perspective. There is no doubt that this experience gave him the confidence to run a large company.

Norman's confidence has been justified. Asda's turnaround into what a former McKinsey colleague describes as the 'UK's fastest changing retailer' has been achieved not only through clear strategic vision, which surprised no one, but also far-reaching organisational change. Norman himself believes that business leadership requires vision, personal credibility, strength of personality and driving energy, all of which close colleagues attribute to him.

What has been important in the development of this leading member of the new generation of Chief Executives?

EARLY INFLUENCES

Archie Norman is the second son of five of two doctors. On his father's side, his grandfather and great-grandfather were also doctors. An important legacy of coming from a long line of family professionals has proved to be a strong underlying ethos and set of values, and motivation by a sense of duty.

> Although I'm not a doctor, I'm a professional and my values are those of a professional. I believe in and I feel comfortable with the idea that what I'm doing is a service, not a service in the sense that

dry cleaning is a service, but a service in the sense that otherwise being in public service would be. It's professionally valuable to other people and that's much more important than anything else. I'm not a red tooth entrepreneur and not here to make money for myself. That would be an agreeable by-product. For the same reason, I wouldn't agree to run a large tobacco company or something which is not useful. I think that securing a future for Asda with 70,000 employees might be a useful thing to do.

As the second of five boys, born within eight and a half years, he describes his early childhood as 'fairly socially robust', with a degree of sibling rivalry but more importantly, the need for independence and fending for himself. 'You have to help yourself and be prepared to find ways of getting what you want or influencing other people. I came from a secure background, but people were too busy to put anything in my lap.'

Although school at Charterhouse was not particularly challenging, Norman was influenced by a brilliant economics tutor, Graham Jones (now Headmaster at Repton), who was instrumental in his discovery of economics, and more fundamentally, in exciting him academically for the first time. 'He was the first person who I found academically interesting. Although I didn't have unhappy school times, I found work very dull, totally dull. There were two things that I really enjoyed at school – playing football and economics'.

He decided to go to Cambridge not only because his father had also been at Emmanuel College but because, unlike Oxford, it had a pure Economics tripos. His decision not to follow the family tradition in studying medicine had been determined early by a lack of enthusiasm for the chemistry 'A' level.

Between school and Cambridge, Archie Norman took 'a year off' but not in the way most people understand this experience, as perhaps travelling, meeting people, a free floating experience. As a result of his father knowing a professor at the University of Minnesota, he enrolled in this mid-western university of 43,000 students, took some 'enticing courses', while working and paying his way through. 'That was my idea of taking a year off. Nobody in my family would have expected me to take a year off to lounge around. I didn't believe in it. I never have done. I don't take time off now.'

He chose economics at Cambridge both because he was good at the conceptual analysis required and because he thought 'completely mistakenly' that it might be useful for business or understanding political issues better. His grounding at Charterhouse and Minnesota was sufficiently advanced that he did not need to work hard to pass comfortably through his first two years at Cambridge.

CAREER DECISION-MAKING AND DEVELOPMENT

Archie Norman had a broad early career objective to run an organisation, but this was not confined at first to business. He attributes most of his career moves to chance – opportunities presenting themselves and being taken.

> Coming from such a professional family, and in an era when business consciousness and status was low, my ideas of what the business world was about were totally vague. I didn't choose business – it just worked that way. I didn't want to join the civil service. I wanted to go into politics or into business management. I didn't really choose, the opportunities chose me. As so often in careers you create your own luck and pursue the line of greatest attraction. You have to take the big opportunities when they arise because you never know if the door is going to open again.

He did, however, take active steps to position himself for opportunity, for instance deciding to go to the Harvard Business School.

Archie Norman first conceived of a career in business on leaving Cambridge, first planning to join Citibank, then to study at Harvard Business School, and to take the finance route to become a Finance Director, as the fastest ladder to the top. He joined Citibank in the midst of recession, when choices were few for those seeking 'rapid commercial induction working for quality people', and to earn a reasonable income.

> For young men in a hurry, which we were, there was hardly anything you could enter and go straight on to a fast track. That was the trouble. There was a tremendous sense of ageism and one felt very acutely at 22 that one didn't want to be put down in that way. I just couldn't accept that I had to learn everything in mundane detail before I could take any responsibility. It was the lack of being valued in many manufacturing environments that

really put bright people off and still does today, whereas if young graduates go to Goldman Sachs or McKinsey they are treated like serious people.

I've always had this strong view that I'm not comfortable in British establishment type institutions with all the stuffiness and resentment of youth and success. I felt that Citicorp was a modern professional place to work and that was very important. The notion of a fast track was a feasible idea. The man who ran half the corporate bank in London in 1975 was 28 and that was a powerful example.

The bank was expanding rapidly at this time and as an Account Officer, he was given responsibility for selling Citibank corporate finance products and lending money to twenty industrial companies. He had profit responsibility, made large sums of money for the bank and lost some as well, learning from mistakes.

At this stage he had a tremendous sense of urgency and impatience and two years seemed a long time. 'In those days, your sense of age and time was much stronger and every year really counted. With hindsight two years was the bare minimum. Citibank couldn't have been more generous and they were a tremendous two years.' However, if he has any regret in his working life, it is not taking a year off after Cambridge.

I think if you put me up against the wall I have doubts about whether that early period at Citicorp was right. In your early twenties, you ought to be less serious. With hindsight, now I am stuck, I can't take a year off and go around the world, go to Hong Kong, join the army or something like that. But then I could have done. If I had done so I am confident I would still have found a fast track when the time came. If I was advising me aged 21 I would say, don't be so serious, go and do something you want to do, have fun and then worry about a career at 25 or 27. Go to Harvard Business School then.

His decision to go to Harvard was influenced by colleagues who went to the Business School a year ahead of him. He could see that Citibank was moving him no closer to his objective of running an organisation and Harvard Business School seemed an ideal way to generalise his early financial experience. Harvard was the best business school in the world so the obvious choice.

The most important thing about Harvard is that it's a tremendous builder of confidence. People talk about MBAs coming out of Harvard and elsewhere being arrogant and of course it's true but that's also a reflection of the advantage of it. The strength of the case study method is that you get insight into two thousand different business situations, a belief that each is capable of analysis and that management can make a difference. If there is one lesson out of it, it is that business situations are different from what they seem, always capable of analysis but there is no single 'right' answer. This is very, very powerful because MBAs develop a can-do mentality and you set out to achieve things. The technical knowledge you pick up from Harvard Business School is peripheral. It's useful but not the main advantage. I am a great supporter of the MBA. I believe that it will be more important. There are still very few alternatives – the fast track into commercial life in the UK still suffers from being mostly financial, e.g. Goldman Sachs, a few big companies, then McKinsey and other consultants. Accountancy is technical training but not good management training.

The MBA is one route only and not always worth while. The important thing about MBAs is that there are good schools and very weak schools. There is something about the way British academic and business institutions combine which means they have chronic difficulty in producing a decent applied MBA.

His international experience in the US was of great value in reinforcing a sense of professionalism in management and stripping away 'stuffy British ideas about status, and the idea of management as a hierarchy'.

Although he would have preferred to have spent a couple of years in the US after Harvard, he also understood his future to be in the UK. The value of the MBA was still largely unrecognised in the UK, except by consultants and a few firms like Courtaulds (largely owing to Christopher Hogg's presence, a former Harvard MBA). Only at McKinsey did the offer sound like 'a major step up the ladder'. He also shared an immediate rapport with the people, McKinsey was prepared to pay-off his Harvard debts and he appreciated the strong professional values of the firm.

It wasn't overtly commercial and there was a strong sense of duty, and management professionalism. They were not boffins nor academics, but were working with important clients in the UK to solve real problems. Looking back, there are times in your life when you collect clusters of people who will be friends for the rest of your life and then there are periods when you don't. I know many McKinsey people extremely well and still see them.

However, given his objective to run an organisation, joining McKinsey was not straightforwardly a route to the top. As he himself points out there are very, very few chief executives in the UK among McKinsey alumni. In his view, there are good reasons for this – good consultants do not necessarily make good chief executives – the orientation is different.

> Most partners at McKinsey make very good consultants, but this is temperamentally different from being a good chief executive. Consultants have strong professional values, a very strong sense of independence but they don't like being responsible for lots of people. Being a consultant is the next best thing to being self-employed. That's why when they leave consultancy you find them in jobs of that kind, or running their own business.

As with most people who join McKinsey, Archie Norman did not intend to stay indefinitely. After five years he became the youngest partner ever in the London office. His decision to leave three years later came at a natural point, and was driven by the opportunity that arose at Woolworths Holdings.

He had been working with Woolworths Holdings as a client in 1983 when Geoff Mulcahy (now Sir Geoffrey Mulcahy) was Finance Director. When Mulcahy became Chief Executive in 1984, he asked Archie Norman to help plan the recovery of the company and in 1986, to help organise a successful defence against the Dixon's bid. Mulcahy then asked him to join the company as Group Finance Director, and help him to build the company.

The direct move onto a Board of a major public company is the career objective of many senior consultants or partners at McKinsey, but it is often difficult to achieve because of the lack of management experience – a more common route would be through a corporate planning role, not often at Board level. Norman admits freely that he was not technically qualified to be a Finance Director, but fortunately, neither had Geoff Mulcahy been before him.

In his six years at Kingfisher, the company moved from being an unstable company at risk of takeover to a successful established blue-chip British Company with market capitalisation that had more than doubled, comprising five large companies and a number of small businesses. At this stage Archie Norman felt that the major period of change was over and his task complete. Geoff Mulcahy was only 50, very able and a strong leader.

> I wanted to be a chief executive. I wasn't deeply frustrated. It had become a well-managed comfortable place to work, but I didn't want a comfortable place to work. A number of things came up that year which I didn't follow up and the Asda opportunity seemed to be the nearest thing to the Woolworth challenge in 1983, a situation where a very large company is being written off, in some ways justifiably, where the problems are well recognised and where there is enormous challenge. I would much rather pitch in at the deep end, than take on something smaller, in steady state. I also felt that some companies have a degree of spiritual value, a set of underlying values and purpose which can be a reason for feeling their survival is useful in the community and Asda is one of those.

His first year 'of taking charge' at Asda provided him with a period of great development, reflecting not only the common discomfort of changing companies at the top and being expected to have all the answers, but also the challenge of running an ailing company.

> You go through periods of very steep learning and development where you are under not just the challenge, but the greatest pressure. Some people just back off, but if you're a bit unstable like me, you go into over-drive. Coming into this place at the time I did was like a piece of theatre. There are very few situations where a business as big as this has fallen into a demonstrable situation of disrepair not only in the marketplace, but organisationally. You're regarded as being the answer and potentially the saviour. Everything a supermarket does is in the public eye. It's tremendous fun and it's great pressure. When I came to Asda in December 1991, everybody here was hoping I had all the answers. Of course, the answer is the facts are very hazy. You know certain principles, but the right starting point is to recognise you don't know the answer. The worst manager, particularly in retail, is the arrogant manager. The art is to come in on day one and give people confidence and direction while keeping options open.

Two years later, he had together with a small team of executives recapitalised and refocused the business, changing the management team and revitalising the culture.

> The role of individual responsibility as the centre of management effectiveness comes much easier in America. This is a very pressing issue. Most individuals at Asda used to view their role as to come in and do their functional job, whether it was buying or personnel. Their role was narrowly not broadly conceived. Instead our objective is to create a broader sense of ownership. You want to create a sense in which the individual is responsible to improve the company in any way he can. It takes years to change peoples' values and approach to their work. It has taken two years to achieve appreciable change here. I've witnessed this in at least six different companies, and I remind myself often of this every day. So it's important to tackle it holistically. You've got to breed a sense of urgency and ownership. You have got to demonstrate what you mean through leadership, paradigms and examples. You have to invest in change and get people involved in the change process. We set up twelve multifunctional teams called 'positive action groups' to get people involved to work together. The final thing we do is to change some of the people – we give them a chance, and if they can't change, then, regrettably, they go.

A former close coleague at McKinsey who has advised Asda over the last three years testifies to Norman's success in turning the company around.

> Archie has proved to be an exceptionally effective chief executive. It is no surprise that he took all the right strategic decisions when he went to Asda – after all, he had well demonstrated his strategic expertise both at Kingfisher and when he was a partner at McKinsey. However, the most exciting and sustainable element in the Asda recovery programme has been the changes that he has made to the organisation. He remotivated everybody from employees in the stores to the top management at headquarters and introduced an openness and willingness to be challenged that has become a model throughout the industry.
>
>   Archie didn't just mouth organisational jargon – he really has transformed an organisation that was moribund into the UK's fastest changing retailer.

Although Archie Norman in hindsight does not believe that he has had any significant professional setbacks, in the same breath, he foreshadows how he would deal with not succeeding at Asda.

> It would be a very big disappointment to me if I can't achieve something in this business but if we don't achieve what we have set out to do, with the time, energy and management team, it will be because the odds are stacked against us.
>
> There is a disease that has grown up with the glamorisation of business which means that business leaders are sometimes regarded like football club managers. If your company does well you're a superstar and if the company does badly you're not. The fact is that the success or failure of a company is determined as much by the fortunes of the marketplace as by the management. You can have an extremely good CEO of a failing company. Enhancing the value of a failing company can be just as rewarding and challenging, in fact more so, and more worthwhile than managing a business that has everything going for it. The public value system doesn't recognise this. Understanding of business is pretty low in the UK and at the end of the day if I don't succeed it would be difficult for people to say 'well he's done a good job anyway'. I might have done, I might not but to the man on the street Archie Norman would be regarded as the Chief Executive that didn't deliver. Now can you come back from that – yes you can but it depends on whether people really believe in you, whether there are enough people with sufficient faith to take you on and give you another chance. The financial markets and the media are not very forgiving.
>
> In the USA business awareness is greater. There is a more educated audience in that they understand business better and not the same degree of naivety. Just look at the extraordinary aura of success that surrounded successful UK company leaders in the 1980s. These tycoons may or may not have been successful, but the overstatement was wrong and damaging.

Asda is clearly not the end of the professional road for Norman, now in his early forties. There is no pre-ordained natural time horizon to consider a move from Asda: any sustainable recovery will take at least three years, and a further two may be required 'before we can say that we created a sustained recovery'. In this period, he would like both to restore value to shareholders and only if successful would expect to share in that performance financially. This would give him the freedom to do something next that was not necessarily financially rewarding, perhaps in the public service. It is only in this context that he is financially motivated – his lifestyle is not extravagant, his family small and his financial needs 'not great'.

Given his sense of public duty, early interest in government and his candidacy for the Conservative party in the Southwark Council elections in 1985 and 1990, many speculate that a political career might next attract him.

Archie Norman doubts that he would ever retire 'in the normal sense' unless he is forced to although he does see himself living eventually in the country.

FAMILY AND PERSONAL LIFE

Archie Norman has been married since 1982 to Vanessa Norman, Publisher of the *Diplomat* and *Foreign Service* magazines and proprietor of Diplomatist Associates. They have one daughter. Unlike most other chief executives of his generation he makes no conscious attempt to balance his personal and professional lives.

> Being a very small family, it is much easier to both spend time at work and also see a lot of each other. I don't attempt to achieve balance in the sense of making sure that at any point in time I'm not commited to my work. That would be ridiculous. Obviously for the first nine months at Asda, I didn't do much else. What is more important is to be interested in the broader context. I have a wide circle of friends and connections who help maintain a perspective on Asda. Knowing how unimportant you are is crucial otherwise you become consumed in your own little world. If you don't have that broader vision and outside interests, the small things that happen in your own company become disproportionately important and then it starts to get to you. I still take on many outside engagements and on the whole I tend to take on more than I can deliver. I have a chronic problem of agreeing to do things and I now write as a matter of course to all these people who ask me to serve on something. I tell them at the outset that I probably won't show up. When I joined Asda I tried to resign from everything. Some people were charming and said 'stay on and come when you can' but even this is not very satisfactory.

In spite of heavy demands on his energies and time, Norman has no trouble relaxing. 'I think that the best way to relax is not to get too het up in the first place.' He plays lots of sport and has introduced his own directors football team at Asda. 'It is very good for people to see their Chief Executive splattered on the football field. It takes any sense of grandeur away.' He plays indoor tennis every Friday night, listens to music, is interested in opera and has a small house in Scotland.

He takes about six hours of reading home with him every weekend and therefore does less 'real' reading than he would like.

Archie Norman believes in God, is a sporadically practising member of the Church of England, and his spiritual beliefs clearly inform his business life.

> I think it all connects up. I believe very strongly in individuality and a sense in which people individually in the company are important and the company should help them develop. With Asda people work very hard and at the end of the day the value they add is not only for the shareholders, but the broader community. My work values and personal beliefs are reasonably well aligned. I think that my management values and approach to individuals are consistent with my beliefs about the Church. I have never set out to articulate it and do not find it useful to do so. I don't expect colleagues to adopt my view of life.

LEADERSHIP AND SUCCESS FACTORS

Archie Norman attributes much of his success to luck. 'Business life is a game of snakes and ladders, and I've had to come up two or three fast ladders. I accept that my approach carries with it career risk. My approach is to make explicit the risks we are facing and invite people to support me.'

He is reluctant to talk about his own strengths, 'I think you'd have to ask other people. I do have a very clear idea of what I do well but I don't find it very helpful to talk about it. I think that I am in the right job.' A close colleague describes Norman as 'incredibly bright. He operates at a completely different level than most senior executives and knows more about marketing and finance than most directors responsible for these functions'. In his view, Norman's only limitation is experience. 'When he has no knowledge of an area, he operates on logic which very rarely lets him down'.

Norman believes that chief executives generally are lucky, extremely persistent, and have a driving energy which comes from a 'burning sense of motivation, even insecurity'. In addition:

> Firstly, running a company like this, when I started a troubled company, you've got to have personal credibility. You must say what you mean and mean what you say. That is so important. People want something to latch onto.
>
> Second it is important to create some sort of vision for people and there are different ways of doing that. The critical thing for the leadership role in a large employer is to have a way of effusing leadership so that people sense that there is a clear set of values that goes beyond planning for earnings per share. What we want to be as a company, why this company is an enjoyable company to work for – why it is worthwhile working for this company. That comes from the values the management radiate, and the business purpose you articulate and what you describe as the company's goal in the marketplace.
>
> The third thing is that you must have strength of personality and driving energy; you can't lead and sit in an ivory tower. You've got to be right out there.

Archie Norman is consciously motivated by a sense of duty. Although he talks about a driving desire to succeed, he is uncomfortable with expressing this as 'a need to prove' himself. ' "The need to prove yourself" is a very fashionable way of putting it. Obviously I really want to succeed but whether I have a need to is another matter. I am a very motivated person. To me it's just natural to be motivated.'

He also believes that in most cases, the motivation of the chief executive changes as he grows older.

> When you are in the early stages of being a chief executive, there is no doubt that the driving force is the needs of the business. Business and personal objectives are aligned. When the business objectives are achieved then the personal agenda starts to come out again. That's where people return to the comfort factors, the need for respect and recognition. That is when you start to become less effective.

I think most chief executives place excessive value on their position and status . It would be unnatural to do all this work and not want to be recognised for it. But that doesn't mean that need for recognition is driving them at the outset. Most businesses don't provide a lot of external recognition. They do provide internal recognition. But it's entirely natural if you put in a tremendous amount of work and sacrifice a large part of your life to build the business to want someone to say 'Well done'. What happens is that a lot of chief executives grind through their forties building the business, dealing with difficult situations and sorting them out and then in their fifties they look for recognition.

My perspective is that later in life it is natural that people seek public recognition. The risk is that too late in the day people strive to compensate for the early neglect of their family. This manifests itself in the form of acquiring houses with bits of countryside around them. They suddenly start collecting art and it's a recognition that 'time has passed me by, my family is grown and I've never developed a personal life'. For some there is a danger that at that stage they become very demanding about recognition internally which is very destructive – they need to be driven round by a chauffeur and they need to have a large car – it's more prevalent in this country than anywhere else, and it reinforces the status-consciousness of British business.

Most chief executives don't come from blue-chip backgrounds – they never expect to get so far and public recognition is very important. They work at it. That is one of the great values of the British honours system. It gets people to give something back.

While Norman understands the 'walk on water' syndrome, especially for business leaders in retail, he believes that it develops only because businessmen become excessively consumed with their own success – the leadership role alone does not provide the necessary conditions. As long as the challenge is still steep the risk of failure is very evident and humility prevails.

When you look at most new chief executives they are very well aware of their own weaknesses. The concern is whether you can do the job especially if it is a turnaround. Walking on water isn't the problem at that stage. Excessive self-belief is a problem that sets in following initial success. The risk is that senior executives become

consumed with their own success, lose touch with people on the
ground and stop listening to the outside world.

Rather unusually, Norman has neither had a mentor nor a role model
himself nor is there any one business leader he particularly admires.
He sees a clear difference between his own and the older management
generation.

> I think that in this country the business world is becoming more
> professional, and more demanding on people's analytical and
> conceptual skills and the quality of management is improving all
> the time, so if you look at the new generation of managers, many
> are smarter in this respect – perhaps less worldly and balanced in
> other respects.

He has a clear idea of the qualities required in his senior managers:
'I'm looking for people who are still fighting, who are willing to put
their head over a parapet, people who will disagree with me. We need
people who are smart, energetic, willing to fight and challenge the
system.'

In evaluating leadership potential at Asda, junior executive employees are given logical, quantitative and verbal aptitude tests by an
internal management development specialist. Senior executives are
also assessed externally both as a safeguard and to understand how to
get the most from their talents. 'The power of these tests is to get
people to recognise that many different qualities are needed to make
a management team'.

In advising his daughter about how to make career decisions, he
would encourage her 'not to worry' and to follow her heart.

> A lot of people talk to me because a lot of people are like me and
> would like to do the sort of things I have done. I generally advise
> that it is most important, particularly in the early stages of career,
> to concentrate on establishing only two things: what you do well
> and what you enjoy doing. The latter is the one that really matters.
> There is a tendency, especially with middle-class British people, to
> worry excessively about what is respectable, what is high in the
> value system – for instance, become a chartered accountant,
> merchant banker or lawyer or go into medicine or the civil
> service. In this country, becoming a salesman, or starting your
> own business or running a restaurant or acting or music are often
> not seen as meeting the middle-class idea of a respectable career, so

many talented people miss out what they really want to do. I have friends in their mid-thirties doing things that they never really wanted to do. It is a waste and they end up invariably not doing well at it either. It is especially a British failing.

Archie Norman believes in having broad goals rather than narrowly specific career objectives.

It's very important for people to have a broad idea of what they want and enjoy. If you've got the broad strokes of the canvas then that's all that's needed. It can be a great mistake for people to have very specific goals too early in their careers. Career moves are essentially unpredictable and you never quite know what will turn up and when.

For those people who do have a genuine interest in business, and an ambition to run a company, what advice would he give? There is no single 'model' route to the top. He acknowledges that his own path was unusually fast, 'There is a peculiar natural progression professionally in the UK which tends to take people to the top a bit later'. He believes that this is unlikely to change, although there may be more chief executives in their early forties.

4

Martin Taylor

Chief Executive, Barclays Bank Plc

Date of birth:	8 June 1952
Place of birth:	Burnley, Lancashire, UK
Nationality:	British
Marital status:	Married
Family:	Two daughters
Languages:	French, German, Italian, Russian

Education:	Eton College
	'A' levels in Physics, Maths, Chemistry
1971–1974	Balliol College, Oxford
	BA Chinese

Career:

1974–1978	Reuters
	Financial journalist in London, Paris and Frankfurt.
1978–1982	*Financial Times*
	Lex Column
1982–1990	Courtaulds Plc
1982–83	In Head Office
1983–87	Managing Director, Courtaulds Clothing
1987–90	Managing Director, Courtaulds Textiles
1987–93	Director, Courtaulds Plc
1988–90	Chairman, Courtaulds Textiles
1990–1993	Courtaulds Textiles Plc
1990–93	Chief Executive
1993	Chairman
1994 to date	Barclays Bank Plc
	Chief Executive

Outside appointments: Non-executive Director, W. H. Smith Plc

Interests: Reading, music, travel, architecture

INTRODUCTION

Martin Taylor has perhaps the most unusual background in the study. An old Etonian, he studied Chinese at Oxford and has never had a career goal. Not only were his first eight years of work spent as a financial journalist (including four working internationally) but the idea of entering business did not occur to him until age 30 – an inspiration for those considering a change of career!

Financial journalism in the Thatcher years, however, developed in him a fascination for business and in 1982 he joined Courtaulds because the Chief Executive, Christopher Hogg, whom he knew, offered him a job. One year later he moved into general management in the clothing division and in 1987 was appointed Managing Director of Courtaulds Textiles. With the demerger of Courtaulds and Courtaulds Textiles in March 1990, he became Chief Executive of Courtaulds Textiles Plc. As one of the most highly regarded businessmen of his generation, with an interest in and knowledge of finance from his days with the *Financial Times* and Reuters, he was head-hunted to Barclays Bank as Chief Executive, taking up his post in January 1994.

Martin Taylor has been greatly influenced by mentors, including Sir Christopher Hogg, who has referred to him as a much better manager than he was at the same age.

Martin Taylor has a deeply contemplative side to his nature and his only goal is to take a few years off at some stage to travel and read. Although highly analytical, he particularly enjoys the emotional and motivational aspect of management and trusts his feelings and instincts more than rational analysis. He describes his approach to business as 'feminine'. Certainly he has a reputation for outstanding communication and interpersonal skills and an ability to deeply influence and persuade audiences as diverse as city analysts, shareholders and colleagues.

In many ways he epitomises a new breed of management, characterised by Richard Giordano as a mixture of hard driving 'type A' and more sensitive 'type B' personalities. Another fashionable expression of this suggests that he is both left-brained (analytical) and right-brained (holistic) in his approach. Ironically, perhaps, he describes his attempt to balance his professional and personal lives as 'appalling'.

What has been important in the development of this leading member of the new generation of chief executives and what are his views on leadership and careers?

EARLY INFLUENCES

As is unusually common for chief executives and particularly for successful entrepreneurs, Martin Taylor's father died when he was only eight years old and he was consequently very influenced by his mother. The trauma of his father's death was exacerbated by his departure for boarding school two weeks later. The older of two brothers, self-reliance must have come early, although he sees a 'profound requirement for security' as a fundamental legacy of his father's death.

In saying that he is motivated neither by money nor power, he pre-emptively understands that many people might be sceptical about such a denial.

> I'm not particularly interested in having or spending money. What money buys me more than anything else in the world is the ability to stop work if I want to. I appreciate the freedom that money provides.
>
> That sounds awful, doesn't it? We all know people who are money-mad and say it has nothing to do with money and people who are power-mad who say that they aren't influenced by power at all. In my case, I am influenced by curiosity and fear of boredom more than anything else and just horror of not having enough interesting things to do. That makes one ambitious but only in the negative sense that the most interesting jobs are the most senior jobs usually.

At age nine, his destiny appeared to be to teach Greek at Oxford. 'This probably would have happened if I'd been at school twenty years earlier!' Ironically, as Christopher Hogg had been influenced fifteen years earlier to study classics at Marlborough, when his natural inclination would have been to study maths or physics, Martin Taylor at Eton chose chemistry, maths and physics in spite of a natural interest in languages. As with Hogg, he has no regrets about his choice although unlike him, Taylor chose these subjects in spite of advice.

> I thought I should choose something modern. Although they were the subjects I was least good at, I'm very glad about this choice. My knowledge of technical matters is extremely poor but if I hadn't devoted myself to the natural sciences for a couple of years,

it would have been ridiculous. I absolutely wasn't advised to study science. My masters were horrified.

Again, his 'A' level results were sufficiently good to win a place at Balliol College, Oxford where his natural interests asserted themselves. He studied Chinese at Oxford ('not very hard') because of a fascination with languages and poetics, showing the true intellectual's concern to study the original.

I always find languages very easy to learn and very easy to forget. I wanted to learn a hard language that I would never have the time or self-discipline to teach myself. I was at the time, and still am, interested in poetics as well as poetry. Reading Ancient Chinese verse in the original was an important objective for me. It was a huge pleasure.

CAREER DECISION-MAKING AND DEVELOPMENT

Although an academic career in many ways would have been a natural next step, Martin Taylor knew that he was far too restless.

I was deeply uneasy about an academic career. I love learning but I hate libraries. I can't sit still – never have been able to. But all the people I admired and knew well wanted me to carry on studying formally and end up teaching. I just knew that it wasn't right for me but had absolutely no idea what else I wanted to do because I had no exposure to the world.

He has never had a career goal or plan and attributes most career steps to accident. Certainly, at this stage, a business career was inconceivable.

It simply never would have occurred to me until I was 30 that I could ever have worked in business. The idea that I could be responsible for a large organisation would have seemed to me absurd. One of the most absurd things that was written about my move to Barclays was that I had always wanted to do this since I was 18 which was absolute rubbish!

The only goal he has ever conceived is his current desire to take two or three years off 'before I am too old to enjoy them'.

His first career decision to join Reuters was based on a pragmatic assessment of opportunities for a Chinese graduate in a tough employment market.

> I wanted to go the Far East, partly because jobs were very hard to get in London in 1974, the year I came down, the year of the stock market crash. It looked as though the world was ending. I also thought it would be useful to cash in my only employment chip, which was knowledge of the Far East. Reuters gave me a job. It was great for morale. They let me know that I was the tenth out of ten they had taken in!

He joined as an economic journalist, 'considered very much the junior service, the fact that it now makes a lot of money is a different matter'. He next gained fundamental international experience, being sent to Paris and Frankfurt and receiving 'terrific training in journalism' and in the rudiments of how financial markets work.

After four years, he returned to London to join the *Financial Times*, a well-worn path for Reuters journalists. As with many other newspapers at the time, the FT was not allowed to hire direct from university, unlike Reuters, which ironically counted as a provincial newspaper for these purposes under the union agreement. Consequently many aspiring Fleet Street journalists joined Reuters as a first step and it was a natural progression for Taylor.

He then had a very 'UK based career' for four years writing the Lex column of the *Financial Times*, with Barry Riley and Richard Lambert, who were perhaps his first two mentors.

> They were an enormous influence on me professionally. Not only did they teach me a lot about how businesses work and tell me stories about the early seventies and their business heroes but also made me feel that large companies were glorious things and that was a very important feeling.

Becoming responsible for the Lex column was one of the most important developmental experiences equipping him to become a chief executive.

> For the first time, I felt the humility and sense of enormous responsibility you have to feel when you first take over something. I was 27 and people who knew much more than me actually read and believed this column and one had to be terribly careful.

Also the history of Lex was very distinguished, stretching back for fifty years. For the first time I understood that you owe a huge debt of responsibility to the organisation you work for because it has a continuity that goes before you and after you.

As a financial journalist from 1978–82, he was influenced by two important strands of thought in the early Thatcher years, which would fortuitously prepare him in 1994 for his move into banking.

One was the early experiments with British monetarism, the same time that Volcker was at the Fed. I was dealing with important city-financial-monetary-banking issues which interested me enormously and are relevant to what I am going to do now. The other was that large British companies were exposed to the icy winds of competitiveness with a hugely over-valued exchange rate. I just got very interested in what was going to become of businesses like ICI, GKN, Dunlop and Courtaulds which had huge social importance and seemed to be economically failing.

At this stage, although it would have been a natural move, he was not tempted to go into the City. As a financial journalist, he had met many chief executives and chairmen and had known Christopher Hogg before he became Chairman of Courtaulds.

Chris was a very unusual Chief Executive. He was very young for a start. He offered me a job and it was exactly what I wanted to do. I just wanted to get inside and see where it led me. It's an easy story to relate – it's a story of accidents.

I was able to make the transition from journalism to senior management quite quickly because I was lucky in the company and I had Chris Hogg's backing. The company was becoming much more outward-looking at the time (as is Barclays at the moment, by the way), so it was prepared to give an outsider the benefit of the doubt.

Although Chris Hogg is an 'obvious mentor', Martin Taylor has learned from a lot of people, including more junior colleagues.

Martin Taylor spent his first twelve months undertaking 'various' odd jobs for the Chairman and the Board and getting to know the business. In 1984, only two years after joining Courtaulds and at age 32, Martin Taylor had become Managing Director of part of the clothing business of Courtaulds, which initiated the 'two most important years' of his business life.

Unlike many chief executives, he went into general management without broad functional experience in a company, but he notes that his breadth derived from his experience as a financial journalist: 'I think financial journalism is absolutely super training for business, not in terms of managing people, but in terms of understanding the relevant issues'.

Also he debunks the assumption that one must begin one's general management experience leading a small business unit. 'Although I was managing a business unit of a couple of thousand people, you never really manage more than twenty wherever you are. I think people get very hung up on numbers. It's irrelevant whether you are managing twenty or two thousand.'

As is often the case, Martin Taylor found the hands-on running of a medium-sized business in some ways more developmentally important than more senior roles.

> I was actually first responsible for something, very simple but also immensely complicated. I felt completely out of my depth. I learned about the importance of human relations to business, how to persuade people to do things that they wouldn't have done by themselves. It was an intensely human experience. Actually becoming Chief Executive of Courtaulds Textiles in 1987, although it was probably the most stunning thing that ever happened in my life, more stunning than the Barclays move, because it was completely out of the blue, did not have the same impact. It didn't change my life in the same way.

The next major challenge followed the demerger of Courtaulds and Courtaulds Textiles in March 1990.

> We came out of Courtaulds and were on our own. We were a very young company with old assets and a hell of a lot of debt. This was a critical experience for me and I learned how fast you can do things when you have to.

In 1993 a head-hunter approached Martin Taylor about the chief executive role at Barclays, having first touched base with Christopher Hogg. Changing industries at the top held no fear. Even before joining formally in January 1994, he had met as many people as he could, listening to them, bouncing ideas off them. Since joining, he has devoted himself to changing the culture and the way his people manage and conduct their business.

> At the beginning at Barclays I spent very little time on financial issues *per se* and an awful lot of time trying to understand the dynamics of the organisation and trying to persuade people to do things differently, to look outside more, take more responsibility, understand the consequences of their actions and behave in a more business-like way.

His interest in and knowledge of the financial markets has provided the necessary background for leading Barclays and he acknowledges that it would be impossible to change at the top in certain industries, for instance, computing or motor cars, where he has no interest in the product.

Although he is thoughtful and self-critical, he does not cite any particular failure or setback in his career as developmentally significant.

> I have had some frightening moments and a lot of very frustrating moments. I have avoided a major failure by sheer good luck. We all have failures in our personal lives from time to time, which have an impact on one's confidence professionally. I believe very strongly in the impact of one's personal life on one's professional life. Usually, when things have been difficult for a while, it's because I have become stuck myself. It's not really a function of the outside world. I have unrewarding weeks rather than unrewarding periods!

Consistent with his longer-term objective to take a few years off and the value he places on contemplation, he had hoped to take six months to a year off between Courtaulds and Barclays 'but I've completely failed to do that, haven't I?' The contemplative part of his nature is clearly important to him, providing an insight into his motivation and values.

> I would travel, read, refresh myself. I would find it very hard initially but I would be perfectly happy to stop. I am very influenced by the Chinese philosophical idea of people working for the Emperor, being in favour and then falling out of favour, writing poems in some wretched part of provincial China, and finding equal fulfilment in doing both. I think it's important to cultivate both sides of one's nature. The contemplative part is a

very important part of me and has had to take a back seat for
longer than I would like. My wife would laugh if she heard me say
that – she thinks it's pure fantasy and that I only have to be on
holiday for three or four days before I want to come back to work!
But that's because I don't have the practice.

He gives no thought at all to his next step after Barclays. 'And it
would be a very bad sign if I were thinking about it.'

FAMILY AND PERSONAL LIFE

Martin Taylor is married to a former teacher and has two teenage
daughters. Unlike many of his contemporaries, he acknowledges that
he balances his personal and professional lives 'very, very badly'.

> I don't see half enough of my friends. I devote my personal life to
> my family really and I know they suffer. Like everyone else, one
> comes home tired and cross and without enough energy to do the
> things they want to do. I find it very difficult. I find that the
> demands that professional life makes, not just intellectually or
> physically, but emotionally to be very draining. I don't know what
> the answer is. I work much less hard than other people I know.

Although he is physically at the office at 8.15 a.m. and leaves by 7.00
p.m., he worries about work 'all the time'. At weekends he tries to
limit himself to three or four hours of reading. 'I skim-read. I take an
awful lot home and then I read very quickly because I find it very
dull.'

He neither puts work nor his family first. 'You render unto Caesar
that which is Caesar's and leave the rest for God. One has to be
sensible.'

He is not religious but has a firm belief that 'certain things are
better than other things'.

His interests include reading, music, travel and architecture. 'I
don't read enough because I have to read so many papers. It uses up a
part of the brain that gets tired, not just the eye.' Nevertheless he
reads very widely: 'Novels, not as many as I should. My wife reads
them voraciously and knows exactly what I should read. It's like
someone tasting at a banquet. She's marvellous'. He also reads
history, biography, philosophy, literary criticism and geology.

His approach to time-management is both western and oriental: 'The key is effective use of time but sometimes effective use of time is walking around and mooning about'.

LEADERSHIP AND SUCCESS FACTORS

Martin Taylor is convincingly modest about his commercial abilities – one is persuaded about his sincerity, if not about the conclusion.

> I'm not an entrepreneur in the slightest. I'm not a particularly good businessman – I'm just not. I don't have a talent for business in the raw. I have colleagues who might start their own business and I would back them financially because I know that they would make a lot of money. They are good at the details of commercial life, better than I am. I usually think straight and I'm prepared to draw logical conclusions from what I see. I'm quite good at synthesising as well as analysing, which is harder, or at least, synthesis is what we are not taught to do at school. We were taught to analyse until the cows came home but we weren't taught to bring things together which is what is important if you are trying to envisage an outcome.

It is clear that his real pleasure and reward in management comes from people.

> I have always loved working with people. I am very curious about them and I like them. I also like getting away from them sometimes! I love the emotional side of business, the motivational side. You have to make people want to do what you want them to do. That's what I have turned out to be reasonably good at doing. I don't think that I'm that good at it actually – the problem is that most people are just atrocious at it or aren't interested in it.

A former close colleague notes that Martin Taylor is 'almost too good to be true' and so exceptional that people are unquestionably happy to be led by him.

> It is so transparent that Martin has strengths that others do not, that no one would consider comparing themselves with him. On all the qualities required for business leadership, he scores ten out of ten. He also has the most exquisite management manners.

His relationship with each person on the board is so good that relationships within the management team are also good, because each person feels fully understood and in tune with Martin.

In confirming that Taylor's people skills are outstanding, his former colleague notes also that he can be 'steely and tough' on people issues when he has made up his mind, having taken everything, including people's feelings, into account.

Rather unusually for a chief executive, Martin Taylor's Myers Brigg type is INTP, rather than the more common INTJ. (Although as with many people he has different MBTI results on different days.) The 'P' or perceiving preference suggests that he requires a good deal of information before making a decision and that decisions are often tentative, rather than final. He confirms.

> I'm not an INTJ. What I like to do is to make an analytical decision provisionally and then let things roam around in my mind for a long time. I often find this throws something up. I do believe, not in the sub-conscious, but in the semi-conscious workings of the mind. I also like to operate from feelings. If something seems intellectually right but feels wrong, I would trust my feelings. All your intuition is telling you is that you haven't done your intellectual sums right. There is a dimension that you've missed out. I trust my gut much more than I trust my brain because I know that my brain doesn't have all the information.
>
> Businessmen don't have all the information. This idea that decisions are made based on lots of rational facts is wrong – you take decisions based on 25 per cent of available facts.

He confirms that one of his preferences that changes is 'T' or thinking and 'F' feeling, particularly given his emphasis on emotion, people and his self-described approach as feminine. 'I have a very feminine approach to business. It's a matter of personal preference. I find all-male societies extremely disagreeable and unliveable-in.' (Feeling is the only sex-linked preference and three quarters of women exhibit it.) Certainly he sounds like an 'intuitive feeling' (NF) type, when he notes.

> I find it easier than some people do to put myself into some one else's shoes. This sounds arrogant but it's not. Certainly I fail to do it hugely on some occasions when you miss something because you

didn't have the common sense to think about what it's like to be Ruth Tait this morning. But I'm quite chameleon-like – no fixed convictions maybe!

In selecting high flyers at Courtaulds he looks for the qualities that he lacks himself, an answer he accurately predicts that Chris Hogg would also give. Specifically, 'I also look for imagination, courage, generosity. That's what you need really'.

In answer to a question about the value of being attuned to organisational politics, he notes:

> Political astuteness is necessary only in the narrowest and least manipulative sense. Organisational politics is the bane of most organisations. People who spend their entire time trying to understand people's motives in order to manipulate them are a double liability. Usually they haven't got enough to do. On the other hand, a certain amount of astuteness, letting people know what you are doing, what one might call interpersonal realism is essential.

Martin Taylor emphatically does not believe that the qualities required by business leaders are changing.

> When you look at great political and military leaders, it is perfectly clear what is required – the ability to inspire trust. I will not arrogate this quality to myself because I don't believe honestly that I possess it in any great quantity – this is not false modesty. I know what I can do and what I can't do.
>
> But I don't like leadership in the mass. I'm very uncomfortable with human beings in the mass. Generally the more people there are the more disagreeable they become and that happens over about four people. I like very much to work with small groups or one-on-one. Always have done.

He attributes his own success to curiosity, reasonable intelligence, liking what he does and serendipity.

> Not enough people want to do what I am doing. I'm never sure what sort of people would do it better than me. I just ended up doing it – it was complete serendipity. There must be people who would have been better equipped than me to do the job at Barclays. But they aren't now because they didn't start off in the right way.

Having been both Chairman and Chief Executive of Courtaulds Textiles for eight months Martin Taylor is very supportive of separating the chairman and chief executive roles in a company.

> Having two people leading a business is a very good idea, with the Chief Executive the more active but the Chairman as more experienced and an effective 'warner'. When it works well, it is terrific. A lot of Chief Executives are irritated with this structure, because they have a desire to be the unquestioned boss. It needs two people with different and complementary qualities and an understanding of who does what and respect for each other. It would be very tough if you had a fundamental disagreement on where the company should be headed. I've never lived through this but it could cause a lot of tension.

Although his own career path clearly prepared him for his move to Barclays, he does not believe in approaching one's career more strategically or drawing lessons from his experience. 'If my career path had been different, then the next step would have been different', suggesting that it would have been equally rewarding.

Martin Taylor's advice to ambitious young people is consistent with his own approach to his career.

> Don't think about it. I suspect that people who at twenty have an ambition to run a large public company are the ones who never get there and are almost certainly unsuitable for the job because they are ego-driven. If you are interested in business, it is certainly all right to hope that you will do well and succeed but I believe that the aim of running a large company is an inappropriate ambition for a twenty-year-old – you should at that age be concerned about learning more about yourself and the world.
>
> It is essential to do things where you are learning. It is also important not to make bad choices because if you do you will probably make poor business decisions too. It's a question of understanding where something is taking you – I don't mean upwards – but whether it is broadening or narrowing you. Is it going to open doors or shut them? It is really a matter of interest more than anything. One spends so much time at work, one might as well do things that are interesting. Back to the fear of boredom. I have always been terrified of being typecast at what I do.

He believes that it is essential in a modern business career to have experience working internationally as well as experience working in a highly people intensive function or industry and to develop a high comfort level working with financial information systems.

This doesn't give you a model career path. It is only experience that you can't do without. If you can't do those things, you will constantly be on the defensive or running to catch up. They must be very easy for you. Other people might think other things are important – for instance, strong knowledge of technological processes, which I certainly don't possess. I think there is something missing in my brain. I am like the woman buying a car. I am much more interested in the colour.

5

Gerry Robinson
Chief Executive, Granada Group Plc

Date of birth:	23 October 1948
Place of birth:	Donegal, Eire
Nationality:	British
Marital Status:	Divorced, remarried
Family:	Two sons, two daughters

Education:
  1958–1964   Catholic Seminary, Lancashire
                             'A' levels: Latin, Greek, English, Maths
  1971   FCMA

Career:
  1964–1971   Lesney Products
                             Cost Accountant
                             Works Accountant, Hackney Factory
  1971–1983   Lex Service Group Plc
                             Management Accountant
                             Financial Controller
                             Finance Director
  1983–1987   Grand Metropolitan Plc
                             Finance Director, Coca-Cola Soft Drinks
                             Sales and Marketing Director, Coca-Cola Soft Drinks
                             Managing Director, Coca-Cola Soft Drinks
                             Managing Director, Grand Metropolitan Services
  1987–1991   Compass Group Plc
                             Chief Executive
  1991 to date   Granada Plc
                             Chief Executive

Outside appointments: Caradon Plc, Non-executive Director
                             Trustee of Common Purpose

Interests: Painting, golf, opera, reading

INTRODUCTION

Gerry Robinson has been Chief Executive of Granada Group since 1991, and has transformed the Group from what was considered to be a heavily indebted 'mess', over-reliant on television rental to a highly profitable conglomerate with tightly managed businesses in television/leisure and business services.

In March 1994 Robinson succeeded in a hostile bid for LWT, in one move making himself one of the three most powerful men in television in the UK and taking Granada into the top forty UK companies.

Gerry Robinson had been head-hunted to Granada because of his impressive track record in management turn-arounds. In 1987 he orchestrated the largest management buy-out that had yet been seen in the UK when he bought Grand Metropolitan's contract services for 163 million pounds (it is worth four times that now). Four years later he sold the renamed company, Compass, making himself fifteen million pounds.

Gerry Robinson accepts the psychoanalytic view that leaders are motivated primarily by the need to prove themselves, based on an insecurity or lack of feeling loved or validated in childhood. In his case, as the ninth of ten children of a carpenter in Donegal, there would understandably have been competition for his parents' attention. At age 11, he entered a seminary in Lancashire to become a priest, a disciplined and rigorous environment that drove him to relentlessly hard work and academic excellence and inculcated the high standards that would take him steadily to the top.

Indeed, Gerry Robinson has never had a career objective or plan but has relied on chance, uncompromisingly high standards, tenacious work ethic and 'doing the job well' to take him to the next step professionally. Early in his career, he was also significantly influenced by older mentors.

The first twenty or so years of his career were spent in going from strength to strength in the finance function. Only in 1983, at age 34 was he given an opportunity to head up sales and marketing at Coca-Cola Soft Drinks and a year later to move into general management as Managing Director. With Grand Metropolitan's sale of Coca-Cola Soft Drinks, Robinson was chosen to head up the company's contract services business, which he turned around and making an active intervention in his career, duly bought out!

Gerry Robinson believes that above all leadership, like parenting, requires consistency. He also views business as essentially straightforward. He is known for his 'Irish charm' and obvious decency – a nice guy, as well as for his clear strategic vision, overall competence and financial and commercial acumen. He also has a reputation for toughness – when David Plowright, the 'grand old man' of Granada television would not submit himself to the rigours of accountability, Robinson famously fired him.

Since selling Compass, Gerry Robinson has moderated his working hours to a civilised eight-hour day, proving that it is possible to work smarter, not harder and still succeed as the Chief Executive of a leading public company. Remarried with a four-year-old daughter and one-year-old son, he makes time for family and personal pursuits such as painting, opera, golf and reading.

What has been important in the development of an Irish-born, one-time-aspirant to the priesthood, and leading member of the younger generation of chief executives and how would he advise others about getting to the top?

EARLY INFLUENCES

Gerry Robinson is the ninth of ten children of an Irish-Catholic carpenter from Donegal. His early education in his small town in Ireland was 'fairly demanding. You learn to read and write and you learn that Ireland's the most important place in the whole world and then you discover that it isn't really'.

At ten, his family moved to England and after a year, he went to the Catholic Seminary in Lancashire to become a priest.

It was the ultimate aim of any mother's child to be a priest. Certainly my mother was very religious, and there was an element of doing the right thing by entering the priesthood and also a total belief in what it all meant on my part. It's so difficult to be absolutely certain about causes but I suppose every damn thing is influenced by your mother in truth, isn't it? It becomes clearer the older you get.

Although he finds himself dismissing it now, he was zealous about the priesthood at the time. The benefit was a very disciplined, highly focused education in an environment where everybody achieved 8 'O' levels and 3 'A' levels. 'You had to drive and strive for it.'

He hated every minute at the seminary from aged fourteen onwards, but had the 'good sense and fear of change' to stay the course until he had achieved his 'A' levels. Relentless effort no doubt contributed to his achieving 'A' grades in all four subjects. At sixteen or seventeen, it was very clear to him that he was not cut out to be a missionary, and he at last resolved his internal battle by choosing to leave.

It was a terrible dilemma intellectually because when you start to examine religion, the whole bloody thing falls apart. Yet there you are, in a highly educated environment with highly intelligent and able people being quite unable to have any kind of debate in any sensible way as to what religion is about. I got to the stage where I thought I just couldn't go on with it. It really wasn't for me. It would have been much more serious if I had gone on to university sponsored by the Holy Ghost Fathers and then taken Holy Orders. I came out without knowing what I wanted to do in any serious way. I just hadn't a clue. I was kind of naive.

CAREER DECISION-MAKING AND DEVELOPMENT

His first job was the fortuitous result of a single visit to the Youth Employment Office who sent him along to be interviewed by Lesney Products as a cost clerk. As he was placed in the cost office and encouraged to study accountancy, it became clear that the 'right thing to do' was to become an accountant although it had never before crossed his mind. There was no element of active choice involved. 'It was absolutely classic. If they had sent me along to be in personnel, I would have followed the personnel route.'

He spent nine years at Lesney Products, progressing from cost clerk, senior cost clerk and eventually becoming a works accountant in one of the factories. The experience was extremely positive, both because of the entrepreneurial, dynamic nature of the company and because he found a support and mentor in Bob Tanner, his boss in later years.

Lesney Products had been set up as a die-casting business after the war by two ex-servicemen, a salesman and engineer. At one stage, they ran out of orders and started to make a few toys, and soon found that they could not keep up with the orders.

> It was a very raw company, with not much sophistication and therefore a very good way of getting exposed to the harder end of business. If you're exposed to three thousand East End women making toys in Hackney, you have seen most things. They were a tough lot, they really were. It was terrifying!

He was given tremendous encouragement from Bob Tanner who was paternal, very capable in a quiet way, clear in his expectations and also in his interest and support of Robinson.

> A single story about him comes to mind. We used to come in on a Saturday morning and work overtime. We would work for two hours and spend an hour and a half having a game of cards while having our sandwiches. We got caught. I always felt awful about letting this guy down.

His next career move was almost equally accidental – he saw a job advertised, and was attracted to it because it came with a car. 'I thought, "I must have a car". It was as simple as that.'

In 1971, at 23, he moved on a much higher salary to Lex Service Group as a management accountant and progressed over twelve years through financial controller to finance director for the Lex hire and distribution side of the business. His career at Lex followed a similar pattern as at Lesney, with intrinsic interest in the company, hard work and a mentor in Alan Costin, Financial Director of the Volvo sales part of the business.

He found Lex to be very straightforward, uncomplicated, professional, with a 'tremendous buzz' and very hard driven. They paid well and attracted the best people. Alan Costin was influential in his support, his ability and the complementarity of his approach.

> In some ways he was the opposite of me. He absolutely ensured that every 'i' got dotted and every 't' got crossed. I was terribly impressed with that kind of attention to detail. I just don't have the consistency for that and I'm still not good with detail. He is a very able financial guy.

He was also influenced by Ken Burr, the Managing Director, who was very clear-headed, 'feet on the floor', and extraordinarily well-liked.

Although he was undeniably ambitious, Gerry Robinson never had a career objective or even a clear sense of the next step instead following the same approach as so many others, by concentrating without distraction on the task in hand.

> I just did what I was given to do well and was quite pushy in terms of getting things right. It didn't feel any more complicated than that. I was ambitious without a shadow of doubt. But the ambition falls out of wanting to be the best at whatever it is that you do, which in my case is probably to do with having the ninth set of trousers! It leaves a mark on you in some way. I can't think of a single time when I have thought 'I'm going to go on and do this or I'm going to achieve that!' Success probably comes from concentrating on what it is that you are doing in a narrow way. I think it was Hardy who said that most great strides forward are made by thinking narrowly.
>
> Business is actually a rotten intellectual exercise – the essence of business is very straightforward. A lot of great things are the result of an incredibly narrow focus and great drive and a lot of bad things have come out of enormously complex and sophisticated strategising.

In considering difficult professional periods, Gerry Robinson identifies several times at Lex when he was passed over for jobs that he thought he should have got, but ultimately was philosophical about his own childlike response, being 'miffed and hurt' and the importance of not whinging.

> I just waited for the next opportunity to come along, as they always rapidly did at Lex. I always tried to put myself in my bosses' shoes – I would be very turned off by someone who was working for me who came and whinged. I have gone away and been unhappy about it and cried my tears but it's rarely a personal situation, so I never complained.

After twelve years at Lex, a former boss, Eric Walters, who then was running CC Soft Drinks for Grand Met's Coca-Cola franchise enticed him to join as Finance Director. 'Frankly, it was impossible not to.' Two companies had been brought together, resulting in an accounting nightmare of double billings, customers not being billed and debts not paid which Robinson sorted out in a year, with a team of 120 people.

Eric Walters was supportive, straightforward, unpolitical and very clear in his expectations. 'Achieve what you set out to do, in which case you were well-regarded and well-received or you failed, in which case you either got a bit of help or you went.'

After a year, Walters gave him his first opportunity to move out of Finance as Sales and Marketing Director.

> I enjoyed sales and marketing immensely because very quickly it became clear that there was nothing particularly different about it. We had a good group of people, we had a market to sell into, we had different parts of that market and all we had to do was to make sure that we got ourselves facing the right way. The sun shone, new systems were introduced and the company had a terrific year.

As Allen Sheppard concludes, 'Gerry Robinson is one of those accountants who is a better marketeer than most marketeers'.

When Eric Walters was promoted, Gerry Robinson became Managing Director, still reporting to him, and for the first time in four years the company made a profit. 'It was the largest profit CC Soft Drinks had ever made – £3.154 million, and my bonus depended on that!'

At this stage, the Coca-Cola company bought CC soft drinks for £35 million from Grand Met, to sort out their franchise operations in Europe.

> I was absolutely livid. We had done all these wonderful things, built up our team spirit and suddenly it was sold out from under us. In truth, it was the right commercial decision for Grand Met but it left me feeling high and dry.

Allen Sheppard then moved Robinson over to run Contract Services which was 'losing a fortune', an illogical mixture of catering, a few hospitals, an M&E company and a number of international businesses in the Far East, Middle East, South America, the USA and Europe. An £11 million loss was converted into a £5 million profit the first year, then £10 million profit and then Robinson bought the company. 'Which wasn't too smart, was it? We could have reversed the order!'

The strategy had been straightforward – keep the sound core businesses such as catering and hospitals and divest the rest. When he approached Anthony Tennant about buying out the division, Tennant was against it. 'If he hadn't gone off to run Guinness, I don't think we would have bought the company.' When he approached Grand Met again through his immediate boss, the Finance Director and Allen Sheppard, the new Chief Executive, it was agreed that the company should be sold. The management had competed against outside players for the company, and ultimately bought it for £160 million in 1987.

The buy-out was extraordinarily exciting and probably the most satisfying time of my career. It was totally new territory, and there was always the uncertainty of whether it would succeed or fail. Apart from obviously being financially rewarding, more than anything else, it was a very exciting time. In a way all you do, is just repeat a formula. Clearly one has to get things to come into place and that means reading people right and encouraging some and losing others. But it is the same formula.

We had a fantastic amount of luck in the timing. You couldn't do a buy-out like that now. It was arranged terribly easily in six weeks. There were no assets, other than thirteen million pounds in hospitals. By the time we bought it, it was down to four businesses, the largest by far was catering in the UK. This was catering in other people's premises, so you owned nothing. All you had was a six month contract. But if you did it well, your customer kept you for a long time, and we set out to do it well. In a catering operation essentials plod on no matter what happens, and provide a terrifically sound base for producing cash. It turned out to be a terrific success and we took it to market by December 1988. A lot of buy-outs after that went wrong and we were all very cocky about ours doing well.

Although both catering and hospital businesses grew rapidly, it became clear that there was little left for Robinson to do. The shareholders had rejected a bid for Sketchleys, because they wanted the company to stick to the knitting.

There is a point when you have to stop interfering because I absolutely hate it when someone wants to manage me. Anyone who is any good has to be given space to get on with it. The decision not to buy another company means that you have to clear off. Otherwise you overmanage and interfere or end up buying something because you want something to do.

For most of the year he went into the office only a couple of days a week and, after an initial adjustment period, started to enjoy spending a lot of time painting and reading.

When head-hunters approached him to run Granada, he was 'ready to just get in and sort something out again'. He studied the business, the people, the finances and what had gone wrong, 'getting the feel for it'. He concluded that the tumbling profits could be turned around quite quickly.

> Whatever else we do, in the long run the business must be based on a growing profit. I have a simple belief that if you get to the stage where you are panicking and think that you have to acquire something to achieve growth, you're in deep trouble because you make silly acquisitions.

And grown profits he has. On a turnover of £941.4, Granada had profits of £103 m in the half year to April 1994 – up 51 per cent. Granada also in 1993 bought Sutcliffe, catering and laundry business, for £360 m.

His tenure as Chief Executive has not been without conflict and pain however. In February 1992, David Plowright, Chairman of Granada Television and elder statesman in the industry, was asked to resign because of disagreements with Robinson. The press reported the move as a victory for the forces of commercialism represented by Robinson over those committed to quality.

Certainly, Plowright's removal is experienced by Robinson as a failure on his part, but the parting was the inevitable outcome, not of Robinson's disagreement with the strategic direction of Granada Television but with Plowright's refusal to be accountable.

> It was a pity but inevitable. It was clear to me that it would go one way or the other – either David was going to fall in line and get on with sorting television out or he was going to go. He was a nice guy and an interesting guy, but he couldn't knuckle down. I have no axe to grind about him. If I were in his position, I would have had the same difficulty. At 61 he was not going to stand for some smart arse coming in and wanting to know what he was doing, asking for plans and reviewing performance.
>
> That's what the conflict was about, a management process that didn't suit him. It wasn't really about different directions because I didn't know anything about television. I know a great deal more about it now and still wouldn't want to set any kind of strategic

aim for television. That has to be done by people who know the detail and understand the business. My aim was to make sure that we were managing the business in the right way because the whole industry structure has changed and is much more competitive. We had to accept that and make sure that we were as efficient and hard-nosed as possible, while still producing good programmes well. Above all, we had to make money out of it and not just be a passionate broadcaster.

David resented that I wanted to review what they did when I knew so little about it. But it was my job to review the business, and I wouldn't have taken the job in the first place if I wasn't prepared to tackle this. David misread it. He thought that he could win through, and escape management scrutiny. It was impossible for me to accept that.

In considering mistakes in his career, he forthrightly identifies his handling of David Plowright's departure.

I felt desperately upset and still do that it ended up the way it did because to me that was a personal failure. He shouldn't have gone out like that. He should have gone out as a grand old man of television. I ask whether I could have handled it differently.

He believes to a certain extent in business that it is difficult to clearly identify mistakes and therefore to learn from them.

You have a bash at something and there almost isn't a right or wrong way. If your judgement is reasonable and you feel that you are right about it, you make it happen. It might have happened better another way, but you will never know. I can't think of an absolute failure that nearly floored me.

Even disappointments that were experienced as failures at the time, such as Tennant's refusal to allow the Compass management buy-out, in retrospect are not experienced as negative.

Gerry Robinson intends to retire early, by 55 at the latest and to spend at least part of the year 'growing potatoes' in Donegal.

FAMILY AND PERSONAL LIFE

Gerry Robinson has been twice married and has two teenage children, a four-year-old daughter and a one-year-old son. He notes that the experience of having a child at 45 gave him a clearer understanding of his own father who had his tenth child at the same age.

Whether or not his first marriage, as with several of the older generation, was the casualty of overwork, he now has the more balanced life described by several of his contemporaries.

Having already experienced semi-retirement, Gerry Robinson describes himself as 'pretty lazy. It's very important to me that I don't work really long hours.' Consequently he is in at work between nine and ten and usually leaves before six o'clock, also ensuring that he frequently takes Fridays off.

He plays golf, paints and loves to read 'a tremendous mixture of stuff'. Lately he has been reading Freud, impressed by the originality of his thought expressed amid enormous antagonism and resistance. He also is a real opera buff.

LEADERSHIP AND SUCCESS FACTORS

Gerry Robinson fundamentally agrees with the psychoanalytic perspective that people who aspire to leadership are those driven by a need to prove themselves, based on a 'basic fault' in childhood derived from not feeling loved.

> I've thought about it quite a lot and I'm absolutely certain that most leaders in some deep sense are striving to prove something which is unprovable, certainly by the route of business success. I'm pretty certain that they are striving in a negative sense rather than a positive one. There is an element of 'look, mother, I'm running ICI'.
>
> I equally believe that proving yourself is undoable because the need is absolutely insatiable – whatever you achieve doesn't actually give you whatever it was that you were supposed to have had earlier on.
>
> Any real happiness stems from being at ease with yourself and I have a horrible feeling that business success stems from the opposite and is a rotten substitute. There is no relationship between the process of succeeding and any genuine desire to get to know yourself and to understand the roots of whatever it is that makes you strive. But the motivating force to be the best, whether in business, science, academia or whatever field, comes from

wanting to prove how wonderful you are because basically you don't feel that wonderful.

Consistent with this belief, he would advise his own children to follow their hearts in choosing a professional and personal path, rather than one that is valued by others.

> I would like to see them just be happy in whatever it is they decide to do and I'm sure they will decide to do quite, quite different things. There is absolutely no correlation between success in financial/prestigious terms and your own feeling of personal value and worth. If they want a successful business career, good luck to them. It's financially rewarding but a hell of a lot less worthwhile than being a good painter. (On the other hand, I don't want to knock business for those with a genuine interest in it because people are best served by having businesses very well-run.)
>
> I don't push my children hard in an educational sense although they both actually do reasonably well. They should do what they want to do. Children sometimes try to follow their parents. What a hopeless position particularly, for whatever reason, if a parent is especially successful.
>
> Children are separate and will end up with their own trials and tribulations. The hardest thing is to accept that they are going to go through all that. You cannot save them from being hurt. You can just be around. The last thing they need is a driven parent. I find going to dinner parties and hearing people talk about registering their kids at school at the age of two depressing. I don't want any part in that at all. I hope that they will find peace in whatever it is that they do.

Gerry Robinson believes that success in business derives from 'getting on with it' rather than career planning, 'I am quite cynical about someone who tries to find a route to the top in business. Very few make it to the top. I know many very able people who perhaps should have made it, who have not.'

On the other hand, there are experiences that are valuable. Unlike many others, he does not identify international experience as critical but values early general management experience above all.

> It is important quite early to have an opportunity to see the business in the round. Unless you do, you tend to think that the organisation is made up of your little bit and far more complex

parts that you don't fully understand. If you can clearly see your impact on the whole, you begin to understand what it all means, and to believe that it is possible to understand the business.

As with parenting, Gerry Robinson believes that the most important quality of leadership is consistency – so that people know where they are day to day. He gives an example of modifying the behaviour of his daughter when she was ten months old. Every night she woke her parents three or four times, to be picked up or fed until he decided that they would go to her, but never feed or pick her up. After one night, she was fine. 'It's a great clarifier.' At the beginning, people at Granada clamoured for things which he made clear they would not get. 'People then knew what to expect and the organisation settled down to dealing with reality because they know where they are. People like solidity and consistency.'

Vision too is critical to leadership, but he is swift to demystify it as something sophisticated or complex.

> Most visions are terribly simple, such as 'I will rule the world'. Both at a personal and a corporate level, you do have to have a vision, be clear about what you actually set out to do – people must know what success is. I'm a hard-nosed financial visionary.

Consistently, believing that business is essentially straightforward, he does not share the view that high levels of intelligence are needed of business leaders.

> The danger of a high intellect is that it can veer into over-intellectualising a business problem that is essentially very simple. On the other hand, people with nous but average intelligence can be enormously successful in running large companies. You can learn very quickly what the ten key issues are in a company and unfortunately seven of them will be the same every time for every company!

A former Chief Executive to whom Gerry Robinson reported confirms the strength of Robinson's strategic judgement and leadership.

> Gerry is very good at seeing the wood for the trees and ran the business in a cool and clearsighted way. He clearly distinguishes between what is important and what is not. He is also very proactive about identifying business opportunities and developing

the strengths needed to exploit them. Although he takes strong positions and is very self-confident, he is not inflexible and will change his mind if a good case is launched.

Gerry Robinson notes a paradox in the requirements of leadership.

> There is little doubt that being able to communicate with and get close to people is important, but it is also necessary to be able to separate yourself, and at times go out on your own in order to make something happen, even though it is not the chummy thing to do. There is a necessary loneliness to leadership.

His former boss reinforces that Robinson, as with many business leaders, does not have strong affiliation needs and is very direct.

> Gerry Robinson is a very nice guy and certainly not arrogant, but can come across to those who don't know him as a bit cool and distant partly because, in personal contact, he 'doesn't waste words'.

Another former boss and Chief Executive describes Robinson as self-confident, dynamic, bright, modest, with a good sense of humour and advises those dealing with him to be open, upfront and direct if they want to be well received.

Gerry Robinson does not value political astuteness in the office politics sense, although he acknowledges that managing upwards, the communication of what you are doing, is necessary to succeed.

He fundamentally believes that everyone, both customers and employees, are best served by companies that are run well commercially, not 'softly'. Uncommercial decisions result in everyone suffering.

> If you are going to run a business, you should do it extraordinarily well and commercially. You cannot carry lots of people that you don't need, if the business won't support it. I get very angry about the belief that softness in business is the right route because it really doesn't serve people well. We have made a lot of people redundant in Granada and that is a result of having done a lot of silly things in the past. If you are in the role of leading the company and very well paid to do it, you must do it well, be firm and consistent. This is hard but it is what you owe.

Just as he does not accept that high levels of intelligence are required of business leadership, nor that business life is becoming much more complex, Gerry Robinson does not believe that leadership skills have changed fundamentally at all. In his high-flyers, he looks for a track record that evidences the clear-mindedness and consistency that he believes above all to be necessary.

6

Bill Castell

Chief Executive,
Amersham International Plc

Date of birth:	10 April 1947
Place of birth:	London, UK
Nationality:	British
Marital status:	Married
Family:	Two daughters, one son
Languages:	Spanish

Education:	St Dunstan's: 'A' Levels in Zoology, Botany and Chemistry City University BA (Hons), Business Studies, Marketing option ACA

Career:
1965–1970	Wellcome Foundation Commercial Trainee
1970–1973	Spicer & Pegler Articled Clerk – Qualified ACA
1973–1974	Ultramar Marketing – Head of UK Retailing
1974–1989	Wellcome Foundation
1974–76	Finance Controller, Europe
1976–80	Head of Finance and Administration, Continental Europe, Africa, Asia
1980–86	Managing Director, Wellcome Biotechnology
1986–89	Commercial Director
1990 to date	Amersham International Plc Chief Executive

Outside appointments:	Design Dimension, Chairman Green College, Oxford, Visiting Fellow
Interests:	Family, travel, international politics and economics

INTRODUCTION

Bill Castell is Chief Executive of £300 million turnover leading health science company Amersham, at the forefront of creative joint-ventures with the former Soviet Union and the only firm in its industry to operate from bases in Europe, the US and Japan.

Bill Castell is an accountant by training, and spent most of his working life at Wellcome, with a few years break, beginning in finance then gaining cross-functional experience in marketing and operations before his first general management appointment at age 32 as head of Wellcome Biotechnology and then as Commercial Director on the main board at age 40. When John Robb was appointed as Chief Executive of Wellcome in 1989, Bill Castell was approached through search consultants to head up Amersham as Chief Executive at age 42.

From an early age Bill Castell had a general goal to be a successful businessman in the world of science and has been active in acquiring the skills and experience required to achieve this. An infectiously enthusiastic, very open extravert, he was deeply influenced first by the breakdown of his parents marriage and then by the active support and ambitions of his father. Initially an underperformer at school, he describes himself as driven by personal dissatisfaction. His open approach to self-understanding and self-criticism provides a particularly fertile ground for life-long development and learning. Physically energetic, emotionally open and his own severest critic, he positively welcomes feedback, whether positive or negative, as an opportunity to learn, to change and to grow. More than any other person in the study he has been influenced first by older mentors and then by contemporaries he admires and trusts.

Representing a significant group in the younger generation, Bill Castell exemplifies more clearly than any other the tendency to place equal, and in his case greater, importance on family rather than professional life.

What has been important in the development of this exceptionally open leader and Chief Executive of the younger generation and how would he advise others about reaching the top?

EARLY INFLUENCES

The greatest single influence on Bill Castell's early life was the instability caused by the separation and later divorce of his parents

77

when he was five. He and his older sister lived intermittently with his mother who was in and out of hospitals and over eighteen years he had fourteen different homes, living sometimes with relatives, sometimes on his own, sometimes with his father. His mother's central aspiration was to provide a home for her children, and he fell under great pressure to provide her with support and stimulation. This instability and his mother's expectations created for him an early clear priority to have a good marriage and a stable home life. In reaction to his mother's dependence, he would seek a wife who was not only stimulating but also had her own career, ultimately marrying a general practitioner. Happiness at home remains incontrovertibly his most important objective.

The second profound influence on his life was his father, who as he grew older became his best friend. His father was a successful businessman who grew a small hosiery business into an international textile company and was Chairman of the Liberal party funds when Jeremy Thorpe was the leader. He was a person of great drive and high energy and enormously ambitious for his son. During the few hours they would spend together every second Sunday morning, his father would show a compelling interest in his life and his future:

> He would talk about those unrealistic things he hoped I would achieve that he hadn't achieved. He was determined that high offices in the City should be things that I should aspire to. I once said to him 'Now that you have taught me to be so highly motivated that adrenalin drips from my fingernails, what will I do now?'

At the same time, Bill Castell was seriously underperforming at school, feeling rather left behind by his father and devoting himself to sport, rather than school work. A pervading sense of failure provided the dissatisfaction with self that continues to drive him today.

> If you ask what really motivates me, it's a personal dissatisfaction. I don't like myself every day of the week. It goes back to my youth. My father did well, he left me at a minor private school in South East London called St Dunstan's. I watched him move into a different level of society. I could have gone to boarding school but I chose to stay home with my mother. I was in the 'G' stream at school. It wasn't a distinguished school. I took a long time getting

my 'O' levels. I got French 'O' level on the sixth occasion, having worked in St Tropez as a waiter. After serving Jeanne Moreau breakfast in bed I decided that I had better get a bit more ambitious and I passed them all second time! I was looking at the world of opportunity through my father's eyes and slowly realised that unless I woke up I would miss that world.

When his parents divorced, he was given some money and became absolutely determined to be 'mega rich'.

I used to do property deals. I would get on the phone and hassle 'I've got this graveyard for sale, what's my commission?' At 21 I thought 'what the hell's it been for?' It was a good experience. I realised that emotional satisfaction was much more rewarding than financial satisfaction. I could be very wealthy and very unhappy, I knew that. I don't know how people who are born with a silver spoon in their mouths motivate themselves. I don't think I could. I would probably have never finished my 'A' levels at school and been a layabout.

Although his financial motivation now is less ambitious and certainly not primary, he admits that money continues to motivate. 'I am always overspent. I have a nice house, a comfortable lifestyle and enjoy taking my family on trips, giving them different experiences.' As an extravert motivated by personal dissatisfaction, recognition of his success by those he respects is also admittedly important to him.

I do like to be recognised. I find it disappointing that people who used to deal with me don't deal with me any longer because I have moved to a smaller business. I enjoy creating a network which facilitates international business. I worry when I lose it. It isn't public recognition that matters but respect. I've been asked to do three or four articles and programmes by the media and I always say no, because the personality cult worries me. You make one mistake and you're dead. I'm not after that sort of recognition but if I can be respected, then I'll be very happy. I don't have to be liked by everyone but if I feel that someone I respect doesn't like me, I get worried.

At school his ambition was to emulate his hero, Jacques Cousteau in a science-related career, specifically sea farming and marine biology. When he was 17, his father sent him to the US for the long vacation to work in marine biology laboratories, but he quickly realised that he was too extraverted for a career in scientific research.

Although Bill Castell had failed his 'A' levels in science first time around, with the encouragement of his future wife he surprised his headmaster by passing them the second time and being offered a place at Aberystwyth to do a degree in marine biology. At this stage, however, 'Two women kept me in London. I felt that I should stay with my mother, rather than leave her on her own. I also had a very strong interest in my then girlfriend who is now my wife'.

CAREER DECISION-MAKING AND DEVELOPMENT

Bill Castell had been offered a five-year apprenticeship with the Wellcome Foundation, which included a sandwich business degree. A future in science and business in London proved irresistible. 'My clear driving goal was to be an effective businessman in the world of science and to develop the skills required for that role, not only the professionalism of law and finance, but also increasingly the discipline of organisational psychology so fundamental to business.'

Toward the end of his business degree, by this time one of five people on the personal staff of the Chief Executive at Wellcome, Fred Wrigley, he was informed that the company intended to send him on stints to Central America, the US and then as Sales Manager to Spain. Recognising for the first time how little control he had over his life and career, he decided to acquire a professional qualification, both to gain independence and also to prove that he could discipline himself. He chose accountancy, because it would give him credibility, get him into 'long trousers' quickly and give him an edge over the competition of his own age group. Finance proved to be the 'luckiest' choice he made professionally.

> That gave me the long pants. It made me a professional. If you are a lawyer or an accountant then you can go and deal with a 45 or 55 year old and they will accept you because you are a professional. If you go in with a marketing degree they won't accept you. I knew I needed the professional discipline if I was to succeed as a generalist.

In resigning from Wellcome, he burned no bridges, writing to the Chairman to say that he was leaving in order to develop himself but hoped to rejoin. He chose next to join accountants Spicer & Pegler, because of the breadth of the clientele and the opportunity to work across different industries.

Risk aversion and lack of faith in himself led to his betting with an old Etonian that he would fail his exams. If Castell passed, he paid £1200 and if he failed, he was paid the £1200 that would allow him to try again.

Upon qualifying he joined oil company Ultramar for a year in marketing management. At this time, his father, now in his fifties, suffered a business reversal and together they launched a company dealing with avalanche and snow control. When his father became ill, Bill Castell was given a leave of absence to run the business. At this stage he was considering not only business as a career but also Conservative politics.

However his original interest in science prevailed and he returned to a financial role at Wellcome, as a stepping-stone into general management. 'After that my career decisions were really made for me by Wellcome.' His career at Wellcome over sixteen years took him across all the principal functions – finance, operations, marketing, R&D – at levels where he was directly involved in decision making.

Bill Castell's career at Wellcome was powerfully influenced by mentors, beginning with his father-in-law Harry Mendleson who was first Personnel Manager, then Personnel Director of Wellcome.

> He was a fervent Labour party supporter, with very strong people values who helped me to develop a strong social conscience. I none the less observed the inconsistencies in his values and lifestyle as he drove me to work in his Jaguar! From the time my own father died in 1980 until Harry Mendleson's death in 1982, my father-in-law was my best friend.

On his return to Wellcome, he was in addition deeply influenced by Claudio Matons, Director Europe, Africa and Asia. 'He trusted me, gave me considerable responsibility and grew me as a man confident in many environments.' Finally, Chief Executive Alfred Shepperd taught him intellectual discipline.

Two further people influenced him profoundly in these years. Sir William Henderson, Chairman of the Agricultural Research Council and former head of the Pan American Health Centre, sat on the Wellcome Biotechnology Board for seven years and shared his 'supreme understanding of science and of people management'. Ian Taylor, a consultant and former Veterinary Senior Manager at Wellcome would closely observe his behaviour and tell him openly

when he was falling short, or abusing his powers and characteristically, he relished this feedback.

Two important scientific influences were John Beale and Norman
Finter who qualified as doctors soon after the war, went into medical
research and were his 'friends, colleagues and fellow enthusiasts' for
nine years when he was responsible for Wellcome Biotechnology.

More than any other business leader in the study Bill Castell
acknowledges being influenced by older mentor figures and continues to be influenced by contemporaries he respects. He positively
welcomes negative as well as positive feedback as an opportunity to
learn. Deeply self-critical, he is a life-long learner who relentlessly
reaches out to understand how he can do better and is generous in
acknowledging the impact of others on his experience and development.

At age 29, Bill Castell's career took an international route at
Wellcome taking financial and administrative responsibilities for
continental Europe, India, Pakistan, North Africa, Kenya, Nigeria
and Japan. For five years, he was away three weeks in four. 'I enjoyed
the challenge of promoting a common product across different
cultures, and the opportunity to become a management chameleon.'

In 1981, Alfred Shepperd, the Chief Executive asked him to head
up Wellcome Biotechnology. Characteristically unconfident, it took
him six weeks to accept the role.

> I told him, 'I don't know anything about science – surely I should
> stay in the financial stream where I can make a contribution.' He
> said to me, 'When the Chief Executive tells a young but competent
> executive he should take a job the competent executive usually
> listens.'

This was his first true general management role. As a finance
manager, he had been 'reasonable at negotiations', had enjoyed
commercial deals but had never really felt that he was a good
manager. Now he grappled with organisational and motivational
issues and as ever, the challenge of disciplining himself. 'Motivating
individuals hasn't been a problem because you motivate people by
being as natural as possible. Develop a facade and no one's
interested.'

Six years later, he was appointed to the Wellcome Board.

> I came back from a visit to Denmark slightly inebriated (it was
> difficult to come out of business functions in Scandinavia without

getting inebriated). I had a rough time at the Capital Expenditure Committee and was summoned to the Chief Executive after that meeting. I thought that I was going to be castigated for poor performance. The contrary was true. Alfred Shepperd asked me if I would join the Board as Wellcome's Commercial Director.

Throughout this period he saw his future at Wellcome, for fifteen years reporting to Alfred Shepperd. In 1989 John Robb was appointed as Chief Executive, which coincided with a re-examination of his life and career.

Robb's appointment must have stimulated the head-hunters because within a few weeks of the announcement two head-hunters called me. One of the jobs was a job in North America in healthcare and the other was to join Amersham International as Chief Executive. I was aged 42, I really felt that Wellcome was a second family, and had a deep emotional commitment to the company, but I also knew that it would be rather disappointing at 60 to have only done one thing, however stimulating. It would not broaden me as an individual.

I had determined before the appointment of the new Chief Executive to change something and I had lengthy discussions with my wife. There are three important aspects of life – family, work and where you live. If you are happy with all three, you will have a very fulfilling life. Our family life has been a good one: to say it is excellent sounds smug. But we had decided to change homes or change jobs.

The challenges were beginning to diminish. You knew who your friends were, you knew the shops and where the street lights were on the road, and you knew your company so well so that it wouldn't necessarily get the adrenaline going at maximum speed.

We moved our home, and when the offer came from Amersham, I decided to change my job. Quite frankly, if you're offered the chief executive position of a public company at 42 you have to think very hard about ignoring that opportunity – no matter what the differences in size or scale of operation, or what the fortunes are in the relevant companies because you may never get the same offer again. Grab lady luck when it arrives. Better to have tried and failed than never to have attempted it at all.

Bill Castell is open about the difficulties of becoming chief executive of a company completely new to him.

When I started at Amersham, I just didn't know what the hell to do. It's very difficult walking into a firm as a complete stranger, not knowing anything about the business, not knowing anything about the people. Next time (hopefully there will be a next time), I'll know better what to do. I just didn't know where to start.

He feels much more comfortable now, and has brought in a few key people whom he trusts, Ron Long from Wellcome as Commercial Director and 32-year-old New Zealander Kirk Stephenson from Morgan Stanley as Finance Director.

His loyalties are strong. Of Ron Long he says

I've got an old pal called Ron Long who taught me how to manage myself in 1982. My father-in-law had two boys he liked – Long and me. He introduced us when we were 25 and said, 'You two should get along because you'll work well together'. And we didn't like each other, and didn't get along for eight years. Then we worked together for three years. When I moved to Amersham I called him up and said, 'I've got a job for you. I need help, please come' and he said, 'Right I'll come!' We are very good friends.

His choice of Kirk Stephenson was equally personal and gives an insight into the strength of his instincts.

Then I recruited a man who had helped me on the first major task at Amersham, a young New Zealander, 30 years of age. I liked him so much but I couldn't get him to move across to Amersham. So I thought, 'How do I keep him on the tab?' I said to his boss, 'I'll retain you to help us with this deal in North America but I want Kirk to do it.' I kept Kirk on board that way and managed to persuade him to join. And he comes home and plays tennis.

Bill Castell has a powerful contemporary network of advisers/friends who provide stimulation and support. This network includes Dennis Stevenson, 47-year-old Chairman of GPA and the Tate Gallery and head of his own consulting agency, who provides him with advice on corporate strategy, and acts as devil's advocate. 'He has got a superb intellect and is a superb supporter. He phones me every Sunday and says, "What have you done wrong, what are you doing and what should you do?" And I confess.' Wally Olins, Head of the Olins Design Group, has been a friend since 1982, and was the influence leading to his first hiring Dennis Stevenson.

He is also close to Bill Muirhead who runs Saatchis US and increasingly to John Studzinski who runs Morgan Stanley in Europe. He appreciates people who will be frank, open and if necessary, critical. 'When we were selling the clinical business at Amersham, John Studzinski phoned me up and said, "Bill, I think that you are abusing your position as Chief Executive, you're not getting the best for your future shareholders and I'm deeply disappointed with you".' Characteristically, Castell took Studzinski's concern seriously, advised his chairman of the call and ultimately all were satisfied with the outcome of the deal.

On joining Amersham, he told the Chairman, Sir Edwin Nixon, that he would leave at 52 because of a conviction that no one should run a business for longer than ten years. His objective at Amersham is to ensure that the company's technical skills make a contribution to advancing health sciences in the next ten years and that he leaves a robust professionally managed company behind him which is self-confident in an achievement culture.

Sir Edwin Nixon rates Castell's leadership as 'superb'.

Selling our Amerlite business (which was based on a non-radio-active technology) to Kodak was crucial to Amersham's recovery. Bill Castell came in and made it happen. We also bought the US subsidiary of Hoffman la Roche which took us back to our roots in radioactivity and yet we were able to reduce our gearing to zero.

Bill inherited what I call a 'McKinsey matrix of management' across the world, in which there was no accountability. He made a quick study, simplified the organisation and pinpointed responsibility.

He has also successfully established a mission and culture from the bottom up at Amersham. I went to one of our offices overseas not long ago and someone had spontaneously put the words of our mission statement 'leadership, integrity, performance and excellence' up on the wall.

An obvious source of satisfaction for Bill Castell has been spearheading Amersham's pioneering role in joint ventures in Russia, first as a partner in Amercard, one of the first British-Soviet healthcare joint ventures with a consortium of soviet partners led by the Cardiovascular Institute in Moscow which now provides diagnostic kits to more than ninety-five clinics. Amersham also set up the British Healthcare consortium with the Moscow Narodny Bank, Glaxo,

Wellcome and Smiths Industries to help build hospitals and provide health care and a desperately needed immunisation programme to control epidemic-level tuberculosis and diphtheria. Most recently, Amersham has entered a joint-venture exporting isotopes from Mayak, the largest of the former nuclear cities, transforming nuclear reactors making warheads into centres for making radio-isotopes for use in hospitals around the world.

He explains how he initiated the desperately needed vaccine business in Russia. 'As a Chief Executive, you are privileged. Doors open, you meet with Ministers of State in this country and overseas. You can start to build an industrial network of individuals, that can help you create wealth. I approached one Chief Executive to provide us with the technology. We then approached the World Bank to provide financial support for the new vaccine plant that will bring a decent level of immunisation to Russians.'

Increasingly he is interested not only in furthering the progress of science and industry in the world but also contributing to the economic/political debate.

Moving beyond the commercial, Bill Castell last year approached the Japanese to find out on what terms they would buy back the Kurile Islands from Russia.

I approached the Russians to determine what would move them politically and financially to sell, and bankers about how to recycle Japanese money to Russia through the IMF so that the IMF in effect could buy American goods, re-stimulate the US economy and allow the US to drop its trade war with Japan.

He notes that his motivation is at heart commercial and clearly sees a need for business to be more responsible corporate citizens and for government to more actively provide an attractive environment for business to grow.

I would like to improve the lot of humanity, not from a philan-thropic point of view but from a commercial point of view. I hope that industry takes a greater responsibility for the welfare, not only of its employees and their families but also for the communities that they work within. We are at a turning point in our lives where global business and global financial markets have changed the responsibility both of businessmen and politicians.

Politicians paradoxically have a greater responsibility now for securing democracy than they had in the past. Politicians must be less concerned with controlling and restricting industry than attracting and promoting it. Otherwise, the country will lose industry and jobs to cheaper wage economies and democracy itself will be undermined to the extent that it is not underpinned by a healthy industrial sector. I understand the arguments against protectionism and in favour of competitive advantage, but I'm unconvinced that lowering trade barriers will not result in a loss of jobs and a reduced standard of living in the higher wage economies such as the UK.

I don't think that we should necessarily ship technology to Korea and China because in five to ten years time, they will become the cheap producers. I get confused by the GATT. You don't derive quality of life from having the best use of worldwide economic resources because it means that this country could become absolutely impoverished. My industrial structural views are strengthening so much that I'm seeking more challenges from academic professionals who can tell me why I've got it wrong.

Bill Castell also hopes that shareholders will start to look for a 'caring approach to capitalism' and that Boards of Directors will look beyond earnings per share and 'to contributing to an economic and social system that builds a society which provides a culture which allows for self-respect even amongst the unemployed and marginalised communities'. Sir Edwin Nixon notes that Castell has 'very unusually' instigated a policy giving his directors five days off a year to devote to community service.

At this stage, Bill Castell has no plans for the next step of his career but sees a number of areas outside the industrial sphere where he might make a contribution.

I'm not a good reader – the vision of retirement sitting down with a good book and doing my gardening is not a vision that I can embrace, but retirement where some of my experience could beneficially be passed on to a developing generation I would find very rewarding.

Bill Castell is critical about his innate conservatism and risk aversion which is often misread because of his enthusiasm. With hindsight he regrets missed opportunities and is concerned that his caution not lead to under-exploiting the skills of Amersham.

On the other hand, the mistake he regrets the most is allowing too many projects to run when he was Managing Director of Wellcome

Biotechnology 'applying too much altruism and not enough reality. In being too enthusiastic and not making the tough decisions to cause focus and concentration of effort, I lessened the opportunity of converting ideas to real product.'

Generally, he is philosophical about his mistakes. 'If you are prepared to make decisions you have to be able to live with your mistakes. They can't all be successes.' He recognises too that the source of some of his regrets positively fuels his efforts and open approach, for instance, his sense of loss at not experiencing Oxbridge college life:

> I have always felt underprivileged that I never experienced Oxbridge campus life at university, although the spin off is that now my life is my campus, which may not have been true. If I had had this experience at university, I might have been a less motivated individual.

FAMILY AND PERSONAL LIFE

Bill Castell was unique in putting family details first on his CV and stating upfront that his family came first which is of course consistent with his early priority to have a stable and happy home life. 'There is no doubt that if it's a choice between the family and work, then it is the family. We got very close to this choice when I was at Wellcome but the quality of life has improved in the last three years.' None the less he works long hours, leaving home at 7.00 a.m. and returning by 8.00 p.m. or later. The month we spoke he had been to the US twice and Japan once.

His outside interests include design in the community and taking design to primary and secondary schools, inspired by Wally Olins who first got him involved in design bursaries at the Royal Society of Arts and then in design education. In 1990 he went with the Prince of Wales, on a BITC visit with four other chief executives to a run-down mountain village in Wales. The Prince of Wales said, 'This is the worst thing I have ever seen in my life. What do you think?' Castell responded that he thought it was better than downtown New York 'which he found a bit hard'.

He has since taken a special interest in this underprivileged village with 95 per cent unemployment, 25 per cent population turnover every three months, and devastating health and social problems such as Aids and heroin.

> I don't do enough. I go down three or four times a year and spend a day networking for the churchman who cares for the town. He appreciates the support, even if I can't do much. I went there one Saturday to the dedication of his church. There were eight denominations there and the place was full. Yet no one goes to this town because of its terrible reputation. I got to the top of the stairs and he came and put his arms around me and said, 'Thank you so much for coming, my good friend!' I felt very humbled and very moved.

Although Bill Castell is not religious, he believes strongly in an ethical framework:

> Strong personal and family values are very important and making sure that you have made the best with what you've got. I don't go to church, but I like to be able to look at myself in the mirror and my wife in the eyes everyday. To be true to oneself, to the family, to one's colleagues and friends has to be the acid test.

He relaxes little and badly – with his children, mowing the lawn, tennis, a bit of sport. He also reads little outside of work, except the papers – the *Financial Times*, and the *Sun* he borrows from his driver, Gary. He enjoys taking his children to different countries on holidays and reads about the country intensely while he is there.

LEADERSHIP AND SUCCESS FACTORS

In spite of Bill Castell's deference about his early academic achievement, a close fellow business leader confirms that Bill Castell is not only 'very clever' but unquestionably has the clear-sighted grasp of the big picture, strategic vision and outstanding personal qualities required for true leadership:

> He is clearly one of the best business leaders of his generation. He has done at Amersham what many thought was undoable – changed its focus, identified opportunities, taken risks and made it happen. He is also, to an unusual extent, a real human being,

excellent on people issues and the reverse of self-promoting, very honest and exceptionally open.

It is certainly true that the insecurity which drives him and his own capacity to examine himself, to change and to learn have been instrumental to his success, as well as the inevitable luck.

In advising his three children at 15, 18 and 19 about how to make life and career decisions, he would say: 'Be true to yourself, set goals that are achievable but will stretch you and try to match your skills realistically to whatever walk of life you wish to pursue. And don't feel that greatness necessarily gives happiness.' He also encourages them to finish their education in order to have the freedom he enjoyed.

There is no ideal path to the top, and application, wisdom, luck and a bit of leadership and sound personal qualities are above all necessary.

> The easiest route is to be consistent, sincere and to have integrity. Playing politics doesn't work in the long run. I am sure that people look at me and say Bill was always over-ambitious and highly political. Bill looks at himself and says, 'I have always been ambitious but in order to influence, not for power for its own sake.' Most importantly I believe that I have squared with people and I've never wilfully played political games to gain a stronger position for myself.

He cites the example of Ronnie Cresswell, his boss at Wellcome from 1982 to 1986, who asked his advice about whether to go or to stay in the company. Castell advised him to go for various reasons, but also pointed out that he had a conflict of interest in advising him, as he was himself in a possible position to gain from his departure with a Board position. Bill Castell is open to the point of vulnerability, and it is not only difficult to imagine his being political but his reputation belies this.

His bias in favour of education and continual learning is also unambiguous.

> It is vital to acquire a degree, whether a 2:2, 2:1 or a first. A business or finance degree gives the necessary understanding of cash flow, prices and costs to enable you to run a market stall, which will eventually be necessary. However, getting a senior job in

science is less about qualifications than experience, continuing to be at the cutting edge of scientific understanding and understanding how to nurture scientific genius.

Although Castell acknowledges that the manager who has moved through three or four different companies or industries is going to be a greater generalist, he believes that western trends toward greater mobility will remove a sense of security that will ultimately disadvantage western business.

Somehow or other we must build the experience curve but within a family – within an organisation. When you come to critical decisions, you tend to turn to the man who you can rely on, whose integrity and culture you understand rather than the new specialist with absolutely no idea of how to interpret your company's style and values. I rely on people who are strong achievers and good corporate citizens.

Although there is no single ideal path to reach the top it is necessary by your mid-thirties to have moved beyond a narrow speciality.

There is a critical time in the executive's development between 32 and 36. If by that time you haven't been identified and put through a pattern of jobs which gives you generalist experience, then your suitability for Board directorship is much less and you are therefore ill-prepared for general management and chief executiveship. The Japanese do things much better than we do. I would much prefer to have a functional specialist who is also a generalist. I really like my Head of Purchasing to have had a stint in marketing and maybe production before he becomes Head of Purchasing. It doesn't mean you can't go up a functional ladder and become Director of Finance or Director of Marketing but it is much better if you have had other functional responsibilities along the way so that you can understand the other point of view. Age 32 to 36 is a good time to go out and head-hunt. Many able young people are left in a function awaiting dead man's shoes at that age and their chances of succeeding are much reduced.

7

Liam Strong
Chief Executive, Sears Plc

Date of birth:	6 January 1945
Place of birth:	Enniskillen, Northern Ireland
Nationality:	British
Marital status:	Married
Family:	One daughter, one son

Education:	Portora Royal School (three subjects at 'A' level equivalent) Trinity College, Dublin BA (Philosophy)

Career:

1967–1971	Procter & Gamble Brand Management
1971–1988	Reckitt & Colman Product Group Manager, Household Products Planning Manager, Group Headquarters Marketing Director, Leisure Businesses General Manager, Leisure Businesses Vice President, Sunset Designs, California, USA Director, Pharmaceuticals President US Food Business, New Jersey, USA
1988–91	British Airways Director of Marketing Director of Marketing and Operations
1991 to date	Sears Plc Chief Executive

Outside appointments:	Inchcape, Non-executive Director London Health Partnership, Chairman
Interests:	Reading, opera, theatre, walking, sailing, bicycle riding, shooting

INTRODUCTION

Liam Strong took over as Chief Executive of the £2 billion retailing group Sears in 1992 when it was reputed to be the 'biggest mess in British retailing' and 'one of the London stock market's favourite takeover targets'. With a strong marketing and operations background and as one of two possible heirs apparent to Colin Marshall at British Airways, he was approached by Sears to revitalise their large but moribund retail business.

Two years later, with net margins up from 4.5 per cent to 6.2 per cent, a pretax loss of £48 million had been transformed into a £38 million profit. Strong has a long-term programme to make Sears an outstanding retailer and has already introduced massive change – 50 per cent of the top 200 managers are new, four businesses have been sold and standards redefined throughout the company.

At the heart of Liam Strong's success is not only his intellect and ability as a strategic thinker, but also a genuine curiosity that leads him continuously to learn and to 'collect new ideas'. He actively looks outside his own company and industry, and maintains a network of contacts worldwide who keep him informed of best management practice. It is no doubt this life-long learning approach to his work that has enabled him to change industries so often and so successfully – from consumer goods to pharmaceuticals to airlines to retail.

Northern Irish, Liam Strong was educated at a progressive liberal grammar school and has a philosophy degree from Trinity College, Dublin. Although he has never had long-term career goals, his approach to planning his next career move has invariably been based on careful analysis and understanding of options. The result is a classic blue-chip marketing background with Procter & Gamble, followed by alternating senior staff and line roles for seventeen years with Reckitt & Colman (including two assignments to the US), and two years as the high-profile Director of Marketing and Operations at British Airways.

Strong describes himself as principally motivated by the challenge of making things work, although he does not discount the importance of money. In his team, he values independent thinking and strength of character, as well as commitment to work, maturity, integrity and the ability to 'bring people to the party'. He would advise people professionally above all to follow their interests, play to their strengths, and not to worry excessively about their career.

Liam Strong is happily married with two teenage children, and consciously strives to maintain a balance between personal and professional lives that may tip 'either way', but overall is relatively even.

What has been important in the development of this inquisitive chief executive of the younger generation and what are his views on decision-making, career development and leadership?

EARLY INFLUENCES

Liam Strong grew up as the eldest of three children in a village in Northern Ireland, an environment where money was relatively tight and key factors were an ambitious mother and a progressive school. 'As is usual in such cases, I had quite a strong-minded mother but she later said to me – "I wanted you to do well, but it didn't mean you had to go and leave Ireland as well!"'

Undoubtedly, the most significant influence in his early life was his school. Portora Royal School was an old school, with a liberal tradition and broad view of the world, at that time with students from both Northern Ireland and Eire, as well as from overseas. His perspective was consequently outward- looking, not least because 'In the part of Ireland I come from people traditionally grew up with the intention of leaving. It's always been an emigrants' sort of place'. In understanding his life and experience, Strong believes that religion, whether Catholic or Protestant, has not been a significant factor.

Certainly money influenced his very early thoughts about career. His first career thought at school was to become a chemist, as he was the man in the village who appeared to make the most money. 'I was saved from being a pharmacist because my science wasn't strong enough!'

His choice at 18 to study Philosophy at Trinity College was based on inclination not strategy. 'It seemed a good idea at the time.' Halfway through his final year at university, he conceived a tentative interest in becoming a journalist. Concluding that it was too late when his would-be journalist peers had been writing throughout university, he briefly considered the Bar, before rejecting it as requiring too much further training and time. By default, he next chose business.

CAREER DECISION-MAKING AND DEVELOPMENT

Strong's understanding of what drives him is a classic description of what psychologists term 'intrinsic' motivation, derived from the challenge of the work itself.

> It may sound silly, but I get enormous satisfaction simply out of really making things work. I think you are always interested to see how well you can do. When I reach my level of competence then that's fine with me. I will have had a good run and I'll go and do something else.

He acknowledges too that money to a certain extent has always motivated him. 'It's a score card. However, I don't think anyone works for money alone. Certainly, I could have made quite different career choices which would have made me more money, and probably could even now.'

Strong acknowledges that his motivation has changed over time. Recognition from others too is seen in Maslovian terms – once one has it, it ceases to motivate strongly:

> Recognition is important, but it's not a be-all-and-end-all. I'd rather have respect than undying affection. To be seen as some-body who is consistent and straight is important. To put too high a value on what people think of you can distort your actions. Recognition is a little bit like possessions. It seems important to you before you get it, but once you have had a bit of it, the point of difference disappears.

If he fell into business, his first career move was made rationally and strategically. After researching the various business functions, and deciding that marketing 'seemed sensible', he went out of his way to get to know Harvard Business School graduates in Dublin who advised him about the best companies for a business career. In this context he notes 'it never fails to amaze me how little research young people do'. He chose Procter & Gamble as personally the best fit. 'They were very decisive, very clear cut. They were looking for a distinct profile – very bright people who took their work very seriously and who were prepared to go to quite a lot of pains to get things right.'

Although he is impressed with people who follow an early goal, Strong has never had a clear career objective himself, but on a case-by-case basis, analyses whether a move will widen or narrow his career options against some broad criteria important to him at the time. To an extent 'one has to be a positive fatalist and take opportunities as they present themselves. A lot of corporate life is happenstance'.

None the less, he believes that there is inevitably an element of preparation for the next step.

> If you are doing well, a decent job, then at one level you will be looking at the next level and asking yourself what is needed to be successful at that level. If you are a Managing Director of a Division you will from time to time ask yourself questions from a Chief Executive's point of view. You begin to ask 'Could I do that?', which is how you define whether you have reached your level of competence. I don't think people knowingly put themselves into situations where they think they are going to fail, so they must have concluded at some stage that they could do the job above. I also suspect that by the time you get to your forties, you have a reasonably clear idea of the way you want to lead your life, so that you are running your life, rather than it running you. That wouldn't seem like a plan – it's just something that happens over time.

Along with an understanding of the reality of limited planning, Strong is convinced that people rise to the level of their ability unless they are very unlucky.

His four years in brand management with Procter & Gamble, widely regarded as the best training ground for talented marketeers, taught him about the importance of the highest standards, of ensuring that each product had an identifiable and clear competitive advantage.

He left Procter & Gamble because he was interested in an international career and in those days most of the people given this opportunity were Americans. He had also found himself uncomfortable in a culture then dominated by a command and control management style, and sought a more open, direct environment.

His move in 1971 to a product development role at Reckitt & Colman began a seventeen-year career in marketing, development and general management, across the company's businesses and with two international postings to the United States. The themes of these years he identifies as the management of change, and the alternation between line and staff roles: these gave him experience not only in securing performance improvement and managing complexity as a line manager in business units, but also in seeing the business in the round and problem solving from the centre.

During these years too, Reckitt & Colman evolved from an 'amiable but rather old-fashioned company' to a business in the eighties that grew pretax profits each year by just under 20 per cent, under the leadership of John West.

Liam Strong's first two years were spent as a Product Group Manager, developing a new business in air fresheners (now one of Reckitt's largest product categories) and learning the importance of management by persuasion, 'that people will run with your ideas if they have embraced them as their own'.

His next move to Group Headquarters as Planning Manager with Michael Colman, the Group Planning Director, provided him with a broader insight into the business portfolio; how to analyse opportunities, the market and the competition. He worked with some 'great people' including Ian Dobbie, the present Finance Director, and Vernon Sankey, now the Chief Executive, and describes the experience as 'as good as going to business school'.

Next, as Marketing Director, then General Manager of Reckitt & Colman's leisure businesses, his job was to develop market positions and to sell businesses on that were not appropriate.

> This was a crash course in managing change. The critical issue was to hit a pace of change that people could absorb. With people up in the air, uncertain and insecure, I learned that it was essential to be upfront. Even if you don't know yourself, it helps to share that with people. Also, and most important, change will only be successful if there is something in it for everyone.

His decision to go to California with Reckitt & Colman as Vice President of Sunset Designs in 1980 was both risky and a developmental watershed – it took him out of the mainstream, was made against the advice of those pressing him to stay at the centre, and was instrumental in preparing him for key future moves.

> Basically, I went to California because I had always wanted to work in the States. I love the USA. As it turned out, going to California was one of the better things I did, you learn a lot. Out of that I got into pharmaceuticals which I enjoyed enormously, and

which built up my confidence to deal with very technical subjects. I found I was able to understand and enjoy it. This gave me the confidence one job after that to go for British Airways. And if I hadn't gone for BA, I wouldn't have considered a retail company, so there is a certain logic.

Supporting his conviction that much of corporate life is happenstance however, he acknowledges that his move into pharmaceuticals was less career logic than chance, caused by the then incumbent's moving overseas for personal reasons.

His experience in the US not only broadened him culturally, but also initiated a deep appreciation of the importance of teams that continues today: 'The leisure businesses were small with a variable quality of management. Each business had been dependent on single individuals, and it was only through building up management teams that we could rid ourselves of this exposure.'

His next experience from line to staff again as International Director in Pharmaceuticals provided him with a model of how teams should work.

In pharmaceuticals, there was a very collegiate atmosphere; senior functional people ran the business and they had been together for some time and everyone understood their role. People focused on their job without much politics or jostling for position. That is the sort of team we are building now at Sears.

In pharmaceuticals, with large product ranges and complex channels of distribution, his role was to shorten product research lead times, and work with licensees around the world to get compounds to market as soon as possible. At one stage, he visited 21 countries in nine months. After eighteen months he also became responsible for the UK business and prescription and OTC (over the counter medicines).

When Reckitt bought a new food business in the US, Strong was sent to integrate it with the existing businesses. He closed factories, merged sales and distribution, sold part of the business, and put together a new headquarters unit in New Jersey, pulled from the mid-west, upstate New York and also from New Jersey itself. 'We recruited one hundred people in six months, and built a data centre in nine.'

At this stage, he was rung twice to join British Airways as Marketing Director, responsible for all revenue generation, 30,000 people in customer operations, as well as large cargo and charter units. This was an opportunity too good to miss. 'BA were offering me an opportunity to return to England to a service business. It was also a business undergoing considerable change, a high-tech business and very international.' After 14 months he took over the Operations Director portfolio and effectively became the Chief Operating Officer running everything but finance, pilots and engineering.

He is proud of what he achieved in his relatively short stay at British Airways.

> I helped BA to accept what all their data had been saying for about a year; that service levels had plateaued – we had made amazing improvements in the first half of the eighties, but complacency was creeping in and our competitors were catching up. We had to make another determined effort to improve and again widen the competitive gap.
>
> We introduced relationship marketing, collecting the data that allowed us to build real relationships with our high yield customers. We also radically overhauled our decision support and planning systems, the ones that help to keep us on time. Finally we were able to manage our way through and rebound from the Gulf War. And as we did that we used the recession to adjust our manning and cost levels which had crept up in the 1980s boom.

His decision to join Sears was both a positive embracing of the challenge of another large service business that needed repositioning, as well as a recognition of the limitations of his future at British Airways.

> The airline was the creation of John King and Colin Marshall, and one of the great turnarounds in the western world. It was clear that Colin would continue to be hands-on for some time, and I did not relish a waiting game in a company that already had been transformed. British Airways has some of the best people in the world. That quality down the line was probably the only thing I missed from BA in the early days at Sears. As we have increased training and development in Sears, we are finding just as many enthusiastic and effective people as we had at BA. It is just a matter of time.
>
> I have to say also, that above a certain level in the company, BA had more politics than any sensible person would wish. I dislike politics as it focuses people on the wrong questions. I was beginning to think about looking for an opportunity to turn-

around a company, when it was suggested over lunch that I should look at Sears.

Since joining Sears, Strong is particularly proud that while improving short-term profits he has also significantly invested for the future, both in people and in new retail formats. He has increased net margin significantly, changed 50 per cent of the top 200 managers, sold several businesses and redefined standards for all businesses. He sees this as a long-term programme to create an outstanding retail business, and does not personally look beyond this.

Liam Strong sees the value of changing industries as he did, from consumer goods to pharmaceuticals to airlines to retail, as providing an understanding and perspective not possible otherwise, and acquiring 'the skill of learning to learn'.

As with many chief executives of his generation, Strong has never had a mentor, but has learned from a lot of people he has worked with: from Colin Marshall at British Airways, about how to manage a service business and from John West, his Chief Executive at Reckitt & Colman, about how to manage a mature business with a strong bottom line. He admires Jack Welch at General Electric for taking an already successful business and making it ever more successful.

Strong keeps in touch with best practice and the latest management thinking through an informal network of friends and advisers scattered around the world, including at Harvard, MIT and IN-SEAD.

> I like ideas. I continuously collect them. At any given time I have got a pile of cuttings and clippings. I like to stay up with what people are thinking. It is essential to have a sense of where things are moving. There is, for example, a growing emphasis on team-work which will shift thinking and management style in the nineties.

He also believes in a 'healthy sense of paranoia'.

> I'm constantly asking myself 'If it's this easy why hasn't someone else done it?' I regularly think of what could go wrong. Every week or two you just mentally review where everything is; what you think is right; who you haven't heard from; what's looking too good. Does it all fit, is it consistent?

Liam Strong can identify no single cataclysmic failure, but many things that he could have done better, or more quickly. Specifically, his first new product development ideas on joining Reckitt & Colman were far too complicated and ambitious. Also, Reckitt & Colman's development into leisure businesses in the late 1970s taught him the benefits of 'sticking to your knitting'. 'The grass is rarely greener on the other side of the fence.' But he sees his most significant failure, and area of greatest development, as related to people.

> The biggest problem of all, is not being tough minded enough on people decisions. As you get older, it is important to trust your initial judgements and not say, 'Well, we'll let it wait.' Performance is based on a combination of the right people and clear direction. When you have avoided a tough decision on people, it usually costs you, the company and most importantly the people involved, more in the end. Certainly, I have made more than a few mistakes in my time.

On the other hand:

> How do you learn if you don't get it wrong? The first time you change things you don't communicate enough. You learn by the experience of people not understanding, not coming with you. One of the things you can learn about till you die, is managing teams. Putting groups together that really will work effectively is one of the greatest challenges. At Sears, as we change a lot of people, we use Belbin's work on the roles of the various team members, whether as completers, planners and so on, to tell us if a group isn't working right, not why it is.
>
> It's interesting to know whether you analyse the reasons for your success as closely as you analyse the reasons why something failed. I suspect one doesn't think about successes as much as one thinks about the things that didn't work so well. Above all, it is critically important to celebrate success.

Strong is hopeful that tolerance is increasing for people who have had significant failures in business life.

> Frankly, it depends on you. It's to do with your ability to rethink yourself and go out and do it again. We all know people who have come a cropper. You can see the one who has got a chance of succeeding next time and another who basically has lost self confidence. In the US, people who have failed are valued if they are seen to have learned from their failure.

Strong has lived in Northern Ireland, England and the United States and has worked extensively across borders and cultures. As an Irishman, he is 'comfortable' in England, having lived here longer than anywhere else, and it is only when he compares his reactions to the United States with his English friends that he realises he is different. 'I am Irish, not British. I like being Irish. One of the differences between being Irish and being British or English is the way in which you react to America. For me, America is not a foreign country.'

FAMILY AND PERSONAL LIFE

In common with many other 'new' chief executives, balance between personal and professional lives is consciously important to Liam Strong.

> My approach to work is essential to the sort of person I am, and a large part of my life is organised to allow me to work hard and put in the time required. But the other side of my life is to be with my family, and we are very closely knit. I understand how Jackie and the kids are doing in their battles, and they understand how I am doing in mine. My wife is undoubtedly my closest confidante. Her input and advice have been invaluable over the years. I couldn't have done it without her. As a family, we are all very verbal, opinionated people and a lot of my spare time is spent talking and justifying myself as the most absentee member of the family.
>
> I believe you can't really claim success at work if it has been at the expense of a personal life; but realistically I suspect the best to hope for is a gentle tug of war between the two.

Strong works less hard now, but in a more organised and rigorous way than he did in his twenties, although business life strays more into private time. He takes one day off a week completely, reserving one day on the weekend for issues requiring thought.

> The thing that bedevils you in senior positions is how little time you get to think about things, and senior people should add value by the way they see things. Many people implement better than I do. My job is to see things differently; to spot what others haven't picked up.

He also takes time to renew himself mentally and maintain 'some breadth'. He reads 'all the time and everything', at the time we spoke ranging from a thriller on military history, to Joseph Conrad and a book about the Knights Templar. Management books are read only if they directly address an issue that he is grappling with at the moment, 'Otherwise it is a bit like doing a finance course if you don't run a company; you forget it ten minutes later.'

Strong relaxes by walking, particularly mountain walking; shooting; playing tennis with his daughter, and riding a bicycle down the tow-path to Richmond Park early in the morning; and he has just taken up sailing: 'Something new to learn'. He loves theatre, films, the opera. 'I've always had a reasonable feeling for visual style. It's one of the things I particularly enjoy in the retail business.'

LEADERSHIP AND SUCCESS FACTORS

Liam Strong believes that there is no such thing as a born leader, that leadership is contextual and therefore no single model can be provided.

> It's difficult to put your finger on the qualities of leadership because the oddest people can be very good leaders and they can lead in all sorts of different ways. Some people lead from the middle, some from behind, some from the front and some from the side. What you are looking for is someone who can actually build a group of people, and get them to perform. One does well by virtue of working with a number of people, and therefore it is not really appropriate to think in terms of individual success.

Insightfully, Strong believes that the independence and strength of character required to be successful in the second part of one's career, are qualities one survives in spite of initially. Inevitably, one must learn an acceptable balance. 'In the first half of their career people who are challengers of the status quo, and comfortable taking their own decisions, without being part of a supportive group, learn about organisational and interpersonal dynamics, and how far they can challenge the existing order and still be productive. Those who get too out of line with others, cannot lead by definition.'

Leaders are also emotionally mature, with an ability not only to tolerate, but actively to seek alternative points of view. In this context, Strong clearly identifies the danger of leadership.

> The more senior you get, the more you have people tending to agree with you – the walk on water syndrome is insidious. It is critical to give people permission to disagree with you and to create an atmosphere where people are speaking their minds. Sometimes you really have to search out the truth by looking at the expression on peoples' faces and saying, 'Well, I'm not sure that you really agree.' The number of people who are prepared to go to the trouble of disagreeing with you is very few. I've moved from company to company. If you change industries you have to listen even more, you really have to test your thinking and your hypotheses all the time.

Although leaders must be highly motivated, Strong identifies excessive personal ambition as not only counter-productive but obvious.

> To a certain extent you get things because you want them. Running a race, the difference between number one and number two is simply that one person had more motivation than the other. To be self-motivated, to spend a lot of time doing something you take very seriously, you need to be ambitious. But if you are excessively ambitious, then it distorts everything you do. I see people who, as they make a recommendation, think 'Well, that's the business issue, now how is it going to suit me'. Over time it becomes quite transparent and there are limits you put on how far you can trust their judgement.

He believes that those people paying too much attention to organisational politics beyond the 'normal politics of human interaction whenever people get together', are asking the wrong questions.

He believes strongly that intelligence is required to get you to the high levels and keep you there. But it is not sufficient. A strong dose of common sense is also essential.

At the heart of his own success is:

> Never giving up, combined with a structured approach to the business issues that begins with data, develops into a direction, ensures that everyone knows the direction, and builds the skills to deliver. Finally the toughness to make it happen is essential, but must depend on the ability to motivate people. You can't force

people to do things, you can only give them a good reason for doing it, and if you have to order them, then you have failed. The transfer of the idea and then engendering the belief that it can be done, is central. There is a Chinese proverb, 'Tell me and I will forget, show me and I may remember, involve me and I will care'.

He also believes that he is successful because he has been able to use his gifts, physical, emotional, mental and interpersonal, to the fullest, i.e. the work suits him.

I am enormously privileged to be able to really have a go with as many aspects of my personality as I can. It's physically demanding and I am very energetic. It's emotionally demanding and I can put up with a lot of conflict. Intellectually, I get presented with demanding problems, and socially I meet and work with a wide range of interesting, pleasant people.

He recognises that his greatest strength lies in thinking and strategy, rather than in implementation: this conclusion is wholeheartedly supported by one of his close international network of advisers.

Liam's major 'leadership lever' is that he is extremely intelligent, with an incredible capacity to learn and learn quickly. He is genuinely curious, actively looks outside to learn from business leaders in different sectors, and is personally reflective and a good listener. He is also an excellent creative and strategic thinker.

Just as Strong identifies the importance of having the 'toughness to make it happen', so his adviser confirms: 'Liam also applies significant pressure on himself and on others to perform. With this pressure comes the risk of strong resistance. But he is certainly viewed as fair and a person of integrity, even if he's not always described as soft or kind!'

Liam Strong is an ENTJ in Myers Briggs' terms, and very strongly 'thinking' and 'judging', which might account for his not always naturally taking peoples' feelings fully into account in singlemindedly focusing on results (most business leaders have quite strong thinking and judging preferences). As a self-reflective life-long learner, 'with a bit of humour about himself', and a keen understanding of the importance of motivating people, his adviser notes that Liam Strong is more likely than most to develop less-preferred ways of looking at the world, and to change and to grow.

Those people Liam Strong has recruited in the last two or three years as future leaders have a common profile:

> They take their work very seriously, have unquestioned integrity and strength of character, and an ability to bring people with them and to work with the rest of the organisation rather than against it. I look for reasonably strong-minded people and the best I can get. In some ways you are disappointed if the thought doesn't flicker through your mind, 'Am I going to be able to manage this person's expectations?' Some will actually create turbulence, but I would rather have people who will move things and not just manage the status quo. After six months, twelve months, eighteen months you see the benefits. I also look for a real command of their particular skills, a lot of common sense and a lack of what I'd call an inflated sense of themselves. Any job is just a job. Although it may be senior, it's no more or less important than any other role in the company. I suppose it's a certain sense of democracy. While I do love to be in charge, I don't like hierarchy.

Strong believes that the business leader in the year 2000 will be different.

> Organisations will be more informal and workforces more challenging. One will lead from among rather than on top; it will feel more like a network than a hierarchy. Also technical skills will become increasingly sophisticated and rapidly evolving. Chief executives will have to hold their own with staff who are increasingly expert.

Liam Strong would advise people not only to be true to themselves in following their greatest interests and strengths, but also to be prepared to change direction if a mistake is made, not to be in too great a hurry, and to take relevant advice:

> It is most important to do something you really enjoy; something that you are good at, that suits you, that you can really have a go at. If you take a very holistic approach, oddly enough, the least stress is caused, not necessarily by getting into the least stressful situations, but by actually doing something where you can bring most of yourself to bear. That could be being a train driver or a pharmacist or anything. All I say to my children is 'Look, I just want you to be able to use your abilities. I don't mind what you are.'

It is important having found something you enjoy and that you're good at, to be prepared to adjust over time if you don't hit it right first time. Not everyone hits the right line first time round, but there is a line for most strong-minded, capable people. Also, you can take a lot more time in your twenties finding it than many people think. I have probably always been in too much of a hurry. Above all, as you look for your line, take advice. The first step in getting ahead is to listen.

Strong believes that aiming to be Chief Executive of a large company is wrong-minded. 'That is too far ahead to be a workable objective. My advice would be to select a field with some growth in it, one that uses your skills and stimulates you, and then take it from there.'

8

Ann Iverson

Chief Executive, Kay-Bee Toys

Date of birth:	25 February 1944
Place of birth:	Michigan, USA
Nationality:	American
Marital status:	Divorced
Family:	One son, one daughter

| Education: | Arcadia High School, California, High School Diploma |
| | Arizona State University |

Career:

1960–1966	Bullock's Department Stores, Los Angeles
	Department Manager/Executive Trainee
1966–1971	Cohen's Department Stores, Arizona
	Buyer for Ladies' Fashion
1971–1978	Diamond's, Arizona
	Buying Controller for Ladies' Sportswear
1978–1980	Goldwater's, Arizona
	Buying Director
1980–1982	Harzfield's, Kansas City
	Buying Director
1982–1984	T H Mandy, Virginia
	Stores Director/Buying Director
1984–1989	Bloomingdale's, New York
	Operating Vice President
1989–1990	Bonwit Teller, New York
	Senior Vice President, Stores
	Regional Vice President
1990 – 1994	Storehouse Plc
1990–1992	Director of Stores, British Home Stores
1992 – 1994	Chief Executive, Mothercare
1994 to date	Kay-Bee Toys, Massachusetts, USA
	Chief Executive

| Outside appointments: | Laura Ashley |
| | Non-executive Director |

| Interests: | Ballet, theatre, symphony music, museums, shopping |
| | – observing the customer, travel and new cultures |

INTRODUCTION

Ann Iverson, one of a handful of women ever to reach the top in UK business, was brought across the Atlantic in 1990 to bring a fresh new approach to retailing in the UK. She helped to take Storehouse subsidiary BHS from a near loss situation in 1990 to a profit of forty million pounds in 1993. From 1992 to 1994 she headed up Mothercare where she successfully repositioned the business by creating a fun and appealing environment for children. Iverson accomplished two turnarounds in the UK in spite of never having had international experience and never having lived or worked outside the US.

Highly motivated and hardworking, in style Ann Iverson is refreshingly direct, open and frank and she expects the same honesty in her team. Her approach to life and to work is unfailingly positive – she sees the good in every situation. Her strengths lie not only in her hands-on understanding and grasp of retail but also her ability, evolved over time, to think strategically about the business.

Spending most of her working life in the United States, Ann Iverson has had eight career moves, often contributed to by personal considerations and generated by job offers based on her reputation in retail. Her guiding principle has been the selection of environments where her strengths and drive are most nourished.

The first twenty years of Ann Iverson's career in retail were spent largely in buying, and the opportunity to move into operations gave her an unusual edge to move on to general management. Identifying no mentors as such, Ann Iverson has been influenced by many bosses, including a senior woman who taught her to rely on her brain and competence rather than on her gender to succeed. The glass ceiling and discrimination do not appear to have been a factor in her career.

The mother of a 28-year-old son and an 18-year-old daughter, although she has never had a career break, she puts her children first in her priorities.

What has been important in the development of a leading Chief Executive in retail, who has spent most of her professional life in the United States and how would she advise others about how to succeed?

EARLY INFLUENCES

Ann Iverson grew up in a small mid-western town in the United States, the youngest of three children of a successful senior manager in an expanding furnace business. Her father died of cancer when she was five years old, and throughout her childhood she heard sincere praise of his professional and personal stature. 'He was very, very well respected and strongly admired and influenced a lot of people's lives.' Although absent, he provided a professional role model.

Her mother never worked and was not ambitious for her daughter, however she also provided a role model both as a person and in her leadership role in voluntary organisations, and was emotionally supportive.

> My mother was a wonderful at-home person – not the kind who was always baking but the kind who was always there to talk to and really a very good friend. She was a powerful woman in terms of inner strength. Although she didn't work, she was very active in every organisation she belonged to and was either on the Board or was President, so her involvement was very meaningful. So, in a way, she was a good model though she didn't drive me to any professional ambition.

Her relationship with her two brothers, five and ten years older, also promoted early independence.

> Some of my style and aggressiveness (in those days called tomboy nature) came from the friendship with my brothers. It began with very strong sibling rivalry. I was the youngest, the only girl and kind of spoiled. My mother would go out and ask them to take care of their little sister and they would turn out the lights and make scary noises! I learned to stand on my own two feet from them. They wouldn't let me be a sissy or silly.

Over time, her eldest brother became almost a surrogate father figure and she remains very close to both brothers. Overall, she describes her family life as very happy and supportive.

Ann Iverson attributes much of her success to her early upbringing and environment.

> My childhood experience taught me not to give up, not to be a loser, to always go for first place. I used to be a relay runner and a short distance runner in school, and I broke a record when I was in the sixth grade for running! I remembered the tremendous satisfaction of winning and how hard I had worked yet I knew I could

have worked harder. So I was pleased I had won but there was more I could have done.

Ann Iverson attended high school first in Michigan, then for the last two years in California, when her family moved states. In her last year of school, she worked part-time in Bullock's Department Store. She instantly loved retailing. 'I thought it was ideal. I loved clothes, I was making money, got a discount and earned credits towards my high school qualification.'

Although she next pursued a degree in elementary education at the University of Arizona, largely because 'in 1962 it was the most comfortable and accepted path for women to go down', when she got married at the age of 20 she quickly converted her summer experience at Bullock's into a full-time job.

> When I got married I didn't consider staying on at university. I liked university, but I was more interested in actually doing something. I didn't have the patience and didn't see the benefit of sitting in classes all day long. I couldn't see the end result. My family on both sides was quite academic, doctors, lawyers, professors. There was always a strong encouragement to stay in school. I probably rebelled against this. I wanted to find my independence, which came from two avenues in those years, marriage and work, having some financial freedom.

CAREER DECISION-MAKING AND DEVELOPMENT

In most ways Ann Iverson's career pattern follows that of the 'go-getter', one of the five career patterns identified by White, Cox and Cooper (1992) as common for successful women, and characterised by: leaving school at sixteen to eighteen; with a clear idea about preferred occupation; entry on the bottom rung of the chosen career ladder; developing a reputation and proving ability and finally concern with reaching the top.

In Iverson's case, the career orientation and desire to reach the top evolved as she grew more confident with continuing success. She knew early on that she was interested in retail, and initially worked out of financial necessity, with no career goal or plan. Increasingly, her motivation was based on job satisfaction and the gratification of achieving results, until she was working because she wanted to. Although she has two children, she has never taken a career break.

> Our first child came when I was 21, I worked because I needed to. As the years went on I finally discovered that not only did I like it, I was good at it. It dawned on me that I could actually achieve something. I didn't ever have a desire at a very young age to be president of something in the way my 18-year-old daughter has always wanted to be a geriatric doctor.
>
> I didn't think in terms of a career but work was a tremendous motivation. I was challenged to accomplish something better than I had before but I wasn't goal-driven to reach a high level – your goals change as you grow older.

As her career has developed she has become motivated more by helping others to develop, showing the classic shift predicted by Levinson into 'generativity'. 'In the early stages of my career development, results motivated me – results were a combination of extremely high job satisfaction and the financial rewards that went with them. Over time this has evolved into trying to develop an ability to help other people to grow. Passing this understanding on becomes extremely gratifying.'

Iverson's career in retail went from strength to strength, with eight upward career moves, sometimes influenced by personal considerations and increasingly as the result of active job offers from the employer. In all cases, she would evaluate the environment and business culture to ensure that her own strengths and interests would be nourished and fulfilled.

Jobs were selected for their developmental opportunities, taking her through buying, then unusually into operations which together equipped her for general management.

After working with Bullock's Department Stores in Los Angeles progressing to Department Manager, Ann Iverson joined Cohen's Department Stores in Arizona after she had re-married because she was actively attracted to the role of buyer for ladies fashion. Cohen's was a small, family-owned operation. Over five years she grew to know the customers by name and learned the fundamentals of buying.

Ann Iverson next moved to Diamond's, a division of Dayton Hudson, and moved through the ranks to become Buying Controller for ladies' sportswear. This was a much larger transition, with a steeper learning curve. She learned particularly from a senior woman, both about what to do and what to avoid.

> At Diamond's I learned about the very political, big store, public company arena. I worked for a woman who was one of the first women in merchandising and buying in America. She constantly reminded me that there were just a handful of senior women in retail in the country. She was tough, and actually taught her women staff how to survive in a man's world and get along with the notches above in the organisation chart. She taught me how to do the job without gender becoming an issue and that was quite important. She made sure that we were totally prepared so that we were in a position to sell our ideas or solutions to problems, regardless of being a woman or a man. For that period in my life, she was a very strong role model.

Over a seven-year period, Iverson went through several presidents at Diamond's. In 1978 Goldwater's, the leading quality department store in Phoenix offered her a job as Buying Director, a promotion that would have taken longer at Diamond's. For the first time, she had fourteen direct reports and was responsible for the 'whole image of the product' in women's sportswear. Although she had had little strategic experience, by this time she already had learned to distinguish the important from the unimportant issues and to focus on the big issues. None the less, she found the first six months tough, working twice as hard.

> Although I don't hover on perfection, I do have very, very high standards. I had always delivered my numbers. I had always achieved budget and set plans that were what the company needed and that I knew I could deliver. I prided myself on that. I found myself getting really involved in developing and motivating my team, which hadn't been important to me before.

Goldwater's culture was very different from Diamond's, with mostly female staff and Iverson found herself disappointed in the behaviour of some of her female colleagues. 'There were some really bad examples of pettiness, not keeping focused on doing the job and getting lost in the gossip, being a little too emotional and not being committed.'

Two years later in 1980, her divorce freed her to respond to one of the many calls offering her jobs and to move to Harzfield's in Kansas

City, 'It was the most exhilarating experience I ever had. I was ready
to relocate and to take on a new challenge and dimension in my life.'
For the first time, she was part of an organisation that was
committed to people and management development, and received
training complementary to her experience on the job. The development initiative was led by the 'absolutely outstanding' Group
Director of Human Resources, Jim Andress. 'For two years I went
through a tremendous management training programme to develop
my street-smarts into effective management behaviour and the
beginning of leadership.'

From Harzfield's on, Ann Iverson notes a recurring pattern in her
professional life of management buyouts, takeovers, mergers or
'Chapter Eleven' bankruptcies. The parent company, Garfinkels
Brooks Brothers was bought out by Allied Department Stores.
(Iverson had been Executive Vice President of Merchandising of
Harzfield's, a division of Garfinkels.) As so often with takeovers, the
new environment was very different from the one she had chosen.

By this stage in her career Ann Iverson had a very clear understanding of the circumstances she needed to thrive, to grow and to be
fulfilled professionally and her career decisions hereafter were made
to provide her with this 'winning culture'.

When I left Arizona, I was a single parent and for the first time I
could choose where to live, where to work. I knew that I needed to
be part of a winning culture, a driving, thriving environment where
I would be self-motivated, my strengths would be nourished and I
would achieve to my fullest capability. Although external considerations played a part in the next four moves I could easily have
stayed on in each case and ridden the tide. But I evaluated the new
circumstances, and in each case, left only to accept another
opportunity that provided me with more of the positive elements
that I required.

I always advise people to understand themselves and the kind of
arena where they are most motivated, successful and happy. So
many people don't think this through as carefully as they should.
When you move, you must assess what has been good for you and
what you hope never to find again. People tend to be more
influenced by the financial package than the culture when they
move, and this approach leads to career mistakes.

In 1982, as Buying Director at Harzfield's, Ann Iverson had
conceived for the first time a longer-term objective to run a

business. Most of her retailing career had been spent in buying – the 'Queen Bee' position in retailing in America but after almost twenty years, it was providing less and less gratification.

> I had been very successful as a buyer but I was looking for something more. I was losing gratification in the job – sort of like the song 'Is that all there is?' I was also getting burned out on extensive travel and I started looking at what I needed to grow and broaden my experience to position myself to be a candidate on the short list for general management positions. I loved the shop floor but hadn't had any operational or finance experience so I had to put myself in the position of getting that experience.

This careful assessment led to her next move to T H Mandy (a division of US Shoe) in Virginia as Stores Director/Buying Director. Many of her colleagues advised strongly against the move from buying into operations as opting for a professional backwater.

Not only did she enjoy the role of Stores Director, excel at it and learn about store management, but she became instantly more marketable.

> I really didn't know anything about stores management. I got thrown into it and absolutely loved it, because I could talk to all the buyers in a language that they understood and I learned about payroll and below margin expenses and how to design a store to sell the product. As a buyer I hadn't been exposed to these aspects of the business. It gave me a useful perspective and also made me very marketable because there were virtually no women in that position in America. Clearly when you put my experience up against the average experience of a store director, I could run circles around them because they came from an operations, not a customer point of view.

Although overall Iverson's operational experience at T H Mandy had a positive impact on her career, it was also the time of greatest frustration, as she became involved in an inherited management problem.

When Bloomingdale's approached her to join them, she was more than ready to listen. Having by now worked in department, speciality and 'off-price' (discount) stores, she understood her strengths to be maximised in department stores. Marvin Traub, Chairman of Bloomingdale's and Iverson talked at length about how they could develop the branches at Bloomingdale's. Although Bloomingdale's flagship store on 59th Street in New York was the heart and soul of the company, it was clear that the same commitment and high standards had not been pushed throughout the business to the branches.

Ann Iverson became Operating Vice President for the two major Bloomingdale branches in Bergen County and White Plains and 'Joan of Arc-like' became obsessed with making changes. 'You would walk into the store and see thousand dollar dresses lying on the floor and staff wouldn't even pick them up!' She restructured the organisation, introducing and updating reporting systems, developing design programmes and introducing ranges to capture the strengths of the company as epitomised by the 59th Street store.

Her next move was again externally prompted by a job offer, and again met her criteria for challenge and development. David Dworkin had heard of her performance at Bloomingdale's and invited her to join him at Bonwit Teller.

> Again it was the fine clothes and the brand but here the excitement was developing a strategy, developing a whole new customer base, wooing the new generation away from department stores into the speciality store. So the day-to-day aspect of the job was a 'no-brainer' but the exciting piece was being part of a management team that was going to build a strategic plan and turn an organisation around.

As Senior Vice President Stores at Bonwit Teller, she had a wider base reporting to her. Again, parent company The Hooker Group fell into cash flow problems in Australia and there was suddenly no money to pay the suppliers. The company went into Chapter Eleven and although she had experienced three buy-outs in the past, for the first time, Ann Iverson began the process of due diligence.

When Dworkin left Bonwit Teller to run Storehouse in the UK, Iverson agreed to join him as Director of Stores for British Home Stores for three reasons. First, she could see the 'writing on the wall' for retail in the US.

> It was very overpriced, the majority of sales coming from 'red flag specials' or sales items, with added inflation just covering the inability of management to be focused and control expenses. Yet department stores were not admitting the problem or doing anything to solve it. Discounters were becoming stronger, and suppliers' outlets started to sell directly. We were headed toward a

collision course and there was no clear strategy from managements.

Second, she saw clear opportunities in the UK.

> When I came across to the UK I saw tremendous value for money compared to America, a country that wasn't brand driven but design and value driven and that was exciting. It was a nice balance and not materialistic. If you got the offer right you could actually take business from your neighbour where in America it was so overstored that if you were in the wrong location or the wrong pitch, no matter how good you were, you could fail.

Third, she had worked with David Dworkin, had learned from him, had his confidence and was given an irresistible opportunity.

> David Dworkin had been a very good role model for me. He had taught me to sit back and think strategically without losing that tactical requirement for performance on a day-to-day basis which is important for retail. He also had the confidence to have me come across the Atlantic and run a 136 store chain because he knew that I could do it. And he was right, which gave me an opportunity that I would not have had as quickly in America which was important both for my CV and for my development having just had department store and speciality store experience. This experience would make me more marketable if I succeeded and would give me a little more opportunity to write my own steps for the future.

Produce she did. On her arrival in the UK in January 1990, she was confronted at British Home Stores with a lack of focus and strategy and very low rate of customer conversion. She introduced a philosophy of customer care, listening to British Home Stores' customers and responding with the introduction of new store formats in most stores. She brought a new way of thinking about retail from the US to the UK, and without ignoring UK traditions and customer expectations, developed a format which has succeeded in customers wanting to visit and purchase at BHS. From a near loss situation in 1990, BHS in 1993 made a profit of about £40 million on a turnover of £680 million.

When Dworkin in mid-1992 became Chief Executive of Storehouse, he asked Ann Iverson to reposition Mothercare as Chief Executive. Mothercare had become demoralised as the competition

strengthened and market share declined from the late 1980s. In two
years she revamped Mothercare stores, creating a fun and appealing
environment for children as well as meeting the needs of mothers-to-
be and new mothers. She restructured Mothercare, delayering
management levels and creating a more 'hands-on' approach and
customer led culture, developing individual performance related
programmes, reorganising the Mothercare Board which included
three women and focusing on building and retaining customer
loyalty.

Ann Iverson's experience at Mothercare was overwhelmingly
positive and she learned quickly the adaptability of the international
manager, working effectively in a culture not her own, respecting
differences without modifying the energy and approach that had
succeeded for her in the United States.

> From the moment I got off the plane, I never stopped or slowed
> down or changed my normal style in driving the business. But I did
> learn the importance of complementing, not changing the culture.
>
> As an expatriate, I had to step back and look at myself and my
> style. I knew I had to change, to do things another way without
> changing my standards or values. I am by nature extremely hands-
> on and have learned to be hands-on from further away, to delegate
> without losing focus, giving people a clear idea of what needs to be
> done and the power to do it. One of the greatest rewards is
> developing and training our people and I have grown along with
> them.
>
> People in the UK don't react as quickly as in the US. I try to
> speed them up but have also learned to ponder an extra ten
> seconds! I have learned to be more philosophical and inward-
> looking in my thinking. I am just as focused and decisive but there
> is a little more depth.

In June 1994, Ann Iverson left Mothercare to become Chief Executive of US-based Kay-Bee Toys, both because it provided her with an
opportunity to return to the US to be with her family and because the
company was bigger (one billion dollar turnover), in need of turnaround and represented the challenge on which she thrives. Indeed,
she has a clear understanding of the environment she needs to work
within.

> I know I'm very good at sorting out problems and getting the
> business on track but I'm bored with administrative maintenance

responsibilities. I like turnaround situations where the circumstances are working for you – where the company is cash
positive, with a fairly good brand and a lot of upside opportunities.

She is also frank about preparing for her next promotion while
devoting herself to performance.

The best thing I could say about Ann Iverson is that I am always
focusing on what I am doing now and ensuring that I achieve
outstanding results but I don't for a moment lose sight of the fact
that I need to know what the next step is. I don't try to plan the
next three or four steps but clearly I want to know when the next
step is, what I need to achieve to get there and that whomever I am
reporting to for the next few years believes that I am capable of
getting there and will make that appointment when it happens.
Therefore, I need a very strong open line of communication to my
boss, and also with the people who report to me.

Iverson has made it clear that her current role is not the 'end of the
road' professionally for her. A role model herself now for many, Ann
Iverson is conscious of having benefited from the example of many
superiors if not from an identifiable mentor relationship.

Reflecting on her career, she identifies at least one wrong turn but
philosophically accepts the value of mistakes and has no regrets.

Mistakes you learn from. T H Mandy was a mistake. You could
take anything along my career path and suggest a different choice.
But out of every turn or bend in the road, I actually found a short
cut to make up for the time I had lost. I wouldn't re-do anything.
Would I have liked things to have happened faster? Would I like to
be making more money than I am now? Yes! But I don't have
regrets. Every stage in my life has been a learning curve. Sometimes
you don't actually see the benefits at the time.

FAMILY AND PERSONAL LIFE

Ann Iverson is crystal clear in her priorities and expresses them
without the ambivalence of many of her contemporaries.

Even though I have worked all my life, my children always come
first. Work has been second and my personal life last which is

probably why I have married and divorced so many times.

My children came first in different ways at different times in their lives. If there is a school play, you *are* there. When they start growing up and studying and there are warning signals that something is wrong, you must be willing to give up work and time and to do something about it. I always made sure that I attended all school events, was there for all birthdays and whenever they were sick. If I have a very important meeting but they need me, I don't hesitate to cancel. It is important to find quality time which means if you have more than one child that you spend time alone with each.

I would be dishonest to say that you could have a career and children and not miss an important quality of life with your family but I believe it was more my loss than theirs. My children as young adults would say I am very committed to them and to their needs. They are extremely understanding and appreciative of my decisions but as they were growing up they didn't always understand if I was getting on a plane why I was leaving them. Clearly, there was a time when business got my time and they didn't. It would be naive to believe that you can do both but if you're going to be overwhelmed by guilt you will do neither well.

Life isn't easy, you can shelter your children too much. If you can give them controlled exposure, it can help them to grow. If you do go to work then you must be there 100 per cent. On the other hand, if they need you, if they're sick or hurting (which is separate from just saying 'mummy don't go' but really being all right) you must be there. Everyone at work can be replaced and you just can't bring back those times when you were needed by your children and not there.

I also have tremendous admiration for those women who stay at home given the pressures to work now.

Ann Iverson has been married and divorced four times and her most recent marriage did not survive her move to England.

Our marriage wasn't on terribly solid ground when I came across. But my husband was always very supportive of me and my job and said, 'You can't pass up this opportunity. You must go and you must try it, and what happens, happens, both personally and professionally.' Though the divorce wasn't really a surprise, it was still painful.

Iverson is very conscious of the need to renew herself by switching gear.

> I love to immerse myself in things that absolutely force me to concentrate on the moment so that I can slow my mind down. Clearly good theatre, ballet, concerts do just that – in London particularly as the availability is so much greater. In the US it is the movies.

Although she confesses to needing a lot of sleep, her working hours are 'intense and immense'. Some days she will come home and go to bed at 8.00 p.m. to recharge her batteries.

LEADERSHIP AND SUCCESS FACTORS

Ann Iverson is irrepressibly positive and very direct. She believes that business leaders must not only have a vision as to where the company is going and bring people with them, but must also be decisive and scrupulously fair. She is blisteringly scathing about office politics.

> I have no use and no time for office politics. It is my pet peeve. I will do anything to eliminate that kind of self-seeking behaviour, even if I have to get rid of the individuals. I am brutally frank. I try to earn respect and I insist on loyalty. You cannot have politics in this environment. Loyalty requires openness, honesty, an ability to confront when it is professionally necessary. Overall I believe that political behaviour slows you down. There have been times when I have missed promotions because I am too straightforward and too frank – and this wasn't what the business needed at the time. But at the end of the day, a true leader must create an environment where people have the courage to tell the truth and where it's safe to take risks.

Ann Iverson sees her own key strength as strong determination. 'I don't give up. I'm not a quitter and yet I'm not pigheaded enough to push at the expense of important things in life, be it people or shareholders' interests.' She identifies impatience as a significant weakness, as well as her intensity. 'For some personalities my intensity is frightening or a turn-off, and hard to deal with. But I've learned to spot those personalities and I can soften my approach for them. How long I can do that goes back to my impatience!'

Adrian Greenhalgh, Operations Director at Mothercare confirms that Iverson is single-minded and forceful, and also comments on her ability as a retailer, and the loyalty she commands.

> Ann is an ace retailer first and foremost. I have never seen anyone to touch her! She has good vision but she is also very detailed, and good on nuts and bolts – in retail the detail must be right. She is also as 'tough as old boots', highly determined and competitive in the extreme, while being a good team player and very supportive of individuals. She commands a huge amount of respect from our 3500 store staff and when she would go to our stores, she would speak to everyone from the cleaner to the manager. Ann works physically very hard and would arrive on a flight across the Atlantic and go straight into work for 18 hours. She is single-minded and I would sometimes have to shout at her to get her to listen: because she is so forceful she has to be careful not to frighten people off! But the truth is that she does listen and responds well to constructive criticism.

Adrian Greenhalgh describes his expectations before meeting Ann Iverson as being based on a stereotype of the professional American woman but notes that after four minutes, her leadership was clear.

> I will never forget the first time I saw Ann Iverson – it was in Oxford at an away day. I was expecting a Dallas-type, immaculately dressed businesswoman in the equivalent of pin-stripes. She arrived with bright red hair, long red fingernails, large sun-glasses and casual clothes! Within four minutes she had taken over the off-site meeting providing us all with a clear direction and new ideas and it was irrelevant whether she was a woman or a man.

Adrian Greenhalgh also respects Iverson's ability to combine her job with a successful family life and notes that she brings a personal touch to her work which results in people saying to themselves – 'I will really work hard for this person'. For instance, when his son was in an intensive care unit, Ann Iverson dropped everything to drive to the hospital in the country in order to provide him and his wife with support.

In her direct reports Ann Iverson looks for mature, highly motivated, results-oriented and positive people.

I like people who are winners, positive thinkers, for whom the glass is half full, who know how to push hard without having someone fall off the side of the boat as they do it – and people who know how to get the best out of themselves and their people. I like people whose style of management becomes contagious and synergistic.

Since I am such a powerful personality, it's easy to think I want 'yes people'. But I don't. I want to be stopped when I'm wrong and told. Then I want people to buy-in to the final decision, to be committed. I like very strong people around me.

Ann Iverson is not only a fervent believer in the 'ever-so-important golden rule' of respecting others but is also a practising Christian.

People don't see this side of me at work – they see me as tough and decisive. But I need to be able to look at myself in the mirror and know that tough decisions are made with a balance of commercial considerations and those arising from a deep inner faith. If you can't say this out loud, I believe that you are missing an important element of leadership.

Her career advice to both men and women would be identical. Although she did not finish university, she would advise young people 'first to get an education', believing that she 'got away with it' because of timing and the nature of the retail industry. 'Though I would also suggest that you not use education as a long-term vehicle for not figuring out what you want to do.'

She also advises young people to try to understand themselves, and provides practical advice about the steps to take:

It is important to try out different jobs to determine what suits you. At college try different summer jobs, find a good career counsellor and look for role models in professional fields to talk to about your experiences and interests so that you can start to formulate career objectives that match your likes and dislikes at an early age.

Some of the best experience I had was getting out there and working immediately.

Ann Iverson also advises people not to expect too much too soon. 'You really have to work hard to succeed. If it comes too quickly, too easily, at some point in your career it will bite you because hands-on experience is critical.'

Her advice to women professionals is to forget gender. Her policy was always to be completely and unambiguously 'not approachable as a woman at work'. If ever she sensed blatantly obvious discrimination, she would 'shut the door' and straightforwardly express what she had been observing. She acknowledges the importance of ensuring that people know who you are and what you are doing. 'It is all right to take credit, be forward and polish your own apple as long as you don't cross over into the political arena.'

She is herself extraordinarily positive, always seeing the good in any situation, and to be successful, she believes it is critical, as obvious in her own decision-making, to choose cultures where one can be one's best self.

9

Neville Bain

Chief Executive, Coats Viyella Plc

Date of birth: 14 July 1940

Place of birth: Dunedin, New Zealand

Nationality: British/New Zealand

Marital status: Married

Family: One son, one daughter,
                      one step-daughter

Education:	King's High School, Dunedin
	Otago University, New Zealand
	Honorary LLD, M.Com (Hons), (with double bachelors degrees in economics and accounting), CMA, FCA, FCIS, CBIM, FRSA
Career:	
1957–1959	Inland Revenue Dept, Dunedin
	Assessment Clerk
	Junior Inspector
1960–1963	Anderson & Co, Dunedin (now Price Waterhouse)
	Senior Manager
1963–1990	Cadbury Schweppes Plc
1963–75	Cadbury Schweppes Hudson Ltd, New Zealand
	Cost and Management Accountant
	Financial Controller
	Company Secretary
	Finance Director
1975–80	Cadbury Schweppes, South Africa Ltd
	Group Commercial & Finance Director
	Managing Director
1980–83	Cadbury Schweppes Plc, London
	Group Planning Director
	Appointed to Main Board
1983–86	Cadbury Limited, Birmingham
	Managing Director
1986–89	Cadbury Schweppes Plc, London
	Managing Director, Group Confectionery
1989–90	Cadbury Schweppes, London
	Finance Director and Deputy Group Chief Executive
1990 to date	Coats Viyella Plc
	Group Chief Executive
Outside appointments:	Argyll Group Plc, Non-executive Director
	The Gartmore Scotland Investment Trust Plc, Non-executive Director
	Cooperation Ireland, Past President
Outside interests:	Music (plays trombone and euphonium), sport, walking and photography

INTRODUCTION

Neville Bain is the open and enthusiastic New Zealander who took over as Chief Executive of the two billion pound textile and thread multinational Coats Viyella from the Iranian Jewish entrepreneur/founder, Sir David Alliance in 1990.

Bain provides a good example of a Chief Executive head-hunted from a Board position and almost lifelong career in one multinational to head up another leading company in a different industry. He had been with Cadbury Schweppes for 27 years, moving from New Zealand, to South Africa, then to the UK eventually becoming Finance Director and Deputy Chief Executive. He had had multi-functional experience in finance, and sales and marketing and gained his first general management role as Managing Director of Cadbury Schweppes, South Africa at age 38.

The second son of four of a close and supportive working-class family, he early learned the meaning of competition and team-work. Although fundamentally motivated by doing a good job, as an extravert he also welcomes recognition for his efforts. With several degrees and an accounting qualification, he is committed not only to formal study but also to life-long learning and to keeping at the cutting edge of management thinking. Considered by some to be equally at home as a 'management guru' as a business leader, he commits time to lecture on international management issues each year at his alma mater, Otago University where he recently was awarded an honorary doctorate.

Although he has never had an overarching career goal, Bain is open about the importance of planning and preparing for the next career step. His view of leadership is textbook-like – set the strategy, communicate it, get the right people in the right positions, motivate and challenge them and act as team coach – and this straightforward approach clearly works.

Since 1990 Coats Viyella has improved its turnover and profit performance year on year, in spite of the recession, in 1993 reporting an operating profit of £171.7 million up from £90.2 million in 1990. Bain achieved this not only through greater focus on strategic leadership but also by deeply imbuing a culture of performance throughout the company; by successful completion and integration of new acquisitions; an emphasis on management development and training as well as greatly improved internal and external communications. (Coats Viyella won the joint Stock Exchange and Chartered Accountants Award for the best 1992 Annual Report.)

With a reputation for clear 'helicopter vision', and a charisma that leads people to transcend themselves, Neville Bain is also said to exhibit the rare leadership quality of creating an atmosphere where everybody is prepared to be absolutely truthful. A true extravert, he is an excellent upfront communicator and open about his fallibilities, acknowledging that he sometimes talks too much in his enthusiasm.

Divorced and remarried, he now finds little difficulty in balancing his personal and professional lives.

What have been the important influences on a working-class New Zealander now heading up one of the UK's leading multinational companies?

EARLY INFLUENCES

Neville Bain is the second of four sons of a third generation Scots railway tradesman in Dunedin, New Zealand. His family background combined a familiar pattern of working-class aspiration and parental support as well as close-knit and competitive sibling relationships. 'My parents were supportive of education and doing the best that you were capable of, but not in any way driving. They left the individual to choose for themselves.'

Although there was inevitable competition among the four brothers, there was also a great deal of affection and support. 'If one hurts, we all hurt a little.' His father had been a rugby player and the four boys were 'all sports-minded, with a real desire to win'. From this he feels comes an early understanding of strategy and tactics ('Think first about the competition and game plan') and team work. He much preferred team sports.

A good student, he thrived at largely working-class King's High School in Dunedin which provided him with a solid academic background and an opportunity to play the sports he loved, especially rugby – an experience he describes as consistent with his family environment and values – 'no frills – a requirement for honest effort'.

Unlike many in the study with working-class backgrounds, money never appears to have been a primary motivation. With the extravert's natural orientation towards seeking the approval of others,

Neville Bain is none the less also motivated by the intrinsic satisfaction of doing a worthwhile job well. In his words:

> My motivation is complex. I do think that I very much want to be recognised. As a child, I was one of four boys and you have to be recognised occasionally! I have genuinely asked myself whether it is power I want but it really isn't that. And it isn't money. I am paid very well – my salary is a matter of public record but I would happily take a third cut in salary to do something that I really wanted to do. Fundamentally, I want job satisfaction, to do the best I can, to change things. I also like freedom and a degree of control and I do like people to recognise that I have done a good job.

CAREER DECISION-MAKING AND DEVELOPMENT

Neville Bain went on to study at Otago University, one of New Zealand's best universities, undertaking a full-time double bachelor's degree in economics and accounting part-time, an experience he describes as 'A good combination of thorough teaching and a stimulus to expand personal frontiers'. He studied part-time both because he wanted to be financially independent and because he was not confident about being successful at university. Later, continuing with part-time study, he completed his Master of Commerce Degree with Honours.

The decision to become an accountant was conceived with his parents guidance, in spite of it representing an unfamiliar route for the family. 'My Dad could see that I didn't have the skills to become a tradesman. I was achieving quite well at school so he encouraged me to find a good office job.'

It became a toss-up between studying accounting or law. Accounting was chosen because it was easier to do part-time and he had an aptitude with numbers. In hindsight, his choice to do accounting, economics and business studies provided valuable preparation for his business career. 'Accounting was a very useful way of looking into the micro part of the business and also takes you across the total business. The economics approach provided a broader and more macro perspective and the business studies gave breadth in management principles.'

If he has any regret, it is that he chose not to go to university full-time, continue to play rugby competitively, enjoy the social side of university life and also spend more time in this period with his family. Undertaking a full-time course part-time required a gruelling schedule. While undertaking his masters, he would leave work for university at 3.00 p.m., attend lectures until 6.00 p.m., work in the library until 10.30 p.m., ring his children to say goodnight and then go home. This left little room for either social or family life especially as he was holding down a demanding job at Cadbury Schweppes.

However, as so often in life, the flip side of a disappointment or regret was a lasting benefit.

> One of the great things about going to university part-time is that you acquire a sense of urgency. You can't fool around. I had to be focused, well-organised and disciplined to make every minute count, knowing that if I wasted time I was taking away from something else important. Also, the course effectively married the theoretical and practical – by the time I had finished my accountancy exams at age 19, I had three years' work experience.

As a result of his experience, he would advise aspiring senior managers in thinking about education (a) to examine strengths, weaknesses, and interests, (b) to get a very good first degree, (c) to get some relevant, as broad as possible, work experience, and then (d) to consider very seriously a well-structured MBA at a good university. He has no doubt about the value of an MBA but advises:

> The quality of MBAs is variable and you have to choose one that is recognised as first class. The critics argue that MBA programmes lag the needs of the business. There is some truth in that. The MBA programmes that I would criticise are those heavy on analytics and light on the soft issues, such as personal awareness, innovation and leadership which are very hard to teach. The value of the MBA is its structured approach, the discipline, knowledge and what you learn about yourself. In a way, the frontiers of the course are the frontiers of your mind.

Neville Bain describes his career as 'partly organised and partly fortuitous'. He has never had a goal for the whole of his working life, and to the extent that he has had objectives, they have changed over time. To a greater extent than most, he believes strongly in career planning, at least in preparing for the next step.

His decision to study accounting was based on a rational evaluation of his strengths and interests. His first two career decisions, designed to further his training, arose 'partly by chance'. His first job with the tax office was taken because it was a good training ground for people undertaking accounting qualifications, providing time off work for study and exposure to a variety of accounts. His second job with one of New Zealand's leading accounting firms was taken two years later, serendipitously offered by an ex-colleague he played basketball with. He had no long-term interest in a civil service career and he seized the opportunity to specialise in management accounting – his area of greatest professional interest.

His career thus followed a common early pattern of quite frequent moves, although within the same profession. His third and critically important career choice, at age 23, was actively sought for development purposes, with the intention of returning to his accounting firm after a year and allowing him to stay in Dunedin. This decision is testimony to the limits of career planning:

> I joined Cadbury Schweppes because it was the only place in Dunedin (where I wanted to stay) that was big enough and international enough and they were actually looking for a cost accountant. I intended to return after a year or two but got fascinated with the industry and the products and in the end decided to stay and make my career in Cadbury Schweppes.

Ironically of course, having chosen Cadbury Schweppes to stay in Dunedin, his career with the company would take him irrevocably away from New Zealand.

For the next 27 years, career moves within Cadbury Schweppes were again made with a combination of careful planning and preparation and serendipity. He is unusual among our business leaders in advising people explicitly to anticipate their next career move and prepare for it.

> You must always try to be well-positioned and prepared for the next step – the job you would most like after this one. I have never tried to lay out a ten year plan, but simply looked at the options for the next job and tried to prepare.
>
> The element of luck always plays a large part in careers and this is certainly true in my case. Therefore, we need to manage chance. We need to take advantage of luck. You cannot leave your career development solely to your employer – he just is not good enough to manage this for you!

His chosen example of anticipation and preparation however seems to provide some support for the anti-planners, who believe that excessive planning can be counterproductive. When he was the Financial Controller of Cadbury Schweppes in New Zealand, the Secretary of the company was due to retire within a year.

> The Company Secretary was the most senior job not on the Board. The incumbent was retiring in a year's time and there were three people who could have been considered for that job. The obvious candidate was somebody who had been there a long time and had done finance. Without being wrong about it and saying it out loud too much, I thought to myself, 'I have got more potential and capacity than this person has got. I have certainly got better qualifications so if I am going to look at that job, I need to become a better candidate in the next two years.'

As a result, Neville Bain completed an accelerated secretarial qualification in 18 months and was offered the job. Ironically, he hated the job which lasted for only nine months. 'Actually, I wasn't right for the job. The issues were historical and dead rather than living and people oriented which was what really turned me on about management'. Of all his professional experiences, this appears to have been the closest to a failure, although he believes that colleagues looking at his performance from the outside could see that he brought something different and valuable to the job.

Although many business leaders expressed that it is actually counter-productive to plan careers too carefully, believing that one thing leads to another if one focuses single-mindedly on the job, Bain believes that in the UK, successful people are often not open about the extent to which they anticipate and prepare.

> There is a slight amount of down-talk about thinking strategically about careers because people don't like to be seen as aggressive or manipulative. I don't think I am either of those things. I accept that I am a bit pushy, but I'm not manipulative. I am a very open person and I don't think that there is anything wrong in admitting that I look to the next stage. Not that it's a grandiose thing. For instance, I never wanted to be the boss of Cadbury Schweppes UK, other than when I was just beneath that position.

Certainly this strategy of preparing for the next step worked for him over time and it is arguably a logical and even natural approach to a career within a single organisation. After becoming Secretary of

Cadbury Schweppes in New Zealand he realised that to become Finance Director, he needed to gain a wider business perspective including buying. As Finance Director, aged 29, he gained cross-functional experience in sales and marketing to prepare himself for general management, becoming the obvious choice for Managing Director in New Zealand.

However, before becoming Managing Director in New Zealand, he recognised at age 35 that he also needed experience outside the country. Although he had joined Cadbury Schweppes with the intention of staying in Dunedin, he now asked for a move and was sent as Group Commercial and Financial Director to South Africa. This was a point of no return, as his next move to Managing Director, South Africa was a bigger role than that for New Zealand and from here his future lay either in England or outside the group.

As a result of his success in South Africa, restructuring the unprofitable soft drinks interests, building up market share and profits and substantially increasing earnings per share, he was asked at age 41 to join the main board of Cadbury Schweppes as Group Planning Director in London. This move was another example of how impossible it often is to predict career paths:

> I never thought I'd be on the main board at Cadbury Schweppes. It totally astonished me because (a) I was foreign and the company had never had a foreigner on the Board and (b) I had only been in the country for nine months and as Strategic Planning Director, I wasn't running anything. It was a very brave, and if I may say, and it sounds presumptuous, a good decision. I was different and very committed and when the company needed someone to step in and run the UK operation after Dominic, they had given me three years' Board and strategic planning experience, and I was pre-pared.

In two years he introduced a new system of strategic planning that was relevant to individual business units and helped the group to focus on strategic alternatives, a contribution that reputedly is still remembered by colleagues at Cadbury Schweppes. He was also directly involved with acquisitions and disposals.

The next six years were spent managing major businesses within the group, first as Managing Director of £450 million turnover Cadbury Limited in Birmingham, and then as Managing Director of Group Confectionery in London with worldwide sales of £1 billion. As MD of Cadbury he substantially reduced costs (staff numbers slashed by 2500 to 5500) while increasing market share by 2 per cent. As MD of Group Confectionery, he restructured the confectionery business lifting profits from £46 million to £120 million in two years by organic growth.

In 1989, Neville Bain was made Group Finance Director and Deputy Group Chief Executive, responsible for finance, group research, information technology, deputising for the Chief Executive and initiating group strategy. Less than a year later, he was head-hunted to become Chief Executive of Coats Viyella, one of the largest textile groups in Europe, one of the world's leading thread producers and successful retailer with such brands as Jaeger, Viyella, Van Heusen shirts and Wilton carpets. His decision to leave Cadbury Schweppes was a difficult one, confronting him with an assessment of his priorities.

> I had to think very hard after 27 years with one of the best companies in the world about what was important to me. Every five or seven years, I had been lucky enough to change either geography or job type. I had worked with Dominic Cadbury at the top of that company for seven years. We were both at that stage a little under 50 and we retired at 60. It concerned me for the company that the two most senior people should be together for potentially seventeen years and I suggested to Dominic that we needed to think about that. If he wanted me to retire early, I didn't want to be told at 55 that he would like me to go within six months. We would need a couple of years to prepare for that, because I was quite relaxed about going at 55 and doing something else. Equally, I was quite happy to stay on to 60. Certainly he didn't want me to retire early.
>
> But what I really wanted was to run my own company with my own team. I wanted to put into practice directly my own approach to management.

His first response on being approached by Coats Viyella was reluctance to leave Cadbury Schweppes. However:

> Then I looked at the company and the more I looked, the more interesting I found it. It needed a huge amount of change. It had seven major business areas and a strategy that was not clear and needed refinement. It had some good people and some who were not performing quite so well. It operated across fifty-five different countries for at least two product groups, so the complexity was a

challenge. I thought that I could really do something, along with the top team.

Given the breadth of his experience, he was not only able to change corporate environments after 27 years in the same company, but also successfully to change industries at the top from a relatively simple drinks and confectionery business to a complex agglomeration of groups of many small businesses in textiles, thread, clothing, fashion and precision engineering.

> It is certainly possible for capable chief executives to change industries, if they have had the sort of experience that does not make them a one-company, one-country person. It's a question of matching the needs of the job with the individual's strengths, and understanding where you might be exposed. It's also a question of style and personal characteristics and the chemistry of the top team. New people can bring a freshness and an analytical approach that challenges the not-invented-here syndrome, the accepted truths that need updating.
>
> The manager changing industries must of course be a professional person with the necessary tools and experience. It can be frustrating, because it takes a little while to get up to speed, and it is difficult to challenge 'industry experts' within who say it can't be done.

Characteristically, he found one of the few books on the subject of taking charge of a company by John G. Gabarro at the Harvard Business School, who traced the different stages of taking charge and gave him some realistic time frames to work within. (Characteristically too, he had summarised it and gave me a copy of the summary.)

Neville Bain's approach was to undertake a preliminary analysis, very quickly identify a few key issues and bring in trusted outside consultants LEK to undertake a detailed study within three months. 'We did not have a strategy in this organisation. We were doing all sorts of different things. People were running their own empires and little fiefdoms.' Bain devised a strategy with input from his top team and the consultants, he communicated it, made people really responsible for running divisions and created a statement of values as a framework for decision-making.

Depending on what stage the company has reached, Neville Bain plans either to stay until 60 as Chief Executive, or to leave a few years early, ensuring the right succession is in place. In the 'third age' he hopes to exercise his deep interest in corporate governance in non-executive chairmanship and other roles. He also expects to have more time to 'give back' to business through business education and developing young managers.

In evaluating his own career path, he would see it as no more than a 'flexible model' for others.

> Set rules are not going to apply for every person. First, it was incredibly enriching at an early stage to be in a small enough business to not just see a narrow part in great depth, but to see across the whole business. Although Cadbury Schweppes NZ was one of the top thirty companies in the country, New Zealand is a small economy. Also, I was very lucky then to move across disciplines first into selling then into marketing, although I wasn't qualified for either. I then had the challenge of moving geographically within my own discipline, finance (it is incredibly difficult to change both location and function at the same time) and having mastered that, to get my first general management job. I've had jobs that have changed in nature at least every five years. The ideal is to have at least three years in a job so that you can really measure the person in it. A fast-track person should spend no longer than five years in a job.

Although he spent most of his career in a single company, Bain believes that this will be increasingly rare with successful managers moving across companies a number of times.

Although no single person has influenced Bain as a mentor, several of his bosses have been influential in supporting him, giving him freedom to perform and expand, constructive criticism and helpful examples of leadership styles. Specifically, he has a deep respect for Sir Adrian Cadbury.

> He is one of the finest chairmen that I have ever met in terms of how he runs meetings. He has an outstanding style that elicits a unique contribution from every person around the boardroom table and makes the person feel good. Yet he has put me down a few times, when I have been too brash and said things that have been wrong or rude and I know that I have made a mistake.

He also respects Sir Graham Day, Sir Adrian's successor as Chairman, for his ability to quickly cut to the core of things and 'make so much out of so little time'.

The other person who influenced him greatly was his first boss at Cadbury Schweppes, Ted Barringer who was hard working and sales led and had two memorable sayings that have had a lasting impact:

> One is maintenance of the objective, which is an old army principle. Regardless of what is happening around you, you must continue with the objective. The second was that Barringer felt that he could never be the cleverest chap in the meeting, but he could always be the best prepared. I still try before any meeting to have thought through the issues, have an idea of what it is that I hope to achieve in a meeting and what my bottom line is likely to be.

He also admires Sir David Alliance, current Chairman and founder of Coats Viyella for his success as an entrepreneur and his ability to see a deal.

Neville Bain has not only lived and worked in his native New Zealand, South Africa and the UK, and worked extensively across borders with Cadbury Schweppes and Coats Viyella, but as a New Zealander both appreciates cultural differences while working comfortably within them.

> It is an advantage being a New Zealander in many ways. People respond well to a different approach and as long as you are professional, will accept differences in style and recognise the uniqueness of the contribution. I'm relaxed about not being English and people who report to me are relaxed about it. As a consequence, I'm not locked into the old boy network. I do have a few people who ring me up to ask whether I'm free to do non-executive jobs, and I say no, because I can't do more than I'm doing. So being a New Zealander hasn't interfered with being successful in the UK.

FAMILY AND PERSONAL LIFE

Neville Bain's family provides a valued ballast for a demanding life, and following the failure of his first marriage, partly due to overwork, he is careful to preserve a balance.

Although he works 65 to 80 hours a week, and travels one third of his time, he tries to keep weekends for his family, aiming to arrive home no later than Saturday morning and never to leave before Sunday evening.

He has two grown-up children, Susan and Peter from his first marriage, and a teenage step-daughter.

> I am very lucky with my wife, Anni, who is both very supportive and an excellent foil for me. She is also happy with the balance of time I spend at work and positive about the time I am away. My output would be impossible without this marvellous support.

At the end of the day, if there were a conflict between family and professional priorities, he would put family first, but in his experience, both needs can be met through flexibility.

> The needs are never quite as black and white as that. It's always possible, for instance, to send someone to the US for a meeting and have a follow-up meeting here in London or to cut corners in other ways, if it's absolutely necessary.

For relaxation, he walks, writes and plays the trombone and euphonium.

Without being a churchgoer, he believes in God, and until recently gave time to chair a charity devoted to increasing cooperation and understanding between Protestants and Catholics in Northern Ireland.

LEADERSHIP AND SUCCESS FACTORS

Neville Bain defines leadership in terms of what the business leader does:

> The leader must have a vision that is clearly enunciated and communicated in a simple way. It is then very, very important to have the right people in the right jobs, to give them room to do their jobs within a framework and to motivate and challenge them. I keep thinking of sporting analogies. The captain of the team decides the team he is going to field, the strategy against the opposition, and motivates his team to do their best.

In speaking of the leaders he has admired, Sir Adrian Cadbury, Sir Graham Day, Sir David Alliance, Lord Sheppard, Sir Anthony Tennant, Sir Robin Irvine, Chancellor of Otago, he points out their differences and the importance of timing.

They are all so different in style. What does it say to you? It is best to be uniquely yourself. Don't try to mimic anybody else and there will be a right style for an organisation at the right time. Anthony Tennant wasn't given the job heading up Grand Met, yet he went on to do a wonderful job with Guinness and Allen Sheppard is hugely successful at Grand Met. As for myself, I'm better with a business that is expanding and growing and not the right person to unbundle an organisation. The best book on leadership that I have read is by John Kotter, who makes the point that leadership is really about example and doing a few good things quite well. Business leadership needn't be heroic.

Consistent with his view about leadership being about vision, communication, selecting the right people, motivation and coaching, he sees himself as first a team person. Of his own approach to leadership and management he notes:

My style is open and straightforward. Appraisals are very important and I provide direct, frequent feedback – both good and bad. I believe in thoughtful preparation in keeping with the size and complexity of the issues, but there is a high premium on speed of response, not analysis paralysis – more ready, fire, aim, with fine tuning on the run. Continuous learning and development is a must. One must continue to journey and never arrive. I work hard, have high standards both for myself and for others. I like the big picture: ideas capture my imagination, but I don't always follow through on fine detail and I need a good completer beside me.

He also shows an ability to be self-critical and is unquestionably an extravert: 'I agree with a lot of negative things people say about me. I can come across as full of myself, enthusiastic and pushy.'

A close colleague at Coats Viyella describes Neville Bain as 'truly bright' and outstanding as a leader, with the capacity to run an even larger, more complex company than Coats Viyella. His strength lies in his 'helicopter vision', his ability to rise above things and also a charisma that leads people to transcend themselves. He exhibits the rare leadership quality of creating an atmosphere where everybody is prepared to be absolutely truthful. Although his colleague supports the view that Bain sometimes talks far too much, he believes that this fallibility is endearing in the context of the man's strengths. He notes that Bain also has a low boredom threshold, and needs someone around him to deal with completing and finishing detail.

In evaluating high flyers at Coats Viyella, Neville Bain looks for people who not only have strategic vision, but are 'hungry for success' with track records demonstrating that they can achieve stretching objectives. He also looks for people who will provide a different dimension and balance to a management team. He wants 'irritants' in the best sense of the word – people who will be original, challenging and confrontational if necessary.

He is very aware of the dangers of leadership. 'You have got to really believe in what you are doing but not fall over the edge of being so sure of yourself that you can't (a) admit that you are wrong or (b) that you are insensitive to other people's views.

In evaluating people, he looks for practical intelligence, but from personal experience, does not rely on tests to make a judgement about intellect.

Education was critically important to Bain not only in giving him knowledge, and technical qualifications, but also in giving a working-class kid from New Zealand confidence to succeed. He remains devoted to keeping at the cutting edge of management learning, relishing the opportunity to research and give lectures for the business school at Otago University each year.

> Chief executives have got to constantly update their knowledge base because it depreciates like anything else. People criticise me for two things – one is that I am always telling them that we are not managing well enough here (I am self-critical too). The other is that I am always challenging them not only on best practice based on the practical, but also from a theoretical base and they see this as 'preaching business school speak'. I have no problem with that. It is good practice.

Bain believes that the Chief Executive in the year 2000 will be an expert presenter and communicator, not only to employees, but to the outside world. People preparing themselves for future senior management should develop strategic skills to cope effectively with change and communications and computing skills, in order to use data effectively without being drowned in documentation and analysis. As organisations delayer, increasingly leaders are going to have to cope with a greater span, more direct reports and therefore have clearer objectives, instil greater trust, and exercise greater delegation.

10

Charles Mackay

Chief Executive, Inchcape Plc

Date of birth:	14 April 1940
Place of birth:	Congleton, Cheshire, UK
Nationality:	British
Marital status:	Married
Family:	Two sons (one deceased), one daughter
Languages:	French, Dutch, German

Education:
1957	Cheltenham College
	'A' levels in Economics, French and History
1962	Cambridge, Queens' College
	MA (Law)
1969	INSEAD
	MBA, High Distinction

Career:
1957–1969	British Petroleum Plc
1957–59	Commercial apprentice
1959–62	University apprentice
1963–65	Algeria – various jobs including Sales Manager, Western Region
1965–69	Commercial Director, Burundi, Rwanda, Zaire
1969–1975	McKinsey & Company
1969–71	Associate, London
1971–73	Engagement Manager, London, Paris, Amsterdam
1973–75	Senior Engagement Manager
	Managed Dar es Salaam office for 18 months
1976–1981	Pakhoed Holding NV
1976–77	Director, Paktrans BV (transport division)
1977–81	Chairman, Paktrans
1981–1986	Chloride Plc
	Director
1981–85	Chairman, Overseas Division
1985–86	Chairman, Power Electronics Division
1986 to date	Inchcape Plc
1986–91	Director responsible for Far East and Chairman and Chief Executive, Inchcape Pacific Ltd, Hong Kong
Nov. 1991 to date	Chief Executive

Outside appointments:
1993 to date	British Airways Plc, Non-executive Director
1991 to date	HSBC Holdings Plc, UK, Non-executive Director
1986–1992	Hong Kong and Shanghai Banking Corporation Ltd, Hong Kong, Non-executive Director
1991–1993	Hong Kong Bank, Non-executive Director

Interests: Travel, skiing, scuba-diving, country cottage, tennis, fishing, classical music, opera, chess, computers

INTRODUCTION

Charles Mackay is one of the most deeply international Chief Executives in the UK, both in spirit and experience. As the third son of an Army officer with a colonial heritage, his early motivation was to travel and to explore the world.

He thus joined BP as a commercial apprentice because of the opportunity to live and work in exotic places, and was sent first to Algeria, then Burundi, Rwanda and Eastern Zaire. He undertook an INSEAD MBA to return to the European mainstream and his career thereafter included work in London, Paris, Amsterdam and Dar es Salaam with McKinsey, in Holland and throughout Europe with Royal Pakhoed, in Asia Pacific, the Indian subcontinent, Africa, North America and Europe with Chloride and in Hong Kong and the Far East with Inchcape. As Chief Executive of Inchcape, he is now responsible for operations in over 100 countries.

Charles Mackay has a reputation both as an excellent and energetic manager of existing businesses, extraordinarily ambitious for his company, as well as an unusually expert strategist, capable of astutely evaluating potential mergers and acquisitions targets. His approach to the business has been described as 'both brilliantly intellectual yet detailed'. He is also an immensely likeable man, with unquestioned integrity and deep compassion.

His career history is quite unique, defying the advice of most career advisers, in that all his career moves (from BP, McKinsey, Royal Pakhoed and Chloride) were made after he resigned without a job to go to. It is a tribute to his competence, track record and reputation that his career went from strength to strength, three times orchestrated by head-hunters. However, resigning without a job to go to may have contributed to his becoming Chief Executive relatively late, at age 51. He has also been supported by influential mentors.

His career is further unusual in having gone from twelve years with BP (including two years apprenticeship, four years studying at Cambridge and INSEAD and six years of line management) into consulting with McKinsey for six years, before going back into senior line management.

Although his career moves to McKinsey, then to Royal Pakhoed as Chairman of their transport division, to Chloride as Chairman, Overseas Division and to Inchcape as Chairman and Chief Executive of Inchcape Pacific were largely serendipitous, Charles Mackay has

147

always had a clear sense of moving forward developmentally, learning new skills and experiencing new cultures.

His marriage is unusually close and testimony to the importance to an international management career of having an internationally oriented and interested spouse.

At Inchcape, Charles Mackay inherited a very sound business from Sir George Turnbull, but he has taken this diverse services and marketing company valued at two and a half billion pounds, from strength to strength, acquiring motor distribution and retailing company TKM and insurance broker Hogg and providing new coherence by restructuring Inchcape's activities by 'business stream' – motors, marketing and services – rather than by location.

What has been important in the development of this leading international Chief Executive with a rather unorthodox career history, and how would he advise others about how to reach the top?

EARLY INFLUENCES

Charles Mackay is the youngest of three sons of a brigadier in the Royal Engineers. The legacy of coming from a 'typical middle-class professional colonial background', with father and older brother in the army, one uncle in the Navy and the other in the colonial service, was a single-minded ambition to lead a life of travel. 'We talked incessantly about life in the Gulf, India, Malaysia, Hong Kong, other exotic places. It never crossed my mind that I would not spend most of my working life abroad.'

Although they were not well off financially – a 'constrained sort of genteel poverty' – money has never motivated Mackay. All three boys went to boarding school and there was nothing left from an army salary. His parents did not own a house or a car until his father was over fifty. The family always used public transport, never went to restaurants, never had a holiday. This was common post-war and never worried him. Boarding school also mitigated any sense of relative lack of opportunity.

I always wore secondhand clothes. Even when I was at BP, a mother of a friend gave me all his suits because he suddenly shot up three inches. I couldn't afford to buy a suit. When I joined BP, I was making £300 a year and I didn't make more than £365 for the next five years. I was hard up but I still was not driven by money at all.

CAREER DECISION-MAKING AND DEVELOPMENT

Emerging from boarding school at 17 with 'A' levels in Economics, French and History, the driving force was to lead a life of travel. He had planned to go to Oxford and then into the Foreign Office.

At Easter 1957, before taking his 'A' levels that summer, Charles Mackay realised that he would have to find a job. His father having put three boys through public school, close to retirement and with very little capital, unexpectedly refused to pay for university.

Mackay's choice of BP was entirely by chance, the result of responding to an ad looking for people with 'A' levels to become commercial apprentices. He applied (his only application) because BP was highly international and was accepted.

Owing both to luck and his own persistence and determination, BP was also to give him the opportunity to go to university he thought foreclosed forever. He applied for a new scheme providing a university apprenticeship for arts graduates, for which the personnel department initially refused to consider him because he was already in the company. 'I had to be very insistent, as much as one can be at that age.' Finally, an exception was made and a year later he went up to Cambridge to read Law.

He chose Law because it would be good training for business. He had done 'A' level Economics and 'wrongly, I thought I already knew enough Economics and should learn something else'. He considers Law a very good choice in providing a logical approach to business.

On his return to BP he asked immediately to be sent overseas. A planned appointment in Nigeria had to be turned down at the last moment because his father fell ill. In early 1963, he was sent to Algeria immediately after the end of the civil war in a climate of terrorism and instability. By this stage, he was engaged to his Swiss wife, who shared his love of travel. This proved to be a turning point in his career, and as so often in life, a short-term set-back provided the circumstances for an even better opportunity.

That decision was absolutely fundamental to my career because it got me into the French stream as opposed to the English stream. If I had gone to Nigeria, I would have been just another expatriate speaking English in a former English colony and my career would have been totally different. Because I went to Algeria, I had to work in French. I had done French at 'A' level but frankly I was great at analysing Racine and Molière but pretty lousy at speaking decent French. By becoming fluent in French and very at home with French culture my career took a European route rather than a British route. That was pure chance.

Algeria also offered the excitement, danger and adventure that he sought, his imagination fed by his father and brother's experiences of war. 'I have always tended to take a challenge with a degree of risk, sometimes physical risk, because I find it stimulating. I suppose I would have been a natural army officer or colonial administrator.'

Not only did he learn French, acquire a taste for European and Arab culture, and thrive on the climate of risk, but at age 23 was given very early responsibility in running a sales force of Algerians, most of whom had fought in the war. He also married and had his first child in Algeria.

After two years, he was called back to London and asked to sort out a problem in Zaire, then still the Congo, which was in desperate upheaval. BP were rather vague about the posting. Although it turned out to be based in Burundi, recently independent from Belgium and not quite so unstable, it also covered Rwanda and the Eastern Congo. He only learned this after he had accepted the job. People thought that he was mad to take the risk, with a wife and new baby. From the start, however, both he and his wife wholeheartedly embraced the opportunity. 'My wife has been a marvellous support; wherever I have gone in my career, she has always been very positive and just followed'.

At 24, he was Commercial Director for the whole of the Eastern Congo, Burundi and Rwanda.

> It was early responsibility, it was adventure and it was at times, quite dangerous. My wife and I nearly got killed with deserting soldiers holding us up and threatening to shoot us. Someone I had intended to travel with actually was killed. I went through all sorts of problems with the job. It was my first taste of Black Africa which I liked. It was fun – another marvellous three and a half years. My wife loved it and we had our second child down there.

This was also a turning point in his career; for the first time he became compellingly ambitious to succeed. The catalyst was BP's position at the bottom of the market in the region.

> I had never been that serious about work. When I was first at BP I used to enjoy life like any young man and probably my social life was more important than my work. I wanted to go to university

but when I got there I was pretty idle academically and spent most of my time rowing and socialising. In Algeria, I was just a young man doing my job and enjoying life, but when I got to Burundi and found that BP was behind and everyone was trying to put us down, I suddenly wanted to win.

If I'd gone along in jobs that had not been terribly stretching, I probably would have been just a normal, average sort of guy. What changed me was the feeling of being on my own in a far-away country with people trying to put one over on me, fighting back and winning and getting tremendous satisfaction from it. For the first time, being in a tiny pond, one was known in the community as being successful and I decided I rather liked it. I wasn't driven from an early age to succeed, but found I enjoyed the results and the sense of accomplishment.

Since then, I have always been highly competitive for my company, more so than for myself. If we are going to be in a market, we are going to win. There is no point in coming second.

A close colleague at Inchcape confirms that Mackay's ambition for the company today is extraordinarily demanding and aimed at the best possible result for the organisation rather than for himself. 'Charles has a need to set himself and others targets that are immensely stretching. He needs to feel that the profile of the future is the best that we can possibly make it.'

Mackay's next move back into the European mainstream was strategic, actively sought and based on a fear of being sidelined in Africa, and classified as a 'developing country man'. He applied to BP to do an MBA at INSEAD, as it had a reputation for offering good courses and was trilingual in French, German and English. He was ultimately successful in persuading the company to send him to INSEAD, worked very hard under pressure and topped the year, as had his three predecessors from BP.

The next move was unpredictable, totally unplanned, painful but personally necessary, and a source of some anguish for years. Shortly before he was to return to BP, he asked the Personnel Department about his next career step and was told off-handedly that they would decide closer to the time, but that his salary would be £2000, £6000 less than he had made in Burundi, and £3000 less than when he was at INSEAD. He was furious and insulted.

For the first time in my life, I made a highly emotional decision. I refused point blank to return on those terms. I said to them. 'You

are cutting my salary by 60 per cent and asking me to bring back a
wife and two children to a standard of living which is way below
what I had before. I don't expect you to match it. But I'm 29, I've
been with you for twelve years, I've got a good track record. Not a
single person coming out of INSEAD this year will earn as little as
£2000 a year. I just can't accept that. I am prepared to do a lot for
my company, and take a lot of risks but I won't be exploited in that
way.

The Personnel Department could not be moved, and his resignation
was accepted.

At this stage, serendipity began to operate. A chance meeting at
INSEAD had resulted in a McKinsey consultant, Larry Kem, giving
Mackay his card, in case he should ever consider leaving BP. On
leaving Britannic House, therefore, he got on a tube at Moorgate,
walked into McKinsey's office in 87 Jermyn Street and asked for
Kem. 'I was absolutely shaking with rage. I explained everything to
him and said if he had been serious I would like to talk. He said,
"Sure, we were serious". So I joined McKinsey.'

Although his move to McKinsey was accidental, the consulting
firm's reputation in 1969 was outstanding, and he knew it would offer
tremendous training. Charles Mackay never intended consulting to
be a long-term career. He stayed for six and a half years, was given
early responsibility, because of both his international background,
and unusually for McKinsey consultants, experience in line management.

At 29 Mackay was older than most people joining McKinsey and
his progress was swift. Within a year he was a junior Engagement
Manager and two years later promoted to SEM (Senior Engagement
Manager). His line experience proved invaluable.

> I came through fast not because I was a very good consultant but
> because I was used to managing people and therefore could relate
> to clients more easily and they could relate to me. Certainly many
> people who worked for me at McKinsey were a damn sight
> brighter than I was.

He worked both in the UK and in Paris, specialising increasingly in
shipping related studies. In August 1972, because of his African
experience, he was sent to Tanzania to rescue McKinsey's operation,
which was in a 'bit of a mess'. The rescue was successful, the practice
growing from four to twelve consultants with a large backlog of very

interesting studies, owing largely to Mackay's ability to get on well with senior Africans.

After eighteen months, he returned to France, and then started a one-man study reorganising Heineken in Holland. At this stage, Jan van den Berg, the London Office Manager, told Mackay that he would be put up for partnership in the next round and it appeared virtually a *fait accompli.* However, he realised that if he accepted a partnership, he would feel obliged to stay for three or four years, and his line management experience would become less and less relevant. Meanwhile, he had been living in London, commuting to Paris and Amsterdam, seeing very little of his wife and by now three children. He decided that the toll was too large for his family and that it was time to leave.

For the only time in his life his next decision was significantly influenced by financial considerations. He decided to return to Europe because in 1975 with inflation in Britain at 26 per cent, tax at 83 per cent, and the need to start putting three children through boarding school, he would be unable to live on an English salary without a 20 to 30 per cent annual increase in salary to keep pace.

Also, for the first of three times, he talked to head-hunters who were instrumental in his move. The outcome, however, was very different from his carefully thought-out plan. He wanted to live in Switzerland because his wife was Swiss, the standard of living was high and excellent companies offered good opportunities. He wanted to run a division or a reasonably sized subsidiary. Systematically, he spoke to all the head-hunters in Switzerland that McKinsey had identified for him. Ultimately, the colleague in Brussels of a head-hunter in Zurich proposed the role of strategic planner for Royal Pakhoed, a leading Dutch oil storage, property and transport conglomerate based in Rotterdam.

Although on the surface the position met none of his criteria, he was promised a move into senior line management within a year or two, and he was impressed by the company. It was well run, with an excellent reputation, the biggest oil storage company in the world, the leading property company in the Netherlands and with an extensive but loss-making transport and distribution division. Against his 'better judgement' he accepted the job.

As luck would have it, he never took up the planning role but went straight into a challenging line position, as a director of the troubled transport division, Paktrans, which he was charged to bring up to a position to sell. Mackay ultimately became its Chairman after eighteen months, having taken it off the sell list by turning it around and achieving record profits.

> So you can plan to a certain extent but you have got to be opportunistic. I planned to go to Europe but was certainly not planning to go to Holland. The job I ended up doing was not the job I was going across to do and it was supposed to be one year and turned out to be six years!

At this stage his future with Royal Pakhoed looked promising and he and his wife enjoyed Holland. He learned to speak and write Dutch – though it took him two years. Again, the unpredictable intervened, this time in the least bearable form of personal tragedy.

> In New Year 1981, we were hit by a double misfortune. On New Year's Eve, our very beautiful, thatched house was burnt down. But much worse, two days later, my elder son was knocked down by a car outside the house and died a few days later just short of his sixteenth birthday. The whole family was obviously traumatised.
>
> I told myself 'Now, I mustn't make any decisions in a hurry because we have had this shock.' I waited until the middle of the year. By then I had decided that we really had to leave. The trouble was that we lived in a small place where everyone knew what had happened and we really couldn't get away from the memory. We had to drive past the place where it happened. Quite apart from my wife, our other two children, a daughter aged fourteen and a younger son who was almost ten, had an awful shock. Life would never be the same. So I finally accepted it. I thought we should leave. The children were at boarding school in England and I thought we must be close to them.

Again, he approached head-hunters in England. He finally chose to go to Chloride. The job was considerably less well-paid than Royal Pakhoed but he accepted it because it had a strong manufacturing and product development element, which he lacked, and he would run all operations worldwide outside of Europe and North America, which gave him exposure to new parts of the globe. Finally, he had been working in Dutch, French, Belgian and American companies and welcomed the opportunity to work again for a British company. 'It was probably with misplaced zeal that I thought I could play some small part in the reconstruction of British industry.' He also liked the management team.

Although he was very successful at Chloride, driving up the profit of their overseas operations in tough conditions, he ultimately found himself at odds with the strategic direction set by Michael Edwardes (who had since returned to Chloride as Chairman after his time at British Leyland), including the sale to Pacific Dunlop of Chloride's Australian and New Zealand operations where Mackay had overseen a turn-around. 'That left a sour taste in the mouth.' Mackay pointed out that there must be a better strategy than selling off successful overseas operations to buy time on insoluble problems in Europe and the USA, but found himself a minority of one on the Board.

When the Chief Executive left because of these problems, Edwardes told Mackay that he would not want him as Chief Executive under him because of their different personalities and management styles. In January 1986, for the fourth time, Charles Mackay resigned without a job to go to, giving Chloride a year's notice, although he in fact left after three months.

A few days after he resigned from Chloride, Roger Morrison rang him up to ask him, very unusually, to return to McKinsey to undertake a study for the English subsidiary of a Dutch company for three months, while he looked for a new position.

Ten years after leaving McKinsey, this experience confirmed to him the fundamental difference between consulting and line management.

> If ever I had any ideas about going back to consulting that killed it. No disrespect at all for McKinsey. I was too much of a line manager. I knew what needed to be done. It was a managerial problem and analysing for a weak management what needed to be done was not going to solve the problem. It really was an eye opener.

During this study, Morrison asked him whether he would mind him ringing George Turnbull, the very highly regarded Chief Executive of Inchcape, to let him know that Mackay was on the market. He had been approached twice before about joining Inchcape, and to an extent, it seemed part of his destiny.

When George Turnbull offered Charles Mackay a job running Inchcape's Far East operations from Hong Kong, he had already been offered a job running a public company in the UK. Although he did not want yet another divisional chairmanship, and Inchcape was still in trouble, he took the job, largely because he really liked George Turnbull. Turnbull also made it clear that Mackay could expect to be his successor if he did well, although there were no promises. As ever, Mackay's wife was supportive, and he welcomed the opportunity to get to know the Far East.

A colleague, reflecting on Mackay's leadership in the Pacific notes: 'Charles did a brilliant job, providing the operation with vision and values, changing the business entirely. His people revered him.' After five years it was announced that Mackay would become group Chief Executive during 1992, after a handover period of several months as group Managing Director under George Turnbull as Chairman. When Turnbull unexpectedly became seriously ill in November 1991 and had to retire immediately, Mackay was made Chief Executive with no hand over at all. His original move to Inchcape also reinforced another pattern in his career – the salary offered was the lowest of any offer received.

Just as money has never been a prime source of motivation, neither has a need for security nor status been an issue. Recognition is seen as a by-product of doing a job well, rather than as an end in itself. 'I'm not a terribly stuffy, pompous sort of person. I don't get my kicks out of that. You get status when you do a good job.'

Throughout his career he has primarily been motivated by adventure, challenge and interest – 'Interest in people, the job, the company.' Like Allen Sheppard, he has led his life so that if ever a doctor should tell him that he has only six months to live, he would have no regrets, no sense of time wasted. 'I would never have missed any of my jobs. Each was a lot of fun, and at no stage would I have done anything different.'

Charles Mackay's career history is unique among chief executives in that all of his career moves were made after a resignation without knowing where he would be going next – BP, McKinsey, Royal Pakhoed, Chloride. Yet moving without a job is the one move that head-hunters and career advisers almost universally warn dissatisfied people against. It is sometimes necessary, but usually puts one in a position of weakness – both psychologically, and in terms of outside perception of your position.

How then did Charles Mackay buck the trend so successfully, not only surviving but thriving professionally, and ending up as Chief Executive of one of Britain's largest public companies?

First, he had the skills, the track record and the reputation to the extent that each of his moves after McKinsey was effected through head-hunters. Second, key people believed in him and continued to protect his interests. For instance, Roger Morrison at McKinsey played a critical role in his move to Inchcape. The most important person, his wife, has also been incredibly supportive. Third, he was self-confident and felt at the time that for him this was the only way.

> In my experience you cannot decide that you want to leave, work properly and also look around. I'm very single-minded about my work – I can't drive a company forward while looking for a job. I'm either wholly driving one way or I'm wholly driving another way. I would prefer to clear the decks and concentrate on trying to find something I wanted to do for the next five or ten years rather than play games.
>
> I suppose I must have had the self-confidence that I would find something – it never occurred to me that I wouldn't. All I can say is that I wouldn't recommend to anyone else leaving a position without another one lined up, but it has worked for me.

There were moments, even with his self-confidence, particularly when he left Chloride, when he wondered whether people believed that he had resigned and not been pushed. The circumstances inevitably put you on the defensive.

As for the next step, he has 'no idea' about what he will do on retirement at 60.

> I might take on a company chairmanship if I was offered one or a number of non-executive directorships. I might do something completely different, in the public sector or for charity. I would hate to think that this is it for the rest of my life. It may mean going down to an ostensibly lesser level of importance, but something that was in itself a new challenge.

FAMILY AND PERSONAL LIFE

Although Charles Mackay works long hours 'as everyone does, you can't get away with working any less', his family has an important place in his life, featuring prominently in at least two major career decisions. He clearly has an exceptionally close marriage. He mentions the support of his wife frequently as a positive base. His children still go with their parents on well-thought-out and exotic family holidays. He notes that although they might say that he does not spend enough time with them they would never say he was not interested in them.

I don't think I'm one of those businessmen whose family has grown up and feel their father doesn't understand them. My son is coming here tonight from university and we're heading down to the country and will spend the weekend together. My wife and I are close and always have been. We have very similar interests and are happy to spend a lot of time in each other's company. We have a very good marriage. She has always started with the assumption that she would support what I was doing. Fortunately, we've had an interesting life in interesting places and met stimulating people so it's been relatively easy and she has been able to develop a very successful career as an interior designer.

His interests outside work are wide and inevitably include travel, as well as sports (skiing, scuba-diving, tennis, fishing), music (classical and opera) and the engrossing challenge of chess. He plays on one of his three computer chess sets each night for a short while to 'turn off' and relax.

LEADERSHIP AND SUCCESS FACTORS

Charles Mackay by instinct and by experience is an exemplar of the international manager. His interest in other cultures and ways of life is deep, and a thirst for travel his profoundest motivation. His marriage to a Swiss wife who also embraces new cultures and countries reinforced his commitment to an international life. One of the best definitions of the international manager is one who is at home wherever he may be, one who empathises with and enjoys rather than judges or criticises cultural differences. In Mackay's own words, he 'would throw himself into a change of country and jobs'. In this context a close colleague notes: 'Charles has a very international perspective and a very open mind. He is positively intolerant of the little Englander approach. He has no prejudice that I have ever come across.'

Another important characteristic of the truly international manager is the learning of languages, out of an interest in communicating and understanding. Mackay learned French in Algeria, Dutch in Holland, and German although 'to his shame' he never learned Chinese in Hong Kong.

A close colleague, reflecting on his leadership notes:

I have never known a man with so many and such varied talents. He has an outstanding intellect and an extraordinarily rare ability to operate at strategic levels while having a capacity for meticulous attention to detail. This combination has been hugely successful for him, and his attention to detail is the only thing he must watch in leading a large multinational like Inchcape. Charles also has the humility necessary to be deeply self-critical, to learn and to change that is fundamental to true leadership which transcends a single context.

Another close colleague speaks in almost identical terms of Mackay's extraordinarily 'fast mind', which is both visionary and 'at times too analytical' and of his high level of internal energy, which leads him to spin off ideas like a Catherine wheel.

A leader must think extraordinary thoughts sometimes and Charles relishes people who can tell him directly that some of his ideas are off-the-wall. He will listen and accept readily – he is never defensive about this sort of feedback.

His colleagues also confirm that Charles Mackay is thoroughly nice with great compassion, a person who bends over backwards to be fair. 'He is not a self-seeker, and would never ask people to do what he wouldn't himself. He has no side and treats people at all levels in the company the same. He is also whiter-than-white – a man of enormous integrity and for instance, a real stickler on expenses.' He is also expert at building relationships and networks that are valuable to the business – 'his mind is always tuned to the needs of the business'. Lastly, Charles Mackay works enormously hard. 'Work is his hobby as well.'

Although Charles Mackay feels fairly uncomfortable talking about leadership, 'it's not something that I sit down and think about', he identifies three essential skills or attributes.

First is the ability to determine what it is you want to achieve, second the will-power and determination to get there and third, the motivation skills to make people run with you. Some people have tremendous charm, or charisma, others have brilliant ideas about products or ways of marketing them, others outstanding financial skills. But if you want to distil it down, those are the three essential attributes.

Although he believes reasonable intelligence is necessary, brilliance can drive out other qualities and lead to indecision and the 'absent-minded professor syndrome'.

Charles Mackay believes that future CEOs will require the same basic qualities although the skills and approach may change slightly in favour of more consensus-management, a team approach and a less autocratic style.

In identifying his senior management team at Inchcape, he looks for a balance of strengths, and is very wary of cloning.

> I don't believe there is a model successful manager – many different types of manager are successful. I prefer to have a wide variety of managers who, through a balance of skills, happen to be successful. So I might balance a maverick with lots of flair with a terrific organiser.
>
> We talk about 'producers' and 'organisers' at Inchcape. Good managers have to be ideally both a 'producer' or a developer of business and an 'organiser' or excellent administrator who makes things work. But you're lucky if you get someone who is good at both – most people are better at one than the other. It's important to choose people who complement each other and get them to work together. Occasionally, people can do both and that's marvellous. I'm probably more of a producer and go-getter who makes things happen but either a producer or an administrator could run Inchcape!

As confirmed by his colleagues, Charles Mackay's philosophy about people is based on believing in them and giving them the fullest possible chance. 'I would rather persevere with someone six months, a year, two years too long to make quite sure that they couldn't make it than to make a judgement prematurely. Not so much for them or for me, but for all the others who are watching. It gives people the assurance that this is not a hire-and-fire company – it expects high performance but isn't ruthless.'

Charles Mackay's basic philosophy is that you can not move forward if afraid of making mistakes – it is important only not to make too many mistakes. He believes that his weakness as a manager is in being overly optimistic both about people and the future of companies – the flip side of the necessary leadership characteristic of believing in people to motivate them and seeing business opportunities in sub-optimal circumstances.

I am reluctant to believe that there are people in an organisation who are not actually working for the good of the organisation but are much more interested in their own positions or in organisational politics. That sounds naive and trite, but I was brought up with a military ethos. I am always trying to drive things forward and always assume everyone else is too.

I am also sometimes too confident that I can turn around bad situations. As someone once said to me, 'Charles, you're a great buyer of companies, but you're not a very good closer of companies', and I agreed with that. I hang on because I'm determined to crack the problem and it can waste time. However, I usually don't take the risk except on smaller companies.

Charles Mackay would offer three general guidelines for those aspiring to senior management:

- Concentrate on doing the job well and the opportunities will come. It really is a question of 'the harder I work the luckier I get'. Don't sit there planning each career step. You'll come unstuck if you do. You've got to give absolutely everything to what you are doing now and then be prepared to be opportunistic if something should come up. But it is important always to have a sense of moving forward and not to stagnate, adding to one's experience.

In Mackay's experience, those people who were too highly organised about career planning and promotions rarely made it to the top.

Those people lacked something – they were too mechanistic about it. I do not think life is like that – it would be like a general predicting exactly how a battle would go. Unfortunately, the enemy is out there and you have to be very flexible in your response.

- Strive to be the best – if you are going to do something you may as well do it well. Stretch yourself – don't let people tell you it's too much for you or you are too young. As Hugh Parker, the head of the McKinsey London office when I joined, said to me, Alexander the Great conquered an empire by the time he was thirty.
- It is important to have early general management experience. There is no substitute for learning the hard way and making your

own mistakes, finding what works and what doesn't, starting out small and then moving on to something bigger. General management forces you to think of all aspects of the business. The actual size of the unit doesn't matter – developing the ability to think about a number of functions simultaneously, and their impact on profit is what's important.

From his own personal experience, he would add the following advice.

(1) If you aspire to be in charge of a large international company, it is important to gain international experience in the field.

(2) It is worthwhile to undertake an MBA in your late twenties, because it strengthens the ability to think across a number of different functions, but it is absolutely no substitute for practical experience. An MBA can go wrong if someone with three or four years narrow functional experience goes to business school, thinks about business in theory for one or two years, then goes back to another functional area, say planning or finance, for ten years. In these circumstances, the MBA will help him to do a better job, but it will not train him to be a general manager. Ten years after business school you really do not remember anything about the courses you took.

(3) Consulting experience, for instance, at McKinsey, will help you to think on a bigger scale, and teach you to deal with the big issues in the biggest companies. It will not help you to find a line job, because there is still nervousness about putting someone straight into a line job from consultancy. An outstanding consultant will not necessarily be an effective line manager or chief executive. Consultants are very good at analysing problems, but not necessarily effective at making things happen in practice.

11

Sir John Egan
Chief Executive BAA Plc

Date of birth: 7 November 1939
Place of birth: Rawtenstall, Lancashire, UK
Nationality: British
Marital status: Married
Family: Two daughters

Education:	De La Salle College
	Bacup and Rawtenstall Grammar
	Bablake School
	'A' levels: Maths, Physics, Chemistry
1958–1961	Imperial College, London University, Caltex Scholarship
	BSc Petroleum Engineering
1966–1968	London Business School
	MSc Business Studies (Shell Award for outstanding
	contribution)

Career:
1961–1962	Bahrain Petroleum
	Petroleum Engineer, Bahrain Island
1963–1966	Shell Petroleum
	Engineer, Holland, Qatar and Iran
1968–1971	General Motors Ltd
	General Manager, AC Delco Replacement Parts
	Operation
1971–1976	British Leyland Motor Corporation
	Managing Director, Parts Division, Specialist Car Division
	Parts and Service Director, Leyland Cars
1976–1980	Massey Ferguson
	Marketing Director, International Construction
	Machinery and Coordinator, European Operations –
	Rome
	Corporate Parts Director
1980–1990	Jaguar Cars Ltd and Jaguar Plc
	Chairman and Chief Executive
1990 to date	BAA Plc
	Chief Executive

Outside appointments:
1987–1994	Legal and General
1989–1994	Non-executive Director
1994 to date	Vice Chairman
1985 to date	The Foreign & Colonial Investment Trust Plc
	Non-executive Director
1993 to date	London Tourist Board
	Chairman
1994 to date	British Tourist Authority
	Board Director
1993 to date	London First Visitors Council, Chairman

| Interests: | Theatre, music, reading, walking, skiing |

INTRODUCTION

Sir John Egan is rare among leading Chief Executives in having successfully headed up two major companies in quite different industries. A charismatic extravert, he has provided a vision and clear sense of direction at both Jaguar and BAA and energised his people to understand and embrace his priorities. Well known as an excellent marketeer with a fervent belief in the customer, and as an outstanding, enthusiastic communicator, he is gifted at rendering the complex simple and getting to the heart of issues quickly.

Although he has never had a personal career goal, he has always been generally ambitious to succeed and his career decision-making has been a mixture of chance, responding to offers and an active search for the skills and the environment needed to achieve.

His career began with four years' specialised experience as a Petroleum Engineer in the Middle East followed by the actively sought breadth of an MBA. Functional experience in finance was followed by early general management experience at age 30 with General Motors, and further moves at divisional director level to British Leyland and Massey Ferguson. Chairman of Jaguar by age 41 he gained a very high profile in the eighties for turning around the ailing luxury car maker.

John Egan's departure from Jaguar with its sale to Ford in 1989 for 1.5 billion pounds was widely regarded as a success story, although accompanied by some quite trenchant public criticism from his successor as Chairman, Bill Hayden which Egan puts philosophically into context. As Chief Executive of BAA since 1990 he has been incontrovertibly successful, in the first four years increasing its profits, extending its international operations and becoming a world leader in innovative airport retailing.

John Egan's career has been characterised by active learning not only from one or two mentors, but also from the lessons gained from the incompetence of some of those around him which he was determined not to replicate. His international experience in the Middle East, Continental Europe and North America gave him a life-long appetite not only for following best practice but also for pursuing global leadership in his industry.

What have been the important developmental experiences of a leading Chief Executive who has headed up two major UK companies in quite different industries? What advice does he have for those who would reach the top?

EARLY INFLUENCES

The younger of two sons of a garage owner and Rootes dealer in the Midlands, John Egan identifies two important influences on his early development – the easy acceptance of change derived from a father who was an entrepreneur, and the self-reliance developed necessarily from the hardships suffered at a highly disciplined and very tough Catholic boarding school, De La Salle College. 'I learned that even in those very difficult places, there were things that one could enjoy, like reading and sport. I got by and things got better from then on!'

He chose to study maths, physics and chemistry at 'A' level characteristically because they were his strongest subjects.

CAREER DECISION-MAKING AND DEVELOPMENT

John Egan chose to study petroleum engineering at Imperial College on a scholarship partly out of a recognition that conventional office jobs had no appeal and partly from a sense of adventure. 'I didn't see myself at 21 going into an office in London with a briefcase. I wanted to explore many different places and opportunities before I had to do that.'

As with many others, he had a general ambition to succeed, accompanied by a desire for independence, without any specific goals.

> I always thought at the back of my mind that I would do reasonably well but I didn't have any particular goals. I didn't have financial goals, but I had emotional and safety goals. That's not the complete story, obviously money is important. It's the lingua franca of business – the better you do, the more money you get. But first I would like to see the company do very well and as a result of that I would like to see that I did well. I look for challenges. In retrospect, I can see that I am always looking to be the world's best. For instance, I would have stayed at Jaguar and tried to maintain its independence but I just didn't think it could be a global leader on its own.

While he cannot identify in his own life the precise cause of his own ambition, he evidences the willingness to examine himself that is the precondition of real learning:

There is something that drives one on. I have no idea what it is. In my case, depression of a deep kind and elation and exhilaration can both exist in the same half hour. I would never be depressed for long, half a day at most. I have learned to reflect and to use these times to understand what it is that actually adds to my life.

Egan cites with approval some research into the psychology of happiness that concludes that most of the circumstances contributing to happiness are found at work.

Happiness was found to come from doing things that are goal-oriented, doing things where you get feedback, where your skills are commensurate with the task. Yet most people think that doing very little is relaxing. I certainly get my greatest satisfaction out of working hard and doing a good job and I am obviously not alone.

As a petroleum engineer, the first few years of his career were spent in oil companies, first a year with Bahrain Petroleum on Bahrain Island, then three years with Shell in Holland, Qatar and Iran. With no previous experience, his first job 'amazingly and marvellously' was as foreman in an oilfield where he learned not only about practical realities of the work, but about management and humility.

At a very early age the oil industry gives you real and important jobs to do which makes you very self-reliant. I was 21. I had a degree and was theoretically capable, but I'd never given anyone an instruction. I had to learn the actual practice of the job from the Arabs who worked for me. I was getting on quite well: after three or four months, Rashid, my lead man, came to speak to me about planning the workload. In a rather confidential tone, he said to me 'Well, John, I suppose that we are going to do this.' All Europeans were called Sahib, and I said to him in full dignity, 'The name is not John, but Sahib John'. He looked at me for some time and said, 'OK, so I am Sahib Rashid'. I started laughing and said, 'OK, Rashid, so I am John' and we both laughed. From then on, I haven't much liked the mistering and the siring.

The rewards and satisfaction of the field were mitigated by the boredom and futility of enforced time in the office one week every month. He learned early the damaging effects of poor leadership, and resolved to become a competent manager himself and never to repeat the mistakes he witnessed.

> I found those weeks in the office often soul-destroying. Much of it
> was wasted by the woolly thinking of the people who gave you
> various projects that weren't purposeful. Engineers are the world's
> worst managers and my boss was brilliant but a typical engineer.
> He would pile paper up on his desk, we would write reports and
> they would get lost. We used to bribe his Indian clerk to put our
> reports on the top of the pile. I knew that if I stayed I would
> become as bad a manager as he was.
>
> As a result, I hate wasting my subordinates' time. I like to have
> my own thinking absolutely clear so that I am certain when I ask
> someone to change something.

As a result, Egan spent two years at the London Business School to
learn about competent management. The MBA provided not only
theoretical management tools, but a lifelong appetite for keeping at
the cutting edge of management thinking and best practice.

> Business school was very important for me. It gave me a theoretical
> framework with which to tackle the job and was extremely
> powerful in helping me to debug the mysteries of experts. I think
> that people who criticise business school graduates for being
> strategists when they haven't yet learned to lay bricks are a bit
> trivial because you even have to lay bricks with a good strategy.
> Since then I constantly try to ensure that my kitbag of strategic,
> analytical and problem solving approaches is as advanced and up
> to date as possible.

Egan's career moves after business school were invariably initiated by
unsolicited job offers and 'almost accidentally' his first move was the
beginning of a twenty-year career in the motor industry. After giving
a lecture on the use of business graduates in industry, he was
approached by the Personnel Director of General Motors who took
him straight back to the office to meet the Treasurer, Bill DeLong,
who in turn offered him a job on the spot. DeLong proved to be a
mentor, good businessman and effective change-agent who sur-
rounded himself with competent young people.

At General Motors, Egan was able to put into practice business
school theory, particularly in finance and organisational behaviour,
and while responsible for pricing and cost-estimating, he deepened his
financial understanding. By age 30, with the breadth of an MBA,
early operational and international experience and financial grounding, the opportunity to move into general management was a timely

challenge. As General Manager of AC Delco, Replacement Parts Division of General Motors, in charge of two or three hundred people, he most importantly discovered how to manage the industrial relations climate effectively by personally talking to each employee.

Egan moved to British Leyland in 1971 largely for cultural reasons – General Motors had been the antithesis of an international culture.

> I felt as though I was working for an alien culture among all Americans at General Motors who were always talking about 'them', and 'they' were my lot – the Brits! I had become almost an apprentice American and grew curious to see how a British company was managed.

He joined the finance department of British Leyland and quickly became Managing Director of the Specialist Car Division parts operation, moving to become Parts and Service Director for all cars. It was a particularly exciting time to be joining British Leyland, 'John Barber and Lord Stokes were going to rebuild the British car industry', and Egan's experience in working with John Barber, was similar in its impact to Allen Sheppard's. Ironically, Allen Sheppard is remembered more as a mentor than John Barber. To a large extent Egan was in the same situation as Sheppard, running a profitable part of a sinking business, with the same sense of frustration and a growing resilience.

> I learned a lot from Allen. He was a good finance man, and he always managed to add value and create wealth. He is also quite excitable and very graphic in his descriptions of situations. We used to have a lot of fun. I also realised that you could go through very difficult and tough times without getting too depressed, because in fact none of the problems really did crush you.

As at boarding school, in the midst of a tough, emotionally challenging environment, he just 'carried on'.

At the same time, Egan's experience with industrial relations at General Motors stood him in good stead.

> I learned that in spite of an enormous amount of chaos, the job underneath could often carry on unaffected. Although it was very difficult to change fundamentally the terrible climate within the car industry, I became sure that I had some answers for the industrial relations problems at British Leyland and was really quite anxious to start improving basic relationships between people.

It was clear, however, that British Leyland was in trouble, 'rapidly going nowhere at all and would likely go out of business'. After five years, when he was offered a job at Massey Ferguson as Marketing Director of international construction machinery and Co-ordinator, for European operations based in Rome, he jumped. The appeal, other than escape, was financial – based in Rome, his after-tax income would be significantly higher. Although he stayed four years, becoming Director, Corporate Parts, Massey Ferguson was a mixed experience, which gave rise to a deep-seated concern about internal communication and his concept of the 'reflective layer and the notion of muddle'.

> Instructions from senior people are delivered to middle management, who know that at least half of the instructions won't work because they are irrelevant, they don't have the resources or different instructions have been given to somebody else. The trouble is they don't know which half so they tend to ignore all of them.
>
> Problems also come from the bottom up and middle management either don't have the resources or they have to break the rules to solve them so they tend to ignore the problems and carry on as they always did. This is why some organisations are so resilient, but neither can they improve. You can improve a company a great deal by getting the instructions and the problems to line up together and by getting everyone going in the same direction, taking common cause in achieving an agreed objective.

As had the oil companies at a junior level, Massey Ferguson provided a useful model of how not to manage.

> Massey Ferguson was one of the worst managed companies I had ever come across. It made money because of one or two good deals in the past and because they were then operating in a simple and profitable industry. While I was there, the agricultural machinery industry came across hard times. It had been living off subsidies which had been given to the Third World to buy tractors.
>
> I remember a very amusing story. I attended a Management Committee of the company in Toronto and the President, Al Thornborough said, 'In these difficult times none of us has experience losing money, but you, Mr Egan from British Leyland have experience of losing money. What advice would you give?' I said, 'I have some advice, but I know you won't listen. Just because

there is a recession, don't believe that you can make companies that are used to losing money into companies that will make money. Anything that doesn't make money today, you must get rid of it, walk away from it!' He said, 'That means we will have to close down Argentina, Brazil, Mexico, Australia, the US. The only ones left will be Canada, Italy and the UK and the price is too big to pay'. However, if this had been done immediately Massey Ferguson would have been profitable and he would have been a hero.

Meanwhile, Michael Edwardes had asked him to return to run a much larger part of British Leyland, and believing it impossible to save, Egan refused. The next offer to run Jaguar he accepted. 'Margaret Thatcher had been elected and I could see from abroad that things were improving, there was something different happening here. I thought that it was almost impossible to save Jaguar, but it was worth a try.'

Egan began by tackling Jaguar's by then notorious quality and reliability problem and rebuilding the pride and confidence of the demoralised workforce. He introduced quality circles and worked hard on employee communication, screening motivational and informational videos several times a year to all the workforce in groups of two or three hundred. By 1981, quality had improved, two major new models been introduced and Jaguar's public and media image rejuvenated. Two years later, Egan had more than doubled productivity. Assisted by a favourable exchange rate, Jaguar's sales in the US soared.

Egan's greatest professional satisfaction was first making over £100 million profit at Jaguar. 'The British car industry had never really made any money and we actually did it.' In 1985 Jaguar was floated and by 1987, with the pound strengthening, speculation about takeover began to circulate which resulted in Jaguar's successful sale to Ford in 1989 for one and a half billion pounds. Ten years before Jaguar had been offered for nothing to several car companies and the sale was therefore widely regarded as a triumph for Egan and the shareholders.

The Ford acquisition was followed by quite trenchant criticism of Egan's leadership at Jaguar by his successor as Chief Executive, Bill Hayden, who lambasted publicly the primitive factory conditions at Jaguar and attributed Egan's success to marketing and effective public relations. Although John Egan accepts with some reservation

Hayden's evaluation of the state of the factories, he puts this into the context of the dramatic turnaround of the company.

Bill Hayden, as the best manufacturing person at Ford, knew more about manufacturing cars than I did but he did not understand that I inherited virtually no assets at Jaguar. One factory was built during the First World War, the other two were Second World War including Castle Bromwich where we lived like hermits in a very small part of a huge factory. We had virtually no engineering facilities.

What I realised in Jaguar was a really excellent concept, a brand name, a tradition but with very antiquated practices and production facilities. My very simple strategy was to make these beautiful cars work and that is what we did. As soon as we could get them to work, and get the paint and the tyres to stay on, we could sell them. We also created a strong dealer network and selling organisation, probably the best in the car industry.

On the other hand, we were always quite realistic. My objective was to save the company and at the same time to be competitive. Under these survival conditions you leave many battles unfinished and although we tried to do something with the factories, this could not be our only priority. The first priority was a new engineering centre and tooling for new models with a body plant to make them in. The assembly plant was the next frontier; they were quite unrealistic if they had expected world class manufacturing facilities – after all they had paid five times asset value.

I had seen British Leyland very stupidly run out of cash and this had made me immensely prudent. I don't take any big step unless it is very, very safe. In these volatile Anglo-Saxon economies you don't get any Brownie points for being brave. We had double jeopardy, with big capital expenditures and high interest rates. At Jaguar we could see the world changing, we could see recession in the States, a very weak dollar and the pound pegged to the ERM and also high inflation. Added to the arrival of a new Japanese competitor, we called this the Doomsday scenario and prudence dictated that we accept Ford's offer.

He is also philosophical about the nature of professional success, reflecting on the vicissitudes of public profile, both in over-rating and under-rating performance. With scepticism about the fickle evaluation of the media, he has an underlying confidence in his ability to make a contribution to any business.

I think about my career in a calm sort of way. You simply carry on. At one stage in the very early days of the enormous success at Jaguar, the media gave the impression that I could walk on water. There is no doubt my image was overcooked. On the other hand, I know I can do a good solid job, that I can improve the performance of any company I am put into and create value.

Although he prefers not to dwell on mistakes, given his own dedication to best practice, he faults himself at Jaguar for not fully understanding the lessons to be learned from Japan, particularly relating to the design process. He looked, but did not see enough.

I didn't catch on quickly enough to the revolution that was coming out of Japan – although to begin with we were in such a mess that anything I did was in the right direction. But the intellectual approach was far deeper than I first understood. We all got very excited by Japanese factory management, but their greatest success lay in the design process itself.

In Europe we thought of the design process as essentially creative, requiring critical path planning to control chaos, whereas the Japanese had broken it into processes, such as research, design, testing design, testing manufacture, tidying up and then making. The whole complicated design process was seen as a series of processes to be caught hold of, so that the next time you could do it better.

He emphasises that even the introduction of Japanese design processes would not have altered Jaguar's fate. 'I'm not sure that anything we could have done at Jaguar would have made any difference. We would still have been bought by Ford at eight pounds fifty per share in 1989, assuming that there was going to be a recession in the UK and in the US.' He has, however, learned by introducing the Japanese design process into the construction process at BAA, and thus halving construction costs.

Egan next accepted BAA's invitation to join as Chief Executive because of a conviction that he could add value to the company and a belief in the future of its airports.

I felt that the management of BAA were taking it in the wrong direction and specifically, that Heathrow was better run than its image and was much more efficient than many airports. I also saw value in the company that was not readily apparent and thought that it was a relatively straightforward job to realise and improve its performance.

In addition, at 51 he was not ready to retire.

> I had got myself up to such a high pitch of activity at Jaguar, especially at the end selling the company, that I was not in the mood to do nothing. There were all sorts of things that came past that I was interested in trying out.

Generally he believes that it is easier to remain within the same industry when changing companies at the top. 'It must be better if you know a lot about it.' It also obviates the dilemma of having to show leadership while having few answers.

> One aspect of changing industries is very uncomfortable. You come into a company like BAA and know very little about aviation, radar, runways, air traffic control, safety in air terminals. To start with, you feel almost too embarrassed to mention some of your general ideas to the experts. You're starting at the top, so people look to you expectantly for leadership and all you've got is questions. This role of learning from ignorance is harder as you get older and you feel a bit of a fraud for a little while.

On the other hand, changing industries certainly prevents staleness, and as one most comfortable with the big picture rather than operational detail, Egan soon created a clear vision for BAA, about which he speaks passionately:

> My approach to corporate strategy at BAA is very simple and straightforward. It doesn't take more than thirty seconds to describe it to you and most of the people in the company would recognise what we were doing and what I want them to do. I tell them that our mission is quite simply to make BAA the most successful airport company in the world. We must first of course find out what the customer wants and we very quickly learn that they want high quality and low costs. The only way to deliver this is to improve the process through what we call continuous improvement and others may call quality management or process management. Continuous improvement is already yielding big results for our business. It requires every single person at BAA to 'bring their brains to work' and therefore includes programmes of empowerment, training and appraisal. I go round the company

each year on 'roadshows' to debate our mission with all our employees and to see whether managers are indeed managing in the way that the mission statement suggests they should.

John Egan's early international experience in the Middle East followed by working for an American company, and later for a Canadian company based in Rome, working throughout Europe no doubt contributed to this international outlook that not only defines corporate objectives globally but also seeks best practice worldwide.

> My international experience has been absolutely fundamental. In most industries in the UK we are not competing on the world scale and it is all too easy to be content with being the best in Britain or the best in Europe. One of the first things I did when I came to BAA was to go and examine airport operations around the world wherever they had a reputation for doing things well. I found best practice and discovered that there was enormous scope for improvement for us. The notion here had been that as Heathrow was the biggest international airport in the world, it must be the best. I acknowledged that it was very good, but pointed out that others did some things better, and we would be even better if we followed them.

In terms of worldwide best practice, he is proud of BAA's achievements in all three aspects of its business – airport management, retailing and capital project development. Of airport retailing he notes:

> Copenhagen, Schipol in Amsterdam and Changi in Singapore were easily the leaders in airport retailing, but retailing at our airports is now much changed and far more innovative, with quality brand names, the development of near shopping malls/department stores, the notions of 'value for money' and 'never knowingly undersold' and money-back guarantees. In catering, if you don't enjoy your meal, we will give you your money back. All aspects of retail and catering are subjected to rigorous market research to achieve our objective of giving the customer what he wants.

He speaks with equal conviction about BAA's achievements in building terminal buildings.

> If you can preplan what you are going to do and build it very quickly you can halve the cost of building it. We need to plan the

best concept. We need to know about the optimal use of space, and preplan every day of the construction process, to have a procurement chain in place, to predict productivity.

We aim to build high quality, low cost world-class capital projects by completing the design before we start building, using computer modelling as they do in the car industry. We also use standardised components wherever possible, building up good relationships with reliable suppliers and reducing our costs. We design afresh as little as absolutely required, again relying on standardised rather than customised solutions. We have scoured the world for best practice and believe that we will eventually be world leaders in this area.

After four years of Egan's leadership, BAA in 1994 increased profits to £322 million, in spite of the Civil Aviation Authority's tough formula for airport charges, pegging south east (including Gatwick and Heathrow) airport charges at 8 per cent below the rate of inflation.

When asked about plans for the rest of his working life, John Egan answers in terms of a change of lifestyle, although there is clearly scope for another move, or a portfolio of non-executive chairmanships/directorships.

I don't see the rest of my working life in breathtaking clarity. I do intend to spend more time doing other things that I enjoy, for instance, going to the theatre. My wife and I are now Shakespeare groupies. She has recently done a degree in English and Italian at Warwick University and studied the whole of the Shakespeare play cycle so we have seen most of the plays over a few years' span. All performances used to seem grey because my mind was elsewhere. Now I am able to relax and enjoy the performance and I am irritated with mediocrity but extremely delighted when I see something very, very good.

FAMILY AND PERSONAL LIFE

Although his present practice and plans for the future include more time spent on activities outside work, as with most business leaders of his generation his life has not always been so balanced. 'I always tried to spend enough physical hours with my family, but in retrospect, my mind was often somewhere else – it wasn't 100 per cent attendance.' However, long holidays were always spent with his children and they still often go on skiing or beach holidays together. Once a year he and his wife take a walking holiday (last year in the Tuscan hills) and a skiing holiday.

Apart from theatre and music, he also reads voraciously, mostly history. He shares a fascination with other business leaders in military history – not only for lessons on leadership and strategy, but for comfort. 'In the middle of the mud and blood of war, I was always reassured at British Leyland to read that things could be much worse.'

Although his attitude towards religion is ambivalent, John Egan has a well-defined personal and professional belief system.

I had religion drummed into me at a very early age so you never escape that. I don't fully understand this yet, but if you were to shoot me in thirty seconds, I believe that early religious education and belief in God would come back in full force. On the other hand, I find the whole ritual of religion and theological concepts and language very difficult to accept. The music is very beautiful of course but it would have been wiser to have kept the Latin liturgy and allowed its full mystery to take over. Trying to bring God into regular life is very difficult.

On the other hand, I do believe that there is a very clear distinction between what is right and what is wrong. I would never get close to running anything doubtful. I need always to be able to explain fully what we have done to our employees, customers and shareholders. It is also important for companies to believe that the guy at the top of the company knows the difference between right and wrong; if they believe that then they will try harder.

LEADERSHIP AND SUCCESS FACTORS

Above all, John Egan believes that there is no single notion or stereotype of a leader in business. Far from believing that the skills and approaches of future chief executives will be different from those required today or in the past, he affirms 'They will be exactly the

same – the ability to learn, to change, to motivate'. Egan seems to
have an intuitive understanding of the world of Tom Peters' *Thriving
on Chaos* or Rosabeth Moss Kanter's 'post-entrepreneurial society',
where change is constant and flexibility key:

> The rate of change in, for instance, the computer industry is
> incredible. One Japanese computer company executive told me
> that technology was changing so fast there that they hardly dared
> have any permanent employees at all, because they could not
> identify the skills they would need over time. People would be
> unemployable for them unless they are willing to learn a whole new
> set of skills every two years.

In selecting future leaders at BAA with the ability to learn, to change
and to motivate, he looks above all for people who will take
responsibility for achieving corporate objectives. He concedes that
he is poor at letting underperformers go which is complicated by his
own tendency to delegate too little in those areas where he has a
particular interest.

> If I have got one fault I tend to do too much of the job for some
> people, particularly in those parts of the business where I have a
> special interest. I sometimes assume that I know what people are
> doing, while I have been doing too much of it for them. Sometimes
> those areas that I am not interested in do a great deal better
> because people know that they have to get things done themselves.

A former close colleague believes that Egan's own success as a leader
is based on a combination of intelligence, infectious enthusiasm and
apparently boundless self-confidence. He notes that Egan is also a
persuasive salesman who could sell iceblocks to the Eskimos and that
he has successfully avoided what might have been a danger in his
earlier days of taking himself too seriously.

John Egan's advice to those who aspire to be business leaders
echoes the experience of most chief executives in the study – success is
not about planning or politics.

> I have a strange feeling that ambitious young people should be
> reasonably patient and hold the success of the company as more
> important than their own success. If they believe in the company
> and really do try hard, they shouldn't be surprised if they do very
> well. Doing a good job is the way to the top.

He has himself changed companies six times in his career, but does not believe that such change is necessarily valuable. It is however absolutely necessary to keep learning.

I always make sure that there are a number of days each year where I am basically learning – from peers, from educational places, wherever. I would advise people to ensure that their personal training programme keeps them up to the cutting edge of skills they need.

12

Sir Christopher Hogg

Chairman, Courtaulds, Courtaulds Textiles, Reuters

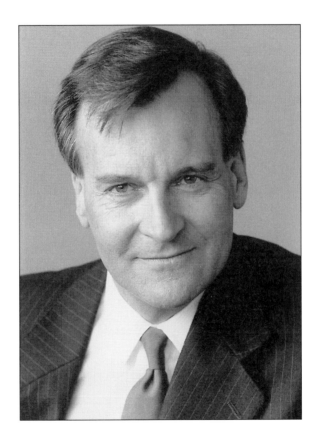

Date of birth:	2 August 1936
Place of birth:	London
Nationality:	British
Marital status:	Separated
Family:	Two daughters
Languages:	French

Education:	Marlborough College
	'A' levels in Latin, Greek and Ancient History
1957–1960	Trinity College, Oxford
	MA with 1st Class Honours, English Literature
1960–1962	Harvard University
	MBA with high distinction

Career:
1955–1957	National Service
1962–1963	IMEDE
1963–1966	Philip Hill, Higginson, Erlangers Ltd (subsequently Hill Samuel & Co Ltd)
1966–1968	Industrial Reorganisation Corporation
1968 to date	Courtaulds Group
1968–1972	Director, International Paint
1972–1973	Chairman, British Celanese
1973–1978	Chairman International Paint and Main Board Director
1978–1979	Deputy Chairman
1979–1980	Chief Executive and Chairman Designate
1980–1981	Chairman and Chief Executive
1991 to date	Non-executive Chairman

Outside appointments:
Reuters Non-executive Chairman, 1985 –
Bank of England, Director, 1992 –
Courtaulds Textiles Plc, Non-executive Chairman, 1990 –
Member of the International Council of J P Morgan, 1988 –
Board of Trustees of the Ford Foundation, 1987 –
SmithKline Beecham Plc, Non-executive Director, 1993 –

Interests: Reading, theatre, walking

INTRODUCTION

Christopher Hogg's background exemplifies what many consider to be the 'model' of the traditional Chief Executive. Headboy of Marlborough, graduating with a First from Oxford and a Baker Scholar at the Harvard Business School, he was early marked out for leadership and success. He had a clear, if general, objective for a career in international business, and a career path designed to equip him for very senior management – the army for character-building, Harvard Business School for confidence and management theory, a year in Europe with leading business school IMEDE, three years in a bank for financial grounding and two years at the Industrial Reorganisation Corporation, the centre of government policy making for industry where he met his mentor Lord Kearton.

Next followed eleven years of senior management positions at Courtaulds working across all aspects of the business, becoming Chief Executive at age 43. Far from being a stereotype, Hogg is one of few in our sample who spent so long with a single company. Well-educated, with several early career moves, apart from his lengthy tenure at Courtaulds, his profile could be that of the 'new' generation of chief executives.

Highly regarded in the business community for turning Courtaulds around and courageously splitting the company into two profitable enterprises, Courtaulds and Courtaulds Textiles, he is also deeply respected for his thoughtful, cerebral, life-long learning approach to management and for his integrity. Is there something special about Christopher Hogg's early development, his approach to career decision-making or the pattern of his career itself that have contributed to his success? What makes him tick?

EARLY INFLUENCES

Christopher Hogg grew up in a middle-class home, the second child of four of Anthony Hogg, owner/managing director of theatrical publisher, Samuel French. Hogg describes his childhood as fortunate. His parents were supportive, providing him with early independence: 'They delegated the management of my life to me from a young age'. His education was the 'traditional, privileged one', boarding at prep school at seven and a half, then Marlborough where he was headboy and on the cricket and rugby teams.

The most important influence on his early life which perhaps provided the necessary 'grit in the oyster' and drive was striving to emulate his older brother Daniel.

> Why I should have been trying to emulate him quite so hard is a different matter; it still puzzles me. He's eighteen months older than I am and actually a completely different person, but in terms of the British educational system he was a high achiever because he was a brilliant athlete. That was much admired and I suspect that was the principal driving force.

An intriguing aspect of Christopher Hogg's development, of which he is very aware, is the extent to which his choice of subjects at school and university went 'against the grain'. He notes that his personality type (a clear ISTJ in terms of the Myers Briggs Type Indicator) is one that produces accountants and engineers. In spite of being more 'numerate than literate' he was influenced by a schoolmaster to study classics at school and English at university.

> Studying classics was decided for me essentially. The Housemaster of my junior school at Marlborough said that classics was the right thing for able boys and future leaders to study and who was I to disagree? I was a very law-abiding little boy, so I read classics. I think I'm right in believing that with my personality type I would have been a better mathematician or something like that. I didn't want to do classics at university because although I enjoyed studying Latin and Greek, I didn't enjoy it that much. English I did enjoy very much and I thought wrongly that English was one of the few things that I could have read other than classics. With hindsight, the university would have let me study history or economics, but it really doesn't matter. I am more broad-minded in a cultural sense as a result of having read English than I would have been otherwise.

Someone less gifted might have under-performed in choosing subjects that so clearly did not call for his preferred way of looking at the world. Yet Christopher Hogg won a classics scholarship to Oxford and received a first-class honours degree in English.

Before going to university, Christopher Hogg spent two extremely influential years undertaking an unusually violent national service, which included eight months fighting terrorists in Cyprus, being parachuted into Port Said during the Suez crisis and killing at first hand before he was 20. He was confronted for the first time with his own fallibility, a powerful lesson he has never forgotten, and which began a habit of self-examination and self-criticism that has never left him.

> National Service shook me as an experience. I had thought that I would be the perfect 'organisational participant', very happy to conform to the military's requirements; but I collided with the army – I really didn't like the strait-jacket. I was a good soldier and did the conventional things right but I discovered that I was not very good at leading men of a different class. In fact, I was a poor officer compared to my brother – I was too intense, too ambitious and intellectual. I also got very frightened which was sobering. I learned a salutary lesson – I might have thought I was God's gift if I hadn't had my army experience! I have never forgotten that feeling of fallibility.

CAREER DECISION-MAKING AND DEVELOPMENT

In spite of his own early experience of going against the grain in deference to authority, in advising his two daughters about how to make decisions about their own lives and careers, he is most concerned that they pursue their natural gifts.

> The ancient Greeks had it right. The words that were written above the gate at Delphi 'know thyself' are a wonderful piece of advice. You have got to live with yourself the whole of your life. You shouldn't run your life to please anybody else, or according to anyone's totems, taboos, fashions or anything else. You must try and understand yourself in the light of all that you see around you, of course. But take it as a guide and try to pick out what it is that's right for you. If you don't do that you will get into trouble. You'll be unhappy or you just won't fulfil your potential or anything like it.

If his adolescent and early adult decisions about education were 'law abiding' and determined by the outside world, his early professional objective to go into industry was rationally chosen based on self-knowledge, and unusual among his Oxford contemporaries.

> My decision was caused by a clear recognition that the value of industry to the economy was not matched by the calibre and

number of the people it was attracting. I think I knew where I was likely to make a contribution most clearly and most easily and would have sensed the disparity between the calibre of people who went into the wealth creating part of the economy and those who didn't. So it was a combination of expediency, pragmatism and a recognition of where I ought to go. I think that's genuine. I don't think that's *post hoc* rationalisation. That's just me. Of course I'm self-interested. But part of that self-interest is wanting to make a useful contribution in one's own eyes – which begs the question of what is useful. Some people feel that being a civil servant is very useful. I felt that being useful was going into industry, which was something that not many other people were doing but which clearly needed to be done, and then doing it well. You could say that's a combination of high-mindedness and self-interest but I certainly wouldn't underplay the self-interest.

Although Hogg's objective was clear, ultimately predictive and certainly guided his decisions about appropriate career development moves, it related more to the nature of the work itself rather than the management level to be reached and consequently allowed generously for the operation of chance or serendipity. In hindsight, to an observer, his career could not have been designed much better to provide the breadth of skills and perspective necessary to be an effective chief executive.

My career objective wasn't a vision which specified what I wanted to run. But I was clear that I wanted to be in general management and I was clear that I wanted to be in an international organisation and I was clear that I wanted to use my abilities fully and in a wide perspective, but how high that took me in business remained to be seen. I didn't start off by saying that I want to run the biggest organisation for miles around and I never have, but on the other hand I have had a restless desire all the time just to keep moving and to keep giving myself challenges and it's that which has pushed me through all the time, rather than a specific desire to run this, that or the other.

You could say, however, that most of my career moves have in a sense been calculated. There is a serendipitous element, but what happens is that opportunities come at you all the time and you select some and discard others. I don't know whether you call that calculated or not but there was a conscious process of selection going on in my case. Again, that's not *post hoc* rationalisation, I'm very clear about it.

You can see it in my job objectives in my curriculum vitae which I wrote at Harvard in 1962, when I was 25 or 26 and I hadn't had any work experience at all. They contained as clear a prophecy as you could get in three or four lines. It was what I then went off and did.

He had gone to Harvard on the advice of the head of the Oxford University Appointments Board, winning a Harkness Fellowship 'the single biggest piece of good fortune in my working life'. As a great believer in a business school education he goes as far as to conclude:

Any success I've had is because I did a business management course. The case study method applied over two years and at high pressure leads *inter alia* to the acquisition of a wide body of factual knowledge akin to what one might obtain from say five to seven years of management consulting. The MBA provided some knowledge about all areas of a company's activities, a valuable analytical framework and an ability to look at complex situations from a general management viewpoint.

Hogg acknowledges that there are necessary experiences that the MBA does not provide, specifically intimate knowledge of an individual company and an understanding of how to work with fellow beings. Critically important to his own experience was the opportunity to live in a country with a different social and economic environment, to acquire a deep interest in science and technology as well as 'confidence that I could understand most things, given time and effort'.

The importance of living in the US cannot be overestimated.

The impact of my original time there is difficult to distinguish because I keep going back, so that I am now almost mid-Atlantic. It is another society, a great society. Everybody in their lives should know at least one other society well if they can and the USA has been the one I know best. I find it enormously stimulating.

Emerging with a clear professional goal from Harvard Business School, his career exemplifies in many ways the elements required to get to the top: broad functional experience, early line responsibility, international experience, and also, the influence of a powerful mentor.

Although Christopher Hogg had a general career goal, he believes that it is a mistake to be definitive too early about specific positions sought.

> It is most important to keep learning and to keep broadening your experience. There are no shortcuts to the top. There is one thing that is worse than not getting to where you want to go and that is not being equipped once you get there.

On returning to the UK he learned that ICI, who had offered him a job two years earlier, placed a value of only one hundred pounds on his business school education. (This was standard at the time, as reflected in Charles Mackay's experience when he returned from topping his year at INSEAD to find BP offering him less than he had made before he took the course. Archie Norman ten years later found the course to be valued in salary terms only by merchant banks and consultancies like McKinsey.)

Christopher Hogg decided to join the teaching staff at IMEDE, a leading international business school in Lausanne, extending his international experience from North America to Continental Europe, visiting different companies in several countries, to write up case studies.

One way to overcome the lack of recognition of the Harvard MBA was to join someone who also held one, which was the foundation for his joining bankers Philip Hill, Higginson, Erlangers, later to become Hill Samuel. Here he 'learned not to be frightened by large sums of money. I worked for an extremely professional man who taught me a great deal about the handling of large, complex financial problems and how to think them through clearly. It was an invaluable grounding for moving across to manufacturing industry, which I did in 1966'.

After three years he seized the opportunity to move on secondment to the Industrial Reorganisation Corporation, established by the Labour government to promote structural reorganisation in British industry based on the mistaken premise that larger organisations would thereby compete more successfully internationally. He specialised in electrical engineering and electronics, building on the interest developed at Harvard and acquiring the sense of technology as a driving force in industry. Lord Kearton, Chairman of the IRC, fortuitously offered him a senior job at Courtaulds thereafter serving as a mentor in the fullest sense of the term.

He was very pragmatic and dynamic and just got on with things. He had an enormous influence on me and trusted me and provided a very good environment in which I could learn. What he did at Courtaulds was a mixture of good and less good and I subsequently spent a lot of time dealing with the less good as well as benefiting from the good, but the same is true for my successor and would be for anyone else.

For the next eleven years Christopher Hogg had a steady and meteoric rise to the top of Courtaulds working in all major divisions of the company. He began as a Director in International Paint, an experience he portrays in a recent speech as unusually lucky, because of the opportunity to acquire experience in operating internationally.

> The marine paint business is about as global in scope and practice as one can get. It requires continuous day-to-day operation on an international scale with endless permutations of the countries involved, so that global thinking and policies are absolutely necessary. I had to travel a quarter of a million miles in two years or so and carry out mergers in twelve or more different countries *en route* to creating a genuinely unified international marine paint business. This business has gone on to be the world's leader, which is not my doing but I helped to make it possible.
>
> This experience has coloured my whole approach to business in the twenty years since and could hardly have been more relevant to the circumstances prevailing in today's business world. To think automatically in global terms in addition to having substantial first-hand international experience, is an invaluable asset for any business leader.

In 1972, Christopher Hogg became chairman of the fibres company, British Celanese, and a year later in 1973, Chairman of International Paint.

It is often true that the most rewarding role in management is the relatively hands-on role of managing a division much as the most rewarding rank in the army is often that of Colonel, leading a battalion. Christopher Hogg did not want to move from being Managing Director of the sixty-million-pound paint company.

> I resisted being moved. Although the higher you go, the more perks and pay you get, it becomes more remote, more difficult to see

what you ought to be doing and to get the immediate satisfaction, which is, I suspect, what drives most people.

He was next given main board responsibility for fabrics and then for consumer clothing products in 1977, a year later becoming Deputy Chairman of Courtaulds and in 1979 Chief Executive and Chairman (the latter from 1 January 1980) at age 43.

In spite of having worked in the company for so long, he initially found the job of Chief Executive to be as difficult, challenging and productive of soul-searching as that of other new chief executives with shorter experience in their companies. He said at the time 'If ever I was promoted out of my depth it was probably in this present job. I have thought "what the hell am I doing this for and can I ever make any real progress". I don't get these sorts of moments now, but in the early days what I ought to do next was so unclear. That's always the real problem.'

As Chief Executive, Christopher Hogg's challenge was to provide strategic direction to a company in crisis, one that had ambitiously moved down-stream from its core business in the chemical industry into textiles, becoming the biggest textile company in Europe employ-ing 165,000 people. As he recently recalled at an international management symposium in Switzerland, it took the whole of the 1980s, the loss of more than 60,000 jobs, and a complete demerger in 1990 of the chemical and textile parts, each into a separate publicly quoted company, to restore reasonable competitiveness and growth prospects.

> In the Courtaulds of 1981, which consisted of some two hundred businesses of varying sizes, most of them in deep trouble, it did not take a genius to see that the right strategy had to be both crude and short term. Mine was simply to insist that every business generated annually net cash amounting to 12 per cent of the book value of its capital employed. The point was that by concentrating on its cashflow above all else, the Courtaulds Group bought the time to begin to address properly the other two great imperatives of business strategy, namely customers and employees.

In the course of the eighties, Hogg's strategy changed from a financial to a commercial one: 'To create Courtaulds as a coherent total business with the whole being greater than the sum of the parts and the customers being served "faster, better or more distinctively" than the competition'. The already mentioned demerger in 1990 resulted in two strong and competitive publicly quoted companies.

In 1985, while Chairman of Courtaulds, Christopher Hogg also became Chairman of Reuters, which provided him not only with an opportunity to become more involved with a subject he loved, electronics, and to learn about a new company but also to gain a welcome perspective upon the demands at Courtaulds.

Christopher Hogg is currently part-time Chairman of Courtaulds Textiles, Courtaulds and Reuters. He made a clear decision to 'go plural' in 1991, relinquishing executive responsibilities at age 55 and thus giving himself the opportunity to specialise with a reasonable time horizon in non-executive roles.

Although extremely confident Christopher Hogg is open about those times which he has personally found difficult. Not only did he express his self-doubt on becoming Chief Executive, he also identifies a period in 1973 when as a result of overwork, travel and exhaustion it was 'difficult to cope'. 'I understood the finiteness of my energies bringing home a Harvard lesson not to make decisions when tired'. He is equally open and clear about the importance of mistakes to development. In *The Heart of the Matter*, a brochure for graduates considering joining Courtaulds, he writes, 'One makes endless mistakes and it is often more important to travel hopefully, enthusiastically and steadfastly than to arrive'.

Most mistakes Christopher Hogg has no trouble living with, indeed no trouble forgetting. Given their inevitability, it is essential to be resilient. 'An important part of the art of being successful is to learn from your failures and not to let them get you down.' However, there are certain mistakes that he carefully avoids exposing himself to because they would certainly get him down.

> I can live with a wrong decision which has been properly thought through. But if I make a big and risky decision carelessly and that's my fault, then I not only kick myself for falling short of standards but I also brood about it as well. Someone who is kicking themselves and losing confidence is just no good to anybody else so I avoid getting myself into those sorts of situations or else I try always to go through a process which lets me off the hook. I go through a process of consulting others. But what other people might call failures wouldn't necessarily worry me at all provided I thought that I had handled them in a sensible way.
>
> Also, I've certainly made poor *business* decisions and I've

sanctioned things which have turned out nothing like as well as I expected them to turn out. I have also made bad mistakes in assessing priorities and wasted a lot of time as a result. Every hour one wastes a lot of time, or is less effective than one should be because one is all the time following out one's own best way of doing things rather than doing what's actually most effective. Fortunately what is most effective is a very elastic concept which no one has got a clear view or opinion about.

I keep coming back to the fact that I am probably my own sternest critic and many times a day I catch myself out. I can laugh at it now and say to myself, 'There you go again. It's because you've got an orderly mind and you just want to be orderly for its own sake. You really shouldn't be doing this, you should be doing that'. I know myself quite well by now.

He is not only self-aware, but open about his fallibilities. In being confronted with his reputation for being intensely ethical, self-effacing and always to be relied upon to do the right thing, he says

I feel very uncomfortable about being talked about in those sort of terms. I am certainly not a paragon. I think I knew that well before the breakdown of my marriage, which in itself did wonders for teaching me more about my fallibilities.

In a sense, the breakdown of my marriage is a failure, of course. But I would argue that to make a conscious decision to separate requires at least a certain moral courage. I know I needed every ounce of moral courage I possessed to do it *and* try to look at myself honestly while doing it.

I found it extremely difficult to see what was 'right' and what was 'wrong'. Charles Handy, who is a very wise fellow, in his book called *The Age of Unreason* (1991) talks about a 'proper sense of selfishness'. The great dilemma in that sort of situation is what the hell is proper? When is it right to become selfish or not? I don't know.

I suspect that the people I work with, particularly at Courtaulds because I have known them a long time, would say privately if you asked them that I am rather more human, relaxed, approachable, comprehensible and likeable now than I was several years ago when I was far too preoccupied, albeit understandably, with the burden of running Courtaulds which could at times seem colossal. I no longer try to hide my fallibilities now.

Christopher Hogg here exemplifies the essential precondition of learning from mistakes – self-examination, self-criticism and self-understanding.

FAMILY AND PERSONAL LIFE

Although Christopher Hogg has separated from his wife, Anne, former Oxford tutor in Spanish language and literature, he does not believe that this resulted from overwork or long hours. Although he works a seventy-hour week, he has always considered home life important and been as disciplined about giving time to his two daughters when they were growing up as he was disciplined about his work. He remains extremely close to his daughters.

He acknowledges however that balance in family life is very difficult to achieve, given the energy and time required in running an organisation. It becomes more difficult over time to relax and the needs of the organisation are necessarily absorbing.

The 'helpful hints' he gave readers in Corinne Simcock's *A Head for Business* (1992) reflect the importance he places on fitness, a positive attitude and hard work.

1. Stay fit.
2. Stay cheerful. Try to see the glass as half full.
3. Listen.
4. Work very hard, with speed and concentration.

It has often been noted that his switching-off activities are solitary ones – reading, skiing, walking – which is perhaps not surprising as introverts generally restore their energies by being on their own. He also enjoys the theatre and reads catholically, including a great deal of history and literature. When we spoke, psychology was the flavour of the moment – he had developed a special appreciation for Jung for having crystallised people's minds – 'a man equivalent to Newton or Einstein – a man after whom things never seem quite the same as they did before'.

LEADERSHIP AND SUCCESS FACTORS

Christopher Hogg is invariably cited by peers as being among the most admired industrialists in the country and among the few British corporate leaders of international stature. What qualities set him apart as a leader? His fine mind is an important factor – necessary but not sufficient in explaining his success. A former close colleague notes how rare Hogg's 'first-class' mind is in senior business management and also how deeply competitive he is by nature, whether on the sports field or in his working life.

People speak of Christopher Hogg being scrupulously fair-minded, analytical, logical in the extreme, and refer to his integrity, thoroughness, loyalty, 'self-control to an almost unnatural extent', self-effacement, lack of pretension and courage. Although this is a deeply appealing and attractive profile, he points out: 'People want to believe in heroes and to feel that those who run their organisations are good and infallible but they're ruddy well not. I've no illusions about that'. Christopher Hogg experiences himself as flawed, certainly too serious and rather boring.

In trying to get to the heart of why Christopher Hogg is so respected, by almost all who know him, he himself provides a clue, in referring to the Myers Briggs type indicator, his own personality type and the book *Gifts Differing* by Isabel Briggs-Myers and Peter Briggs (1980). In another book explaining the Myers Briggs personality types, *Please Understand Me*, his own type, the ISTJ is characterised as highly practical, extraordinarily persevering, quiet, serious and, above all, *dependable*. 'The word of the ISTJ is their bond.... The thought of dishonouring a contract would appal a person of this type.' ISTJs are naturally interested in thoroughness, details, justice, and practical procedures and are gifted at handling difficult detailed figures. They convey reliability and stability. 'ISTJs have a distaste for and distrust of fanciness in speech, dress and home. The ostentatious is abhorred and a neat, orderly and functional home and work environment is preferred.'

Much has been written of 'hair shirt Hogg', with his office being modestly decorated, his dress geared to make people comfortable, his riding of a bicycle to work (for many years up to the end of the 1980s) and his eschewing of the corporate box at the opera and the business lunch.

When Christopher Hogg suggests that he is not fundamentally motivated by money, status or power, he receives support from analysts of his type who conclude that ISTJs 'perform their duties without flourish or fanfare; therefore the dedication they bring to their work can go unnoticed and unappreciated'.

Christopher Hogg does not believe that he is motivated by the need for external recognition.

> I don't know about my motivation. That's an answer which is given very thoughtfully I can assure you – I really don't know. But I suspect that I am trying to please myself fundamentally. I don't think it's external. Maybe it's only the introverts (I) that think that and not the extraverts (E). The extraverts would look outside surely and they would want recognition. The introverts think differently and I'm not sure that one is better or worse than the other. Except in *Up the Organisation* Robert Townsend quotes Lao Tsu who 2600 years ago said something like, 'As for the best leaders the people do not notice their existence, the next best the people praise, the next best the people fear and the next best the people hate'. By that definition the best leaders are introverts.

Hogg himself believes that the three crucial ingredients for an individual manager, apart from the obvious primary skill of being able to handle people, are motivation, open mindedness and analytical competence. Although he accepts the distinction so often made between leaders and managers, he does not know into which category he falls, but suspects that he is a manager.

> I have a managerial turn of mind anyhow. Leaders to me are extraverts and not introverts. They don't *have* to be extraverts but some of the best I've known have been. On the other hand, Lao Tsu's leaders whose existence is unnoticed wouldn't be extraverts. They would be introverts. Maybe there are leaders and leaders, I don't know. I have never had any difficulty getting people to follow me when I really wanted to go somewhere. I am usually pretty clear on what I want to do. I don't have any difficulty making up my mind.
>
> I have one important characteristic. I don't know where it springs from. I haven't rationalised it completely. I am able to put the organisation first automatically. That's enormously valuable because if people see that you genuinely are organisation-centred then they will trust you. If people see that really you are out for yourself, that you are out for the organisation but only in so far as it's going to be compatible with your own goals, then they will look at you askance. I emphatically do not believe that political astuteness in an organisational sense is important.

His dedication to continual learning, to remaining open and flexible to change, extends to examining and adopting best practice internationally, in whatever realm one wants to improve. He is himself an avid reader of the latest management theory. In a speech on 'mobilising corporate energies', he has identified long-term strategic thinking, international perspective and deep people awareness as key for the successful chief executive (although not sufficient) and has confessed his belief that he has fallen short of his own expectations on the third (maximising the contribution of people).

Christopher Hogg is also very aware of the dangers of power, of coming to hear only what you want to hear – the ego trip, the growing taste for flattery, and the disinclination to seek out the very problems and difficulties which the Chief Executive alone can fix. His protection is a detached scepticism.

> I cultivate scepticism about anything that's said to me by somebody who's got an axe to grind directly or indirectly and that includes *all* the people in one's own organisation and *all* the people who may be looking for something from you. Genuinely unsolicited, independent testimonials are few and far between. I think that if I got those from people whose view I respected or I felt were in a good position to know, then I would be very pleased, disproportionately pleased, because they so seldom come one's way.

At the heart of his success lies an optimism, confidence and positive belief in people's capabilities. 'I feel that if you've got sufficient determination there's nothing you can't do.' He is not religious in a conventional sense, although he tried when he was much younger.

> However in Jungian terms, I am religious in the sense that I believe in the collective unconscious. There are forces that move and shake which are outside one's immediate control and outside one's immediate understanding, but those forces can be the accumulation of human wisdom and experience, not to mention genes passing from one generation to another. I don't know if I expressed that clearly. I think that you can be almost religious about the human race, if religion is used to mean that there are more things in heaven and earth than are dreamt of in our philosophy. Certainly I have always felt myself driven by something – rather in the manner of Ulysses as Tennyson depicts him.

That's not religious and I'm not trying to dignify it as such. But that sort of drive applies with many human beings and through them to the human race as well. Incidentally, I am an optimist about the future; one has to be given how unconstructive pessimism is!

I also understand the existence of evil. I find what Jung says about one's 'shadow' self to be very applicable. His vision of the human condition rings very true to me and is movingly earthy and realistic while also being hopeful.

Courtaulds has a reputation of being a 'hirer of talent' – hiring outstanding people rather than hiring to fill a specific position. It is one of the few British companies for instance that understands the value of a 'good MBA'. (Hogg considers that the MBA can provide a conceptual framework that is useful, but that it is not indispensable.)

Christopher Hogg often has selected young professional people and promoted them swiftly – notably Martin Taylor, now Chief Executive of Barclays Bank, former *Financial Times* journalist and Chief Executive of Courtaulds Textiles at 39. Hogg favours youth because of the need for energy, persistence and determination over a sustained period of time in achieving corporate goals.

Selecting those who will run a business, he values great commitment to the products and business, excellent interpersonal skills and a tremendous amount of experience. Intelligence is also crucially important, because business is enormously complex.

Whatever else it is, business is an intellectual exercise. I could never understand how the impression arose that industry was a place for morons. I personally find it fantastically demanding on intellectual resources. You are dealing with an enormous range of variables. You are always trying to make decisions on inadequate information and against time. It means a constant process of selection of priorities.

Hogg also has selected people with strengths that are complementary to his own. In understanding his own strengths to be analytical abstract thinking and strategy, he has needed people who act more spontaneously and are effective at implementation.

In spite of clearly understanding what qualities and experience he seeks, Christopher Hogg does not consider himself to be a 'great people picker'. In common with many Chief Executives, the flip side of being positive and optimistic, is that he has sometimes overtrusted and overpromoted people.

> I am guilty of constant failures of judgement in handling people, particularly in matching people to jobs or to levels of responsibility. But I believe that in this respect in business you have got to keep taking risks, you have got to keep pushing people out of their depth or beyond their reach. Incidentally, the success ratio is comfortably more than 50 per cent but that means that a third or more such decisions are failures to a greater or lesser extent and with those one can kick oneself for not seeing this or that.

His immediate management colleagues have always been Christopher Hogg's principal focus of interest and attention, from the point of view of their calibre, their experience, their training and their team-work. He is a great believer in professional management, management development and life-long learning. Of his time as Chief Executive, he has noted, 'most of my time is spent with my fellow executive directors making sure that the way we work together and the way they are developing their talents is to the best advantage. If you get that right then it will automatically go through the company'.

13

Baroness Jean Denton of Wakefield, CBE

Parliamentary Under-Secretary of State in Northern Ireland Minister for Economic Development, Agriculture and Women's Issues

Date of birth:	29 December 1935
Place of birth:	Yorkshire, UK
Nationality:	British
Marital status:	Divorced

Education:
1948–1955	Rothwell Grammar School, 'A' levels in English, Geography and History
1955–1958	LSE, BSc Economics

Career:
1958–1959	BBC News Information Librarian
1959	Fenwicks, Graduate trainee
1959–1961	Procter & Gamble, Communications Officer
1961–1964	Economist Intelligence Unit Assistant Editor, *Retail Business*
1964	Connaught Rooms, Marketing Manager
1964–1966	IPC Research Department
1966–1969	University of Surrey Hotel and Catering Department, Research Fellow
1969–1972	Racing/rally driver
1972–1978	Huxford Group, Marketing Director
1978–1985	Heron Motor Group
1978–79	Marketing Manager
1979–80	Marketing Director
1980–85	Managing Director, Herondrive
1985–1986	Austin Rover, External Affairs Director
1992–1994	Department of Trade and Industry Parliamentary Under-Secretary of State
1994 to date	Northern Ireland Office Parliamentary Under-Secretary

Outside appointments:
1990–1992	FORUM UK, Chairman
1992 to date	President
1986–1992	Black Country Development Corporation, Deputy Chairman
1987–1992	British Nuclear Fuels, Non-executive Director
1987–1992	Burson-Marsteller, Director
1989–1992	London & Edinburgh Insurance Group, Non-executive Director
1990–1992	Triplex Lloyd
1989–1992	Think Green
1986–1992	Engineering Council
1982–1992	LSE, Governor
1987–1988	Marketing Group of Great Britain, Chairman
1985–1988	Ordnance Survey, Director
1979–	Women on the Move Against Cancer, Chairman/President
1982–1985	National Organisation for Women's Management Education
1986–1988	UK 2000, Board Member
1986–1987	Royal Academy, Member, Advisory Board
1988–1989	RSA, Council Member
1987–1989	Brooklands Museum, Trustee

Awards:
	Honorary doctorates from Bradford University and King's College, Pennsylvania
	Life Peer 1991

Interests:
	Talking shop

INTRODUCTION

Although Jean Denton is one of very few women business leaders of her generation (having been for five years the Managing Director of Herondrive, the £45 million car leasing company of the conglomerate Heron company), her pioneering successes do not end there. She was the British Women Racing Drivers Champion in 1968 and 1969, and is also a committed leader of the women's movement in the UK and champion of 'good causes' (including as Founder of Women on the Move Against Cancer). As a working peer in the House of Lords, first as Minister for Small Businesses and currently as Parliamentary Under-Secretary of State for Economic Development, Agriculture and Women's Issues for Northern Ireland, she is well-known for 'fighting for David against Goliath'.

Jean Denton has met her extraordinarily wide commitments through the Yorkshirewoman's determination to excel, unstinting dedication and hard work, courage, practical common sense and excellent communication skills.

Jean Denton was early motivated to succeed by the support and expectations of a proud father. She is grammar school educated, with an economics degree from the London School of Economics and although she was herself not highly motivated or a distinguished student at university (she swiftly points out) she strongly advises ambitious young people to get a degree.

Jean Denton's early career exemplifies the 'transitory' and un-structured pattern followed by many successful women (in Jean Denton's case, staying fewer than three years in successive jobs with seven different organisations) and propelled by intrinsic job interest, and sometimes, by personal circumstances. (Increasingly, not only women but men will follow such a pattern of lateral job moves as organisations delayer and hierarchies shorten.)

After three years as a racing/rally driver, her career entered a period of relative stability in the retail motor trade, where her previous eclectic experience provided the foundation for her success in senior marketing and general management roles in the Huxford group, Heron Group and Austin Rover. When Austin Rover was taken over, she left to manage an extraordinarily full portfolio of interests which again prepared her for her place in the House of Lords.

Jean Denton's career cannot be readily pigeonholed. For instance, it is unlike that of most of the men in the sample in not having had early senior line responsibility (she was 44 when appointed as

Managing Director of Herondrive) nor broad functional responsibility before moving into general management (although her marketing background and hands-on experience in racing cars gave her the
needed confidence and credibility to succeed as head of a company
car business). Her international experience was limited to racing cars
around the world, and conscious of this developmental 'gap', she
sought later to gain experience working across borders.

Jean Denton has never had a mentor, although was greatly
influenced by Gerald Ronson and throughout her later career has
drawn heavily on networks for learning and support.

Jean Denton's unorthodox and successful working life have proved
her to be a self-motivated, innovative non-conformist with a clear
sense of what is important. She has provided a supportive role model
for other women, who she advises above all not to 'clone' to compete
with men but to express freely their own strengths and point of view.
As with many senior women, she has had no family or 'role conflict'
competing with her workaholism and 'career centrality'. One of her
few regrets has been leaving a good marriage because she believes
that 'team is best' when the relationship is right. She had breast
cancer a few years ago which has since focused her energies on living
life fully with no regrets.

What has motivated Jean Denton to work so hard, what experiences have been important developmentally and what are her views
on leadership and careers?

EARLY INFLUENCES

Jean Denton grew up as Jean Moss in a lower-middle-class family in
a Yorkshire mining village, the elder of two daughters. As so often
with successful women, her environment was aspirational, willing her
to succeed and her father was a powerful influence. 'My father was so
proud of me, I was forever trying to do something to please him. Not
pressured, just proud.'

She also believes that 'Yorkshire blood makes you competitive and
so if there is a mountain to climb, you go and climb it'. She learned
early self-reliance when at 14 she contracted a kidney disease and was
forced to spend a year in bed, reading voraciously, left entirely to her
own devices and learning to give shape to her day.

Her parents were supportive of education, her school unusually
responsive and one of her proudest achievements remains passing her

scholarship at age ten. She had the opportunity to stay on at school when this was unusual in Yorkshire. Her teachers were challenging, providing stimulating extracurricular activities, school camps and an environment of opportunity. 'We never had people saying, "Oh, we're not doing that".' Although these opportunities were unusually rich for a child of her background, she has no illusions about their relative limitations.

> My father was a clerk, very kind, knew there was more to life but hadn't managed to find it. If I'm ever resentful, I resent the fact that if you had an upper-class education, it taught you about art and music. However much you try to learn in retrospect, it's never quite the same. If you're a grammar school or comprehensive school kid you can't necessarily swim, or understand some of the cultural areas you should be able to.

One of the two failures she identifies in her life was her initial failure to attain a scholarship when she was 18. 'Again I am grateful to my parents for backing me for two tries. I don't know why I kacked it, but I did.'

When she decided that she wanted to attend the London School of Economics having never studied economics, her headmaster personally gave her a one-on-one tutorial in economics so that she could qualify. She knew intuitively that Oxbridge would be wrong for her:

> I had somewhere within me a feeling that I would sink at Oxbridge. I don't know where that came from and I suspect that I was absolutely right. So I went to LSE and then had the best of both worlds because I was engaged to somebody who was at Cambridge. I used to do everything in London during the week and then spent at least one day within the rather pleasant surroundings of Cambridge.

Although economics interested her, she was not highly motivated academically and 'suffered from a strong boredom factor' at LSE, to the extent of trying to leave after two years. Not finding anything interesting to do, she stayed the third year and half-heartedly completed her degree.

> When it came to the end, I went into a flat spin because I was sure that I hadn't passed. I didn't deserve to pass because I had played politics and only worked in the last term. My boyfriend went and looked at the board, not me and I got a 2:2 which was fine. So I

found myself a job which didn't need a degree on the basis that I wasn't going to get one.

Although the university experience at the time appeared unrewarding, Denton is a firm believer in the need for qualifications. 'I can't say too strongly how much you need your ticket to open the doors. You can then decide whether you want to go through, but you need your ticket to gain entry.'

Economics proved to be right for her because of its intrinsic interest – she continues to find it fascinating. She describes herself as 'a pragmatic economist' and has over time applied a practical approach to forecasting accurately what she sees as obvious – the shortage of young workers, the opening of car factory outlets in the UK – when experts predicted otherwise.

CAREER DECISION-MAKING AND DEVELOPMENT

Jean Denton emerged from LSE with no career objectives and describes her career as 'totally unstructured'.

> I wonder if it would have been better if it had been structured? I would probably have progressed more quickly if I had done it with more order. On the other hand, I think there is some sense of order underneath it all, which is based on my not going off too often to tilt at windmills. I also have a conviction that things will only happen if you make them happen which has helped.

Indeed, her early career exemplifies the pattern that many women adopt, defined by Driver as 'transitory' (White, Cox and Cooper, 1992, p. 108) (p. 101). This is characterised by no career planning, frequent usually lateral changes, and a flexible decision style. White, Cox and Cooper in a study published in 1992 of women high flyers found that '54 per cent of successful women made a late commitment to their career or had no coherent direction in their working lives'. One possible explanation for 'late starters' was the complexity of forging a vocational identity because of the need to integrate both family and career roles. Although Jean Denton had no family, she did not in the first ten or fifteen years of her working life approach her jobs as a career.

Thus her first seven jobs never lasted for more than three years and ranged from research at BBC News Information, teaching for a few months, a short graduate traineeship at Fenwicks, communications at Procter & Gamble, research at the Economist Intelligence Unit, marketing at the Connaught Rooms, to two years with IPC. She then joined the Hotel and Catering Department, University of Surrey while becoming a successful racing/rally driver for three years.

In these years her career decisions were made quickly, with little information, based often on her personal life and on the level of intrinsic job interest, rather than on where each might lead. Relying on her natural interest in the job however resulted in the development of skills and knowledge that would provide a base for a different approach to her career. 'My decisions were based firstly on the desire to do things that I like (I have so much sympathy for people who fill their nine to five hours doing something they don't like) and secondly on working with bright people and being part of a team.' Jean Denton's spontaneous approach to decision-making and career development is reflected in her own words.

After university, I found myself a job at the BBC News Information, which didn't need a degree, on the basis that I wasn't going to get one. My job was absolutely splendid because it was like being paid to read the newspaper, and the knowledge could stand you in good stead. Then I moved to Newcastle because the man I was going to marry was doing a graduate traineeship there.

Instead of going on the milk round with Procter & Gamble I went in through the communications side. They didn't have a vacancy when I arrived in Newcastle so I taught for a month. When I got home around five o'clock I used to go to bed and recover until about seven o'clock in the evening. I've never been so tired. Then I started a graduate traineeship with Fenwicks who have their main store in Newcastle, thinking retail was interesting. Retail is fascinating because it has a very sharp-edged consumer contact point, but being a graduate trainee in those days was not interesting. You are just an underpaid shop assistant, so when Procter & Gamble said they had a vacancy I moved there.

Then of course we left Newcastle because my husband decided that he wanted to do his PhD in London. I joined the Economist Intelligence Unit, which was really just another arm of the LSE senior common room. There were so many chiefs and very few Indians. But we managed to deliver. I was in the marketing side as Assistant Editor of *Retail Business* and used to write articles on marketing which predicted the next year's market share. People would ring up and say, 'I've just been reading this article. Where did you get the forecast from?' You can't say you stuck your finger in the air can you? It was very much a question of just working it out. I still find it amazing that many marketing people don't seem to know that 100 per cent is the most you can have.

I then went to a client, the Connaught Rooms, and set up a marketing department, gaining some experience within the hotel and catering trade. I moved from there to IPC because it was a wonderful opportunity, being responsible for some of the investigatory work on *Nova* magazine which was the first woman's magazine with text for upper income groups and way ahead of its time. I had an instinct for what I liked – retailing, media and women's areas.

I then learnt to drive, and because I am competitive, started motor racing in the same year. I needed a job where you weren't pinned in by nine to five so I went to do research at the University of Surrey where you could tyre test all day and work on a Sunday. I worked in the hotel and catering department which was headed by Professor Medlik. He wasn't an ivory tower academic, so that I was actually working with industry and have an HMSO publication to my name on manpower in the hotel and catering industry. So it was good in that you weren't cut off.

From there I went into motor racing full time for a few years. At first, I hesitated. I thought 'Oh, God, a girl racer'! I didn't hesitate for long, realising that it was not the sort of chance that comes twice. By the way, if I hadn't had a husband supporting me, paying the mortgage I wouldn't have been able to do it, which is why I can't accept this idea of marriage holding you up. It can allow you to do all sorts of things that you couldn't if you just had one income.

Racing was very good to me. I raced in Europe, I finished the London to Sydney marathon and the world cup rally round Mexico so I can't complain about the life it gave me. And I came back naturally. I realised I didn't want to do it forever. After three years, I knew I was never going to be world champion. There were one or two youngsters coming up with more natural talent than I had. I had attained what I had by working hard. I had an invitation to join the retail motor trade which sounded interesting so I went and did that.

In 1972, at age 36, her career entered a new stage of stability and steady progression when she became Marketing Director of Huxford

Group, a group of garages in Hampshire, which operated the Fiat, Lancia and Ferrari dealerships. It could be argued, however, that her peripatetic experience, particularly as a rally driver, was unpredictably the foundation of her success.

> Having hesitated to do motor racing, it stood me in good stead. I suspect the industry wouldn't have let me in if I could not have driven a car with the best of them. Other people take time off to have babies – I put racing down to high-speed maternity leave. It gave me lots of media contacts and absolute focus because in racing first is first. It also provided a reference point for people who found my new position in the retail motor trade difficult.

She quickly stole the march on a competition that was unsophisticated and inactive in marketing and was eventually able to do her job 'standing on her head', which allowed her at the same time to become the first woman on the National Executive of the Institute of Marketing and to host her own radio programme. Although this was a seven-year period of success and stability she felt that she 'did the traditional female thing', staying for too long when she should have left after four years.

This is the first specific regret of several related to career-decision making. When Denton notes that women particularly are prone not to actively and strategically manage their careers, she receives support from the White, Cox and Cooper study which found that the most frequently mentioned regret among women high flyers was poor career management, with 50 per cent of the women suggesting that this had caused them a slow start, missed opportunities and had led to spending too long in the same position. As with Denton, there was an underlying positive recognition that lack of planning had also resulted in the development of a useful and diverse range of skills.

Denton's success at Huxford positioned her to be head-hunted by Heron as a Marketing Manager, to be elevated to Marketing Director within three months, in charge of fourteen garages and 21 franchises. After two years, Gerald Ronson made her Managing Director of Herondrive. 'I am eternally grateful to Gerald Ronson because he gave me an opportunity to become a line manager. There were only two people who thought I could do it, Gerald Ronson and me – but it was the right two people.' Although she would not call Ronson a mentor, he was an inspiration in giving her the opportunity and the freedom to prove herself.

Ronson's management approach of fully delegating responsibility was developmentally invaluable. 'I had a very early start to independence. At Heron whenever I did anything, I used to ask myself whether I could defend it to Gerald Ronson if it went wrong and if I could, that was fine. At Heron I didn't go crying for help because that could have been seen as a weakness.' As a result she not only learned self- reliance but developed the beginning of an expert ability to exploit networks. 'Networks do work, because you can be open about seeking advice and ask "What the hell am I going to do now?", and have someone who knows advise, "That doesn't work, try this".'

She built Herondrive over five years into a successful £45 million company. It was a tough environment. Every operator had problems with her appointment and she took them out to lunch one by one, proving that she spoke their language. 'You agreed your budgets, agreed your working capital and got on with it.'

At this stage, she knew that she needed international experience, and understanding that Heron's overseas interests were either in property or financial services, she accepted an approach from Austin Rover. Again, she wishes that she had more actively managed her career.

> I shouldn't have moved. I should have sat down with Gerald and said 'what next?' It was a bit daft not to, but I think it's a typically female problem. You don't want to tell people that you're unhappy and need a change, you don't like to push and often then feel if you want to change you have to move. Gerald and I are good friends and I was delivering. I should have said, 'Look, I'm not very good at managing the status quo – I'm good at turning things round – what next?'

Denton was attracted to the External Affairs Director role at Austin Rover not only because it was international and involved with Japan, but also because for the first time she would gain experience in manufacturing. Ultimately she considers this choice to be a mistake because her role was functional, and without power. 'It was like pushing water uphill. Again, it was a female trait to think that you can do what other people are not able to do. I would not leave line again.'

When Sir Graham Day was appointed Chairman of British Aerospace and Rover was taken over, he brought in his own managers and she left. As with many women she was not very skilled at protecting her own interests. 'Being me, I negotiated out without a job. You can't get much more daft!'

Protecting her own interests has never come naturally to her. 'Someone said to me when I started my own company, "Pretend you're doing it for somebody else and you might get it right". And in the same vein, someone else has said, "If you want her to do something, tell her it's free". The interesting things in life *are* free.'

The period after negotiating out of Rover was the lowest of her professional life.

> I don't doubt for one moment that the right decision was to leave but it didn't take the hurt away. During the day I was fine, positive about choosing the next step, but in the middle of the night I thought 'That was a bloody stupid thing to do.' I felt that I could have managed it better.

Although she still feels a sense of failure, she also was reassured that she had behaved professionally when Sir Graham Day later asked her to stay on the Teachers Pay Review when he was the Chairman. 'Why the hell you need a stamp of approval, I don't know but it was quite good to know that I was appreciated.'

For the next five years, she balanced a diverse and demanding set of part-time responsibilities. 'I started to do what Charles Handy calls portfolio management which is what you say on a good day, and on a bad day you could say, "I started to do what men do when they retire".'

She became Deputy Chairman of the Black Country Development Corporation, joined the Board of British Nuclear Fuels, sat on the Health Service Policy Board, the Engineering Council and the Boards of Burson-Marsteller and London & Edinburgh Insurance. In most cases she was approached and chose activities based on interest and 'innate curiosity' – wanting to learn about something she knew nothing about. Sometimes, she initiated activities herself. For instance, 'Women on the Move Against Cancer' was created as a response to one of her fellow motor racing drivers dying of cancer.

> I've had this luxury in almost every case – people come to me. I remember driving to see William Waldegrave and saying to myself 'I am not going to chair a district health authority. I've got too much to do. I don't want to chair a district health authority.' And

Waldegrave said, 'Would you like to join the Health Service Policy
Board?', I thought 'gosh, I can't turn this down'.

During this period she enjoyed meeting people, giving speeches,
getting involved and long term, there was a pay-off as it led to her
current role in the House of Lords which is her 'ideal job'. She
believes that had she planned, she could not have chosen a better fit
for her mix of public and private sector experience and her interests,
'I am using all my experience now but I've always been in a position,
apart from when I negotiated out of Austin Rover, of being so busy
doing what I'd wanted that I hadn't got around to thinking "What
next?".' The only direct action she took that provided momentum for
the peerage was to declare her politics, in putting herself on the
candidates' list for the selection process to become a Member of the
European Parliament.

Being offered a life peerage was the most gratifying moment of her
career 'The first time you stand up at the box as a Minister and
somebody says "could the Minister tell us", you feel like turning
round to see who they are talking to'.

Jean Denton for eighteen months served as Minister for Small
Business, where the role of 'fighting for David against Goliath' suited
her perfectly.

> Government is here for the benefit of the people and not vice versa.
> I resent very much when officials try to make people fit into the
> system and say 'This is the way it happens and you can't bend the
> rules'. As Minister for Small Firms I tried to find an answer for the
> individual, if we could.

Just as she was on top of her portfolio, and making a significant
contribution, she was moved.

> The problem in politics is that there is no succession plan. You sit
> around and wait to be reshuffled! When I was moved from small
> firms, the Prime Minister rang and simply told me that I needed
> more experience. I went to the Department of Environment for
> four months and then I asked to go to Northern Ireland.

In this role, the Secretary of State for Northern Ireland, Sir Patrick
Mayhew, deals with the political implications and Jean Denton as
Under-Secretary is 'simply left to responsibly manage', economic
development, agriculture and women's issues. Consistently, her
priorities are determined by the needs of the individual. 'I run each

service I am responsible for by asking whether this is what I would like to happen to my family, then there is no difficulty.'

Jean Denton does not look beyond her current role, though acknowledges that creating wealth in the private sector is her forte, rather than 'providing the safety net' in government, however challenging she finds it at the moment.

Jean Denton's motivation is a mixture of wanting to do something worthwhile for its own sake, and also a diminishing though still present desire to prove herself as capable. An early conscious desire to be rich never in reality influenced her choices.

> I don't know if it's arrogance, but I have always wanted to do something that made a difference, where something would be better because of my efforts. I did think that I wanted to be rich, but I can't do for I'm not and if I had wanted to be rich I would be. I'm enormously casual about money, but do want to be comfortable. The extent to which money drives me is that it would be nice to buy an air ticket that didn't have a fixed date on it. From choice I have the sort of mentality that likes a fast car parked near the entrance when I go somewhere. When you've bought your Apex ticket, it doesn't work like that. That is my only extravagance. I do like travelling and motor racing gave me permanently itchy feet.

She is performance driven, likes to be measured and recognises still a strong need to prove herself. She drives herself by high standards and a sense of dissatisfaction.

> When I was selling cars with Fiat we had a 14 per cent market penetration when the national average was 4 per cent and I could say 'I told you'. It's an awful thing about needing to prove yourself but one goes on trying to prove that you can succeed. Nobody quite believes this but standing up at the despatch box in the House of Lords is rather like motor racing because you do as much work as you can beforehand but when the flag drops or you're on your feet, it's all down to you.
>
> Every time I stand up and make a speech nowadays, it could have been a bit better, could have been slicker. But because I've always given my best, I don't feel regrets. I might not always have won but I haven't felt that I didn't try which would make me feel guilty.
>
> Recognition is enjoyable but the advantage of age is being able to go out on your own. I have never minded sitting in a room and

coming out with a view which is exactly opposite to everyone else, but increasingly I am conscious that I would hate to come to the end and know that I should have done something but didn't do it – so the fault that it went wrong can only be mine.

FAMILY AND PERSONAL LIFE

As with many successful professional women of her generation, Jean Denton never had children, indeed never wanted them; partly because when her sister was widowed Denton shared in the care of her three children. Divorced, Jean Denton does not attempt to balance her personal and professional lives 'I'm your offender, I'm a real hundred percenter'.

She views walking away from her thirteen-year-old marriage in 1970 as the second significant failure in her life.

> I should have worked at it. I think team is best. (Independence is better than most teams, but our marriage was better than 90 per cent of marriages.) I'm well aware that I would probably relax more if I was part of a team, if somebody were saying, 'That's bloody daft – what are you doing?'

On the other hand, Jean Denton attributes much of her success to long hours and hard work. 'The harder you work, the luckier you get.' She also sees her approach to work as a generational problem and is hopeful that not only women but men will lead more balanced lives.

> We come from a daft generation. We gave up things, we got quality of life badly disturbed. Women who joined on the whole cloned to join so that you weren't actually bringing anything to the table. If you clone you're only going to be less good than the real thing so there is not much point. Women became unrealistic in their expectations. My thinking is straightforward – if your man gets sent to Singapore then go to Singapore, otherwise your marriage is at risk.
>
> I feel good about women's future because I think men are coming towards us. They are beginning to realise that it is absolutely daft to have a family that you only see at weekends.

It is a question of balance – of course you have to go to Tokyo, but do you have to go on Saturday? Of course you have to move around but does it always have to be to Nigeria?

Also globalisation, telecommunications and technology are injecting a little reality. The Hudson Institute recently reported that we now take on in a year the level of information it took one hundred years to take on only forty years ago. As an individual, you get to the stage where you know you can't do it all. Whereas our generation believed that if you applied yourself with industry, you actually could do it all.

To someone who lists 'sleeping' as her recreation in *Who's Who*, she seems unusually determined to need less sleep. Understanding that little sleep was a success factor for Thatcher and Geoffrey Howe, she was advised by someone at Number Ten that the secret was to train oneself to need less. At one o'clock in the morning in the Lords she feels some progress has been made.

One of her greatest sources of enjoyment is her great niece. 'I just enjoy spending time with her. It's great fun and I'm glad she's a girl. She can read way ahead of her time and I was amazed on holiday that she could read the word "fantastically".'

She relaxes by pottering: 'It takes the pressure off thinking, I can tip things out in the drawer and put them back and make decisions about them'. Her work ethic is tenacious, and even when pottering or on holidays, it is not easy to relax.

Four years ago Jean Denton had breast cancer which has not changed the way she lives day to day.

A life threatening illness actually makes you celebrate every day. With breast cancer you go to the hospital, look at the poor sods on stretchers and think 'Aren't I lucky', and so it gives you a change of perspective, without doubt.

I've always been one not to ask God, but to thank God. I do believe in God. I have to believe there's something on my side because I could not have done what I've done by myself. Having had parents that gave me that tremendous break without which I would never have fought my way through also makes me believe. If you don't believe when you go and have a fifteen minute private conversation with the Queen because you're a Baroness-in-waiting, that you can be seen by the people who made it possible then you're suddenly floating on a sea of insecurity.

LEADERSHIP AND SUCCESS FACTORS

Jean Denton describes her own leadership style as based on the Victorian work ethic, and on asking people to do only what she would do herself. She identifies the qualities of leadership as being:

> The ability to know where you're going without doubt – if you don't know where you are going there isn't a chance that you will get there. The ability to share that with people openly and honestly and a recognition at the end of the day, that the final decision is your's, 'I hear everything that you're saying but this is where we should go'. I also work on the basis of delegating as much as possible, trusting people until they let you down and once they let you down, they're foolish.

The leader of the year 2000 will be a motivational and flexible team player:

> Where the good people are now (and they are rare) is where we will be. We've made the major breakthrough from policing to nurturing. We no longer believe there is only one way to do things. It will be impossible to survive without this recognition in the year 2000. Although working through teams is most important now, there are of course still some managers who believe that they can do it all themselves.

Barbara Hosking, former Controller of Information Services at the Independent Broadcasting Authority describes Jean Denton's strengths as embodying the best qualities of a Yorkshirewoman – strength, determination, directness and a healthy competitiveness.

> It is no accident that she was a very successful racing driver. She has a real desire to excel and to win. She is also brave, honest, practical and fair. She is not interested in ivory tower theories but is committed to effectiveness. In government she is like a breath of fresh air. She cuts through to what is important and fights for what she believes in.

Sir William Francis, the Chairman at the Black Country Development Corporation, when she was Deputy, also discerns a common thread through Jean Denton's leadership relating to excellent communication and motivating skills and the preservation of a personal touch.

Jean Denton leads from the front, and is outstanding at interpreting policies and motivating people to follow. She also puts her heart into her work and people respect the human element. Not everyone keeps in touch with their roots and she is careful to devote time to Yorkshire and her family as well as to good causes and the 'task in hand'.

All who know her attest to her workaholism, which contributes to an intensity that may not be mitigated entirely by her ability to enjoy herself.

Jean Denton's leadership in the women's movement in the UK has been as practical and positive as her contribution to business, community and government organisations. Barbara Hosking explains:

> Jean Denton is happy to describe herself as a feminist. She has encouraged and helped women both as individuals and collectively, through organisations such as Women on the Move Against Cancer. She was the obvious first choice to head up Forum UK. Most importantly, women *like* her. We need good strong models who are not Mother Theresa and not saints, models who women feel they have a chance of becoming.
>
> But it hasn't been easy. Even recently, when she took the call to be a Baroness, there was an awful moment in the House of Lords when they read out those old-fashioned words, including describing her as the 'former wife of'. That shook her but she got that practice managed!

Jean Denton is a strong believer in merit and the importance of being measured on performance. 'Otherwise, you drift down to the lowest common denominator. I believe that you should let flyers fly because if we don't let flyers fly how the hell do we protect the weak?'

As with many Chief Executives and Managing Directors she feels most badly about getting hiring/promoting decisions wrong. 'I hate it when I end up firing somebody I appointed because it is a failure on both your parts. They weren't what they promised to be but you didn't get it right.'

Among the people she respects are Baroness Thatcher, Baroness Nancy Seear, Anita Roddick, Sir Patrick Mayhew and Lord Dahrendorf.

As with many of our leaders, Jean Denton would advise young people ambitious to succeed in business to: qualify as much as

possible; gain line management experience where you can be measured ('if you are in a function, everyone has different opinions about
how you are performing'); and to gain international experience.

In addition, she gives strong support to not thinking in a strictly
linear way about one's career:

> You should not worry about the odd diversion because you will
> always learn from it. This includes taking time off to have a family.
> I see young people today trying to cut themselves into so many
> pieces by doing everything, when in fact a breathing space can be
> useful. If women get married, can afford not to work when they
> have a baby, and want to stop for a while, they shouldn't feel guilty
> – they should use the opportunity, enjoy it and continue to learn.

Her advice to ambitious women would differ slightly from that to
men.

> I wouldn't have to tell men to keep moving and planning but it is
> necessary to tell women. Otherwise they become too comfortable.
> If you want to stay where you are that's fine, but if you want to
> move up a corporate ladder, and want a new challenge, you will
> have to look ahead and tell people what you want.

14
Richard Giordano
Chairman, BOC Plc and British Gas Plc

Date of birth:	24 March 1934
Place of birth:	New York, USA
Nationality:	American
Marital status:	Divorced
Family:	One son, two daughters

Education:	Harvard University, BA
	Columbia University Law School, LLB

Career:
1959–1963	Shearman & Sterling
	Lawyer
1963–1978	Airco Inc
1963–64	Assistant Secretary
1964–67	Vice President Marketing
1967–71	Group Vice President
1971–79	President and Chief Operating Officer
1979–1992	The BOC Group
1979–85	Chief Executive
1985–90	Chairman and Chief Executive
1990–91	Chairman
1994 to date	Non-executive Chairman

Outside appointments:
1994 to date	British Gas Plc, Chairman
1985–91	Grand Metropolitan Plc, Director
1991 to date	Non-executive Deputy-Chairman
1984 to date	Georgia Pacific Corporation, Non-executive Director
	RTZ Plc, Non-executive Director

Past non-executive Directorships include Reuters, Lucas Industries and National Power

Interests:	Sailing, tennis, opera

INTRODUCTION

Richard Giordano, Chairman and former Chief Executive of BOC and Chairman of British Gas, is one of the most highly sought after non-executive directors in the country and now leads the classic post-executive life of 'managing a portfolio' chairing or sitting on the board of several leading UK and American public companies including Grand Metropolitan and Georgia Pacific.

The youngest son of hardworking Italian immigrants to the US, he attended Harvard University and then law school at Columbia University. Highly ambitious in a general sense, he never articulated a career goal and attributes career progress to serendipity and hard work but also to consciously acquiring the skills required for the next step. Along with Sir Graham Day, he was rare among chief executives in the UK in beginning his career as a practising lawyer. Pre-eminently a problem solver, his move into business proved immediately successful and was initiated and facilitated by a senior mentor. Characteristically among our sample he had very early line responsibility, becoming Chief Executive of Airco at 37 and more rarely, essentially a one company career (Airco was taken over by BOC in 1979).

Richard Giordano gained early notoriety in the UK as the most highly paid executive in the country as Chief Executive of BOC. However, his success over time in doubling output while halving the workforce at BOC muted if not silenced such commentary.

What have been the instrumental influences in Richard Giordano's career and what are his views on key success factors for business leadership?

EARLY INFLUENCES

Richard Giordano is the youngest son of Italian immigrants to the US, an aspirational environment which imbued him early with a desire to succeed.

It was a family in which mother and father were ambitious for the kids. They weren't necessarily prescribing what to do but were saying 'be good at what you do'. For these immigrant people who came to America at the turn of the century, this was the land of opportunity. They had a set of beliefs related to hard work and success that today are regarded as clichés but for them were real and alive. Of course it was the land of opportunity then and I think it still is.

He went to an all boys high school in New York City, which post-war was a sheltered, almost innocent and hopeful environment, 'We were still very much country boys'. He was both a good student and a talented football player, which helped to make him attractive to the best universities.

His decision to go to Harvard was driven by ambition, 'the idea of going to the best'. Although on emerging from high school he was contemplating engineering as a career, he abandoned this to study liberal arts at Harvard. 'Harvard provided a tolerant environment for an unbelievably immature 18-year-old to grow-up.' During this period his father died and he met and married a classmate from Radcliffe.

Giordano's intention on leaving Harvard was to remain a student, perhaps studying and teaching part-time in India on a scholarship or as an alternative, studying law at Columbia. The scholarship to India was insufficient, and his mother considered this option to be self-indulgent. 'So, I went to law school through serendipity. If I had really wanted to go into law, I would have campaigned for it, and applied to six places as kids do now. It was a more benign period when you could get away with that.'

Giordano thrived at law school, appreciating the intellectual stimulation and intensity of the professional training while viewing it fundamentally as no more than an opportunity to get better educated.

I don't think the law degree qualification makes any difference. What the law degree will do is maybe provide you with skills in analytical thinking and force you to express yourself in writing better than you would. I saw my law school experience partly as a trade or vocational school but also as an opportunity to continue my education beyond the tender age of 22. When I got out of Harvard I knew I was under-educated. They wouldn't like to hear that! Three years in a good American law school was just getting better educated. Any graduate school would do.

CAREER DECISION-MAKING AND DEVELOPMENT

Although ambitious to succeed, Richard Giordano has never had a goal or a plan for his working life, attributing decisions largely to chance.

> Everything that has happened to me has been either accidental, lucky or serendipitous. Not that I haven't worked hard, not that I haven't brought my skills to the game, but it's hardly been a planned campaign to get from A to B. I think that if you look around at lots of my contemporaries you see that is a common story. Not that we were a bunch of choir-boys, suddenly selected. We all had our share of in-fighting, but the major steps that brought a shift change to our careers have been almost all accidental.

Certainly, his two major career decisions were based on the intervention of people known to him, rather than on rational calculation of opportunities.

He joined law firm Shearman & Sterling in New York, largely because his old Harvard freshman tutor was working there. Ironically, a year later the same friend left. The firm was very 'Wall Street – dark grey suits with vests and hats'. Along with the rest of his colleagues he worked eighty-hour weeks and although the work was intellectually interesting, after four of five years, he found the world too narrow. 'You worked with lawyers, you lunched with lawyers and you played squash with lawyers. You dined with lawyers because you worked late nights. I wasn't really cut out for it, not that I knew what I was cut out for.'

The catalyst for leaving was the invitation of a former partner of his firm, George Dillon, who had left to run Airco, a large US industrial gas company. Giordano accepted because he actively wanted a career in business that would provide more excitement, more risk and more challenge. George Dillon was influential as a mentor, believing in him and taking continual risks in rapidly promoting him. 'That's what got me from being a young aggressive lawyer to trying to learn the fundamentals of a business, what makes it run, what makes people run.' He spent only a year and a half in the legal department, before being moved into marketing and by age 32 was running about half the group – the gas, medical and oil businesses.

How was he able so quickly and so successfully to make this transition from specialist lawyer to general manager?

> Each of us comes to our job with a different turn of mind. Even as a practising lawyer, my turn of mind was problem solving. Although I was intellectually stimulated by law I never regarded that as an end in itself and if I were researching a legal problem, I would stop when I found the solution. I would never be a legal scholar. I think problem solving is good preparation for business.

As a lawyer he had had broad experience in litigation, tax and corporate law and had contributed to solving a wide spectrum of problems. His first legal assignment at Airco related to the distribution network which provided him with an opportunity to learn about the whole portfolio of the company's products. 'That's another piece of luck – I might have gone to a part of the business that was much more narrow and my experience curve would have been flatter.' His natural interest in the 'med-tech' products was also an important factor in his development. 'I always felt in my business that I did better when I liked and understood the product. That's why I wouldn't be a very good banker, because I find money absolutely abstract.'

Giordano next plunged himself into solving the problems of the business, rationalising, restructuring, dealing with too much overhead and too many people without 'wrecking people's morale or the momentum of the business'.

After three years, at the age of 32, George Dillon made him Group Vice President in charge of about half the group's operations including all manufacturing, marketing and international business. 'I was way over my head. I couldn't be described as an accomplished businessman. He was bonkers to take that chance but I was a bit like Jack Kennedy – on the job trained.'

Five years later, when his part of the group was growing as the rest of the company experienced problems, Richard Giordano was made President of the Company at age 37.

> In each case of promotion I was utterly surprised – quite the opposite of planning a career. I was running like hell to keep up with where I was. I'm not suggesting I wasn't ambitious because I was but really that which happened was beyond my ambition.

Richard Giordano's single greatest mistake occurred in 1979/80 when at Airco he significantly expanded a graphite business just when world markets for the products were turning down and its major customer, the steel industry, went through a contraction from which it never fully recovered. The company accepted a $117 million write-off. Exemplifying the approach required for learning from mistakes he takes full responsibility.

> I probably should have foreseen that there was really no future in single purpose production facilities for steel. The business had made a bundle of money for years and years and I was seduced by the previous prosperity into thinking that this would go on and on.

His response was to get the failure behind them and move on. 'A lot of people who make mistakes often have their confidence shattered and they really can't go forward. The challenge was to see that the senior management of the company didn't lose its confidence.'

He undertook a quick diagnosis of what had gone wrong and then made sure that the new investments didn't stop. 'It's more important to keep moving forward than to go back and wring your hands.' He also set up a very strong central planning department to provide an authoritative alternative perspective to line managers on issues of strategy.

> It's no good having people questioning you if they are shoe clerks, by that I mean 27-year-old business school graduates. You really need guys with staff of their own, and a power base and stature within the organisation who can step up and say, 'That's not a good idea'. You've got to have people strong enough so that you must make yourself listen to them.

Certainly, in spite of the risk of sounding clichéd, he believes that mistakes are character forming. 'I always ask each candidate for senior positions about his mistakes and am deeply suspicious if he has never made any. He is either an untested character, raising an uncertainty about how he would behave if he made a big mistake or he's not telling the truth.'

Given that people will inevitably make mistakes and cannot always get along with everyone, when are mistakes acceptable and when fatal to rising further?

> If there isn't someone saying negative things about you, you aren't pushing hard enough. You can have occasions when someone doesn't like you at all. It's got to be that others do. You also need to be known, otherwise not being liked by someone can be

very damaging. You can make business errors, but your batting average can't be too bad. Otherwise you are a loser and shouldn't have larger responsibilities. One of the measures of a good leader is that when he makes a mistake, and the company suffers for it, people still follow him. In some circumstances you see someone make a mistake that is not that serious, and the Board and the organisation turns against him and he loses his job. Then you see other guys making a lot of mistakes, but being accepted because people understand that you've lost the battle but not the war. But if you are not a good leader, the loss of the first battle seems like the loss of the war.

In 1973 BOC bought 35 per cent of Airco at Airco's invitation and after five years fight with the justice department over anti-trust issues, BOC acquired more shares in 1978. Then followed one of the earliest bitterly contested takeovers, with George Dillon, Airco Chairman and Giordano, resigning from the BOC Board. Giordano, believing the BOC price to be too low, sought a competing bid from Martin Marietta and BOC finally raised its price to 170 million dollars which was acceptable to Giordano.

With the takeover, he was certain he would be fired, bought a sailboat and decided to realise a dream to sail around the Caribbean and see head-hunters in between. But within three months Sir Leslie Smith, then BOC Chairman, invited him at age 45 to run the whole group in London which 'again was way, way beyond my expectations'.

Giordano came late to international life. Up until his early thirties he had hardly travelled at all, acquiring his first passport at age 30. But in the seventies, he travelled frequently to Airco operations in Japan and Europe and European attitudes were not 'totally strange' to him. BOC, however, was a genuinely international leader in industrial gases, trading in 150 countries with equal presence in America, the Far East and Europe and factories in fifty countries. He came to London in 1979 with some trepidation having found Britain in the seventies very depressing, with the 'language of socialism designed often to disguise an unpleasant truth'.

But it has been a glorious decade, it really has. The environment's been spectacular, and has opened up in terms of people's willingness to work hard, earn money, be wealthy, be slightly vulgar. It was a period of such rapid change in Britain that it took the curse off a stranger coming into a place that really was pretty rigid. I couldn't have managed it in Frankfurt, or Paris or Milan. First of all British management was feeling very unsure of itself. They thought they weren't as good as anybody in the world. The country was very demoralised. Mrs Thatcher's arrival, the pulling back of a lot of the controls, letting people get on with doing things, really changed the whole outlook of management.

After the initial recession in 1982 this became a place of significant self-confidence and openness. It was very welcoming to an American manager, probably more welcoming then than it would be now that British management has restored its self-confidence. But there will always be close ties between the two countries. I found attitudes amongst people very wholesome. There is always a group of people, probably concentrated in the chattering classes, who have a strong fear of American cultural onslaught, but the average guy on the street has very warm feelings toward America. Britain's mind looks east, but its heart looks west.

His role as Chief Executive of BOC during the early years had not been an easy one, however, requiring the halving of the 20,000 workforce in the first four years. By 1993 BOC output had more than doubled to over three billion pounds with over 400 million pounds profit.

Giordano had achieved this growth by streamlining the business and focusing on BOC's traditional areas of strength. He had also introduced a matrix, or in his words 'networking' organisation, by product and geography, newly encouraging specialisation by product and technology lines while ensuring that local companies continued to run their own businesses.

Richard Giordano's first five-year contract was renewed for five more and although he told the Board that he wished to leave after ten years, he ultimately stayed for twelve, retiring as Chief Executive in 1991 and Chairman in 1992. Patrick Rich had been recruited from outside BOC as the new Chief Executive and in April 1994, when Rich became ill, Giordano returned to BOC as Non-executive Chairman, to which he devotes one day a week.

In addition, in Handy's 'Third Age', Giordano has a full-time load of non-executive directorships including Chairmanship of British Gas, Deputy Chairmanship of Grandmet, and Board membership of RTZ and US-based Georgia Pacific. Although he had sat on other Boards when Chief Executive of BOC, and so understood that there is more than one way to solve problems and do business, he nevertheless believes that it is easier now to be flexible and adjust his perspective. 'It's not easy as CEO of one company to sit on the Board of another company because you are inclined to look at the other company's problems and say, "Oh, God, I wouldn't do it that way!" Because you really think your own company's ways of doing business are all there is.'

Fellow Board members testify to the value of Giordano's contribution and underpin why he is so highly sought after as a 'heavyweight' non-executive director. He is not only extremely bright, analytical and incisive in his reasoning but is also direct, clear and 'very much his own man'. Lord Sheppard, Chairman of Grand Met, also points out that Giordano is an enthusiast:

> When we were considering the Pillsbury acquisition, Dick said to us, 'You as the management must present the business case to us in detail and our job as non-executives is not to get excited by the hunt but to analyse the case dispassionately.' Within twenty minutes, he was up on his feet in front of the flip chart saying 'This is what we should do!'

As an individual Richard Giordano is also seen as quite private.

Characteristically Richard Giordano has no plans or objectives for the rest of his life, at the moment enjoying the balance of board work and personal activities he was unable to pursue as Chief Executive.

FAMILY AND PERSONAL LIFE

Richard Giordano has three grown-up children and has recently been divorced from his wife. As with many chief executives of his generation, there is little question that professional priorities invariably took priority over personal ones.

> For guys in my position, work is a very, very jealous mistress. You try your best to have a private life and some do succeed in doing it and some don't. It's not easy. Not only do wives suffer but children suffer. I know that my children missed me and I wish I had seen more of them over the years. I've been lucky though – they are healthy, solid, with no drug problems. Some of my friends' children have real problems produced by a lethal combination of

inattention of parents and privilege. None of my children are interested in business, although they are in business environments. My oldest daughter is a partner with her husband in windmill power generation – they enjoy promoting the life of the machinery and like the fact that it is a green business. My middle daughter is a social worker and runs halfway houses in Connecticut for the disabled.

Giordano clearly sees scope for reduced demands on business people and has a theory that in contemporary international business we travel and communicate too much, the result of a mistaken belief that face to face contact and 'touching the flesh' is always necessary.

Before phones, faxes, airplanes and video conferencing, business still was undertaken pretty effectively. Before the war my father used to go to the West Coast on business. They would spend a couple of days on a train, playing cards but business got done pretty well. In the days of the British Empire they would send a guy off to India and see him once a year. He might get some letters in a packet by steamer but by god he knew what was expected of him. He made all the decisions against a framework that he understood and the people back in London understood. Objectives were clear and values were clear. They knew how to behave, things got done. I have a suspicion that we are doing more face to face than we need to and it is probably wearing people out.

His outside interests include sailing and tennis. Since retiring in January 1992, he has two homes, having bought a flat in New York although, 'New York is almost stranger to me now than London'. He is getting more deeply involved in the United States because his children are there.

LEADERSHIP AND SUCCESS FACTORS

Richard Giordano has carefully thought through the attributes of leadership, as expressed in a speech to Templeton College in October 1992.

My experience over the years has led me to conclude that leaders come in all shapes and sizes. They seldom move about astride great white horses and some are distinctly uncharismatic.

I have also observed that companies with sustained good performance are seldom led by one man. Often three, four or a handful of individuals at the top of an organisation are all leaders and indeed they, by their own example, often encourage leadership at many levels of their organisations.

One of the most important elements of leadership is strategic renewal. Successful leaders are able to step back and rethink their business strategies unconstrained by history or conventional wisdom.

In determining a predictive model for top business people, Richard Giordano identifies: 'Early drive (often unspecified as to goal) is necessary but not sufficient as drive could lead you to being a top criminal or to drink; self-discipline as it must be tempting in a career to branch off, do different things, and lastly, enough emotional stability to stay the course.'

He acknowledges that he is himself driven to succeed and puts this desire to win into the context of leading a large business.

I like to win. I don't think winning means necessarily getting to the top job but it sure means winning the game as defined by where you are. There will be a thousand excuses why you can't win. First it takes a lot of dedication to winning and then understanding the rules of your game. If you are in a game where market share and scale are important then you must chase market share and scale; if you're in a game where you've got to add value for customers in a different way, then make sure you play that game. If you're in a game where technology is very relevant to competitive advantage then for gods' sake don't let your technology erode. You've got to get those strategic judgements right.

It's a risk because the world is not an open book for you to turn the pages and understand what is going to happen. There are a lot of dark alleys, uncertainty – you can't always predict the future with accuracy. The important thing is to be ready for the future – even for a few different futures. You will make mistakes but it is important overall to sustain good performance.

In implementation you have to create an environment where people want to perform and there is accountability for performance. This is difficult in many businesses, like BOC, that are interactive and interdependent. Many a good strategy will simply fall apart by not getting people to want to perform.

People have to like their work. I think you've got to treat people very fairly. I learned more about that as I grew older – it's really important that the organisation be seen as just. Even if we have to take ruthless business decisions, for instance selling a business and letting people go, we treat people well on the way out.

Departing from conventional management practice he does not believe in incorporating corporate values in a written mission settlement.

I don't believe in expressing those things. I think your value system is something that you are expressing daily – the way you treat people, the way you treat customers and suppliers.

Going into a deeper level about people's relationships with each other, I think that we managed at BOC over the years to have a fairly politics-free company. That is the best measure of a value system. We recognised people who were playing games and dealt with them, got them out or changed them. A lot of organisations have politics in a negative sense creeping up in every nook and cranny.

If you asked insiders, they would say that BOC was a good place to work; that they were treated well, fairly; an honourable place. Now that sounds schoolboyish but it's pretty important. People like to be proud of the place they work and it helped that we were successful.

Consistently, Giordano has a reputation not only for having run a politics-free company, but also for toughness in decision making.

In identifying high flyers himself he looks for people who are nice and not predatory, who are objective, cool, analytical, 'don't seem to be flying off the handle or losing their way' and who can make mistakes gracefully. Intelligence is necessary and important, but by no means sufficient. Critically, he looks for 'good personal qualities'.

To the extent that organisations more and more do business with each other laterally, poor qualities will show up quickly. For instance, we all have the experience of subordinates who may relate beautifully upward, a great guy, does the right thing, tells the truth but downward he may be an absolute son of a bitch. Just as you could tell when you were at school whether your friends were trustworthy or not, it becomes obvious whether a subordinate has the right personal qualities.

Richard Giordano believes that the qualities required of senior managers now and in the future are different and that organisations have changed. The organisations where he acquired his early experiences in the sixties and seventies were fairly authoritarian with people relating to each other through hierarchies. There were vast numbers of employees, who expected to spend all their working lives with a single employer. In exchange for employee loyalty and dedication, life-time security was expected.

> The people who made it to the top in the sixties and seventies were what the US psychologists call 'A' types, hard-driving, aggressive, very motivated, very directed but on the other hand very hostile to criticism and quite authoritarian in their ways of going about their lives – the kind of guys who used to bully their children, cow their wives. But they were very ambitious, not just for themselves but for their companies and got a lot done. These guys were identified as heart attack candidates, which was the purpose of the test.
>
> Type 'B' guys were more passive, less hostile, much stronger in lateral thinking and interpersonal skills, able to weather change more easily and in many ways, could deal with adversity without psychological damage.
>
> The 'type A' personality will be substantially disadvantaged in the new era in which dealing with people, and with issues of empowerment and delegation are important. We need a new 'type A' who still wants to conquer the world, but without the negative, aggressive, authoritarian and control characteristics.

The requirements these days of senior managers are complex and even contradictory.

> We push hard-driving successful managers into very ambivalent positions. Outside the company, we want them to compete like mad. All the metaphors we use relate to competition, sport and war – 'Get him by the throat'. But as soon as he comes inside the doors of the company we want him to be benign, co-operative and trusting, giving trust, receiving trust. You can see the ambivalence built into people.
>
> Anyone who is going to make it in the nineties and beyond is going to have to develop co-operative, non-authoritarian skills, the ability to persuade people to do what they should be doing and to get the best from their skills and experience. They will also be

knowledgeable about the political and cultural life of all the communities in which they do business and bring this understanding into the organisation to expand the horizons of their managers and workers.

Giordano emphasises again that both the individual and the organisation must change.

You only learn the new skills by practising them – shifting quality circles, *ad hoc* taskforces, lateral networking all develop these co-operative skills. A young manager who practises these skills is going to see that they work. Sooner or later we do the things that work for us. Necessity pushes you to these kinds of behaviours.

If companies want to get good work out of people the relationship between those people and the company has to change. First of all, people have more choices today; they're more mobile and wealthier. The welfare net gives people a greater sense of security about leaving a job if you are not being well-treated. People are also very feisty if the atmosphere in which they work is not pleasant and are not inclined to just grin and bear it. That doesn't mean we have to run a country club, but all of the systems that surround the environment in which people work need to be seen as effective and fair.

In advising his own children about how to make career decisions Richard Giordano stresses the need for self-knowledge.

They have first to measure their own drive. It's important that they figure out first what they want to be. If they want to be big moguls at business then they've got to set about doing it. They can't work 35 hours a week, take ski trips or a lot of things you do along the way. I don't mean to sound like it's a terrible sacrifice but your life has to be different. In talking to my boy I try to distinguish between ambition and wishful thinking. The children have wanted things, but they want them because they are there. That's wishful thinking which is great at Christmas time. It's not exactly drive.

Giordano attributes his own professional success to luck, timing and getting a very early start on accumulating experience and skills. Although he has not planned, he has clearly prepared himself for being in the right place at the right time and he advises aspiring senior managers to do the same.

The career path to the top is a bit of a race. It is a race against yourself, acquiring skills and judgement as fast as you can, so that by age 35, 40, 45 when you are compared with your peers, you have got more skills and judgement than they do and therefore when it comes to selecting someone to do something more responsible, you will be selected.

I don't think that there is an ideal path to top. A lot of the conventional wisdom about this is baloney. Statistics show that business school isn't the route to the top and neither is consultancy. The MBA can't hurt. It is well documented that it gives people a head start in starting salary but overall MBAs do no better.

You have to have all the attributes. It is better to be tall and good-looking than to be ugly. It is essential to be trustworthy, to have a good set of personal values.

Assuming you are ambitious and have the native ability and talents, including high energy, you need to ask yourself what are tomorrow's managers going to be like, what should they be like, what am I going to bring to my career that's going to make me very useful ten years from now?

If the world is becoming more interdependent, it's obvious that international experience is going to be relevant. It varies by country. If you are British and you want to work for a FTSE thirty company, most are international and you must have international experience. This isn't necessarily true for an American company. Today BOC does business in almost forty countries, and best practice originates from all different parts of the globe.

If the world is becoming increasingly scientifically oriented, you'd better get some foundation in the fundamentals of science, develop scientific curiosity and the ability to turn to a professional scientist or engineer and ask 'How does this work?' and 'Why?'.

You may have had breaks and clearly, will and timing are important. But if you have the natural attributes and appropriate cumulative experience early enough, lightning will strike. If you aren't holding down a pretty substantial job at 40, you are likely to be on a slower track.

He believes that it is also important to stay long enough in each job to actually achieve something and to focus on achievement rather than personal progress.

People who change jobs often need to be careful that they don't become careerists. A careerist is someone who's building the most attractive résumé. Their CV looks terrific, but when you assess their performance, they weren't actually in any place long enough to achieve anything. They are very tough to deal with in an organisation. Their ambition in life is often to undermine accountability, because the CV is going to be damaged by a failure. The careerist will very quickly leave the company when his career runs out of gas and he usually has little patience with corporate management development objectives, if he personally finds himself blocked. At the end of the day we are going to look at the achievement to demonstrate that you have the skills, and we will not assume that just because you were there for a period of time, that you acquired any skills.

On the other hand, variety of experience is a valuable asset. There is nothing intrinsically wrong with changing companies, and indeed the danger of staying with one company all your life is that you can become part of an inbred group who sees the company's culture as the only way to live and that company's problem-solving procedures as the way to solve problems.

15

Steve Shirley

Life President, F.I. GROUP

Date of birth:	16 September 1933
Place of birth:	Dortmund, Germany
Nationality:	British by naturalisation
Marital status:	Married
Family:	One profoundly handicapped son

Education: Sir John Cass College, London
                              Bachelor's degree in Mathematics

Career:
  1951–1959   Post Office Research Station
                              Mathematical Clerk to Scientific Officer
  1959–1962   CDL (Subsidiary of ICL)
                              Systems programmer to Junior Manager
  1962–1993   F.I. GROUP
  1962–1987   Chief Executive sometime Chairman
  1987–1993   Founder Director

Outside appointments:
                              Tandem, Non-executive Director
                              UK Atomic Energy Authority, Non-executive Director
                              Buckingham University, Member of Council
  1989–1990   British Computer Society, President
  1992–1993   Master of the Worshipful Company of Information
                                Technologists

Awards: Institute of Management – Gold Medallist, 1991
                              Honorary Fellowships of City & Guilds Institute and
                              several British universities; also honorary doctorates

INTRODUCTION

Steve Shirley, retired Founder Director of the F.I. GROUP, a leading £45 million computer software house, resembles the rest of the sample in having led a company, but differs from them in having founded the business. Her profile is much more that of the classic entrepreneur than the professional manager/corporate head, and because so many senior women working within companies are choosing to leave the corporate environment to set up companies of their own (certainly this trend is very powerful in the US and is beginning to be witnessed in the UK), Steve Shirley's experience is highly relevant.

Steve Shirley's experience as a child refugee from Nazi Germany during the war provided the 'grit in the oyster' so common in the lives of outstandingly successful and highly motivated leaders. It left a legacy of survivor guilt, an ability to cope with change and a longing for self-sufficiency.

Her approach to her life and career is the proactive objective-setting and single-minded pursuit typical of the entrepreneur. Thus after an early career with the Post Office Research Station and ICL, at 29 she founded her own company in order to provide her with the freedom and flexibility to have children, and to work from home while pursuing a satisfying career. FI was conceived as a software consulting firm to draw on the untapped potential of skilled woman programmers and systems analysts who had left traditional companies to have children. Since its inception, it has pioneered work practices that only recently are gaining widespread acceptance – flexible hours, job sharing, profit sharing and employee ownership. Shirley's greatest personal triumph was bringing the company into staff control in 1991.

A naturally questioning intellectual, Steve Shirley completed a bachelor's degree in mathematics part-time, and is deeply committed to perpetual learning and to the development and empowerment of others.

A self-confessed workaholic, she has balanced the needs of a severely mentally handicapped son with the at times overwhelming demands of growing a successful business. Open about setbacks, she identifies a period during the 1970s recession of significant business failure from which she recovered and learned. Having had no mentor herself she is concerned to be a role model for women in business and she views her own strength as being entrepreneurial leadership, clarity of strategic vision and innovative lateral thinking, rather than day-today management. She attributes her success to sheer hard work and persistence.

What has been important to the development of this entrepreneurial business leader at the cutting edge of management practice, and how would she advise others who would similarly succeed?

EARLY INFLUENCES

Steve Shirley was born in Dortmund, Germany in 1933 as the second daughter of an Austrian mother and a German Jewish father. Her father was a judge and her family middle-class intelligentsia. In 1939, at the age of five, she was sent with her older sister as two of 10,000 unaccompanied child refugees to the UK where they were fostered (in the event very successfully) by a British couple in the Midlands.

Steve Shirley's experience as a child refugee had a lasting impact on her personal motivation, providing a legacy not only of profound survivor guilt and heightened sense of social responsibility but also a need to make a place for herself and to be financially independent. Both the survivor guilt and her approach to money have changed over time.

> Having survived when six million Jews, including nearly a million children, died in Hitler's holocaust, I needed to justify my very existence. Survivor guilt has alleviated over the years, but my strong sense of responsibility has actually increased.
>
> Another very strong motivator has been the desire to make a place for oneself. Few people know what it's like to be a refugee, to have nothing. It was not that I wanted to make money for its own sake but I was not going to be poor ever again. People do not know what it is like to faint from hunger. But even that motivation has changed: I support my son and now have a very positive drive to make money for him. I have set myself a target of how much I am going to leave him and that is a very clear, positive drive.

Her childhood experience also has deeply influenced her approach to business.

> Many entrepreneurs have early trauma in their backgrounds and my refugee experience is quite clearly a major influence on my approach to business. The advantage is that it makes you realise that tomorrow is not going to be as yesterday and it does allow you

to cope with change. It also makes one accustomed to decisions – life and death decisions – at a very early age and probably made me more determined than if I had a more conventional background. By the age of six I was a survivor and as a result I see opportunities not barriers, I see teams, not individuals and I have always focused on strengths, not weaknesses.

The other aspect of a difficult childhood is that my approach to money is very different from that of other people. For a long time I held the company back by pursuing the route of minimum cost, rather than maximum efficiency. I was always used to doing things on a shoestring and often this is not the best way. But it did allow me to be in control, which is what I like.

At her Roman Catholic convent school, Steve Shirley showed a talent for mathematics and was encouraged to apply for a scholarship at a grammar school. Succeeding, she none the less had to attend the nearby boys school as the only girl in her mathematics classes. Her first ambition was to be a mathematician. 'I find mathematics very beautiful and satisfying and it was clear early on that such skill I had was along those lines. I was an intuitive pure mathematician.'

CAREER DECISION-MAKING AND DEVELOPMENT

Unlike many professional managers and in common with most entrepreneurs, Steve Shirley has always had a clear personal goal, although the nature of the goal has changed over the years.

You achieve success, however you define it, by being clear about what you want to achieve at any one time; so for many years I wanted to be a mathematician. Having then come across computers, I changed overnight to wanting to be a computer boffin; later I wanted to be a manager and businesswoman.

One of the distinctive characteristics of entrepreneurs is that we are able to achieve a number of goals simultaneously. So my goal at one stage might have been to achieve maturity of management within the company, or to develop myself as a chairman. My time spans are always very long, and the goal that I had for many years, and achieved after fifteen years, was to get FI into co-ownership. My initial goal was to achieve total ownership by the staff which proved to be impractical.

> So, at any time I have a goal with subgoals. Success comes from single-mindedness, knowing where you want to go and not frittering one's time on incidentals.

She sees herself as always having been driven by 'perfectionism, achievement and wanting to get to the next stage' and although specific goals have changed as she achieved them, her basic motivation has not – 'the classic saying that "as we get older we all stay the same but more so" is true'. Although external recognition of her success has come in later years, and is enjoyed, it has never been an objective.

> There is always a phase in your life when you get recognition for work that was done years ago. In the last years, I have been so honoured by degrees, honorary fellowships, and gold medals. I cannot say I dislike it. It's very nice indeed!

At age 18, unable financially to go to university, she accepted a job with the Post Office Research Station as the employer that showed most interest in her ongoing training. Her commitment to training has never left her. 'Today the whole responsibility for training is much more with the individual. FI's training is far less spoon-feeding and far more the empowered individual taking responsibility for their own training.'

At the Post Office, as a 'glorified mathematical clerk', she learned about how *not* to manage from her difficult first boss and about professionalism.

> I have a great respect for professional skills and making sure that one is competent. When I was the Master of the Worshipful Company of Information Technologists we had a lot of discussion about what it meant to be a professional. To me, professional standards never fall below a certain acceptable level, and that standard has to be high – but not consistently at the heights of brilliance that one occasionally achieves in a manic phase.

With the constructive self-questioning characteristic of the lifelong learner, throughout this period Steve Shirley underwent psychoanalysis to come to terms with her early trauma, which provided her with the strength, confidence and self-knowledge to develop both personally and professionally. In 1959, after eight years at the Post Office and six years of part-time study to acquire a bachelors degree in mathematics, Steve Shirley joined ICL as a systems programmer when she had married Derek Shirley, a Post Office engineer and felt it was not right for husband and wife to work in the same organisation.

She chose ICL, the largest British computer manufacturer, because it was one of the few employers in the computer industry at the time, and in solving mathematical problems through computers she had conceived a far greater interest in the computer as tool than in the solution to the problem. As ever, she relates her past immediately to the present and future.

I am lucky to have that clear interest in computers. Most of us have no idea what we would like to do. This is one of the important reasons behind work experience,. At FI, we offer work experience to girls from the local schools and also some undergraduates. Their understanding of business life is just so different from reality that you realise how important it is to give up your time so that they can see how you spend a day and how people-orientated it is in business.

She stayed with ICL for a year and a half, gaining her first experience in leading a small staff of her own.

It was only when the Harvard Business School prepared an in-depth case study of Steve Shirley's life and career designed to be helpful to young women students that she realised the extent to which her career decisions were influenced by health issues. 'Why did such-and-such happen? Because my son was ill. Why did you do that? Because I was pregnant. Why did that happen? Because I had a miscarriage.'

This began with ICL when she moved to a four-day week, ostensibly because of several miscarriages but also to ensure that she continued to make less money than her husband. At this stage, interested in moving into marketing, she found herself blocked in a technical role and gave notice. Wanting children and some control over her life, she decided to set up her own software consulting firm employing skilled women programmers and analysts who had left conventional careers to raise children, and who could work from home. In a secure and happy marriage, she not only had the confidence but the will to go out on her own.

Each of us as individuals has to either enjoy the pattern of life into which we are born or we have to do something about moulding the future. I have always been pro-active, and was seeking a sort of lifestyle that would allow me to have the time to be with children. The only flexible work opportunities were then very part-time and menial, without intellectual challenge. I felt that with my own company I could create a future that suited me, control my own business life and actually achieve something for other women.

Many people today state similarly negative reasons for going into their own businesses. Because the corporate world does not give the flexibility or support for bright individuals to innovate within the organisation, they feel that they must set up on their own to do what they want to do in the way they want to.

Steve Shirley's success in taking FI from a one-woman cottage industry to a leading IT development company employing 1000 people directly or as independent subcontractors is well-documented, as is her interest from the start in taking the company into staff ownership.

She attributes her early success to persistence and sheer hard work. She worked from a tiny cottage, with one woman in a small spare bedroom, two people in the living-room, the files on top of the piano and Steve in the dining room with baby and babysitter. She also changed her name from Stephanie to 'Steve' when she found her first business development letters to potential clients yielded no response.

By 1970, FI had a turnover of £50,000 with 100 home-based contract programmers and analysts. Her lowest professional period was during the 1970s recession, from which she learned, among other things, the value of staff participation.

We nearly went out of business and I was determined that we should not just be a fairweather company, disappearing when things got tough. I was very, very stubborn. Nevertheless during the seventies I was desperately depressed, and felt absolutely isolated. It was very, very hard.

In the sixties we were focused on FI as a medium for women's emancipation, and after the seventies recession I realised that I needn't have been as isolated and we would have progressed more quickly if we had been more participative. I started to research a lot of companies, including the Mondragon steel works in Spain as a cooperative and as an example of how long things take, only last April did I visit them! So we have evolved from emancipation through a participative phase to workforce co-ownership.

In 1985, FI undertook a staff survey relating to working conditions which revealed that staff wanted to work together more outside their homes because they enjoyed the social interaction.

> This is what people had always told me but being a pretty cussed soul, I pursued home working for many years and pushed it 100 per cent. The survey made quite clear that people did not want to have the electronic office in their home – what they wanted was the flexibility. And we took action on it. Too frequently, one does staff surveys or customer surveys and doesn't take action on unexpected or unpleasant results. From a managerial point of view, you really have to listen and act on the results.

Steve Shirley's source of greatest satisfaction has been taking FI into co-ownership.

> Ceding control of the company to the workforce has given me enormous satisfaction. It took fifteen years, with a lot of preparatory work beforehand. I hold my breath that it will continue to motivate the staff so that they will drive the company forward.

Steve Shirley retired from FI in September 1993, and in Handy's 'Third Age' has a portfolio of activities.

> My aim is to escape from information technology and undertake a national role. I would prefer to do a few things intensively and solidly rather than, as some people do, have ten non-executive directorships. If you don't really commit to an organisation, you're just taking up space.

Until 1993, she was the Master of the Worshipful Company of Information Technologists, the hundredth livery company in London. Although relating to information technology, it was less about technical exploitation, than the strategic and innovative use of information technology and its social and economic implications. Although she was the fifth woman Master of a livery company, three have been Royals and she is proud of having been one of very few practising woman Masters.

Her only other commitment in information technology is as a non-executive director of Tandem Computers in the US because 'Tandem is a manufacturing corporate where my software experience is valuable and as a major multi-national, it extends me in a natural way.'

Steve Shirley also serves on the Council of Buckingham University, the UK's only independent university, very international and experimental, because it is young and small and so needs her skills.

In choosing activities, she looks for balance, but also for organisations with cultures that emphasise people.

Most of her working life has been spent within her own company, but even in her early years at the Post Office and ICL, she never had a mentor. Although helped by many people, she took charge of her own career from the start. She is however, like Baroness Denton, an active networker and not surprisingly, maintains a database of people she has met.

Never having had a single role model herself, she would like to serve as one for young professional women:

> I aspire to characteristics in a wide range of people – a variety of skills from finance to communications to presentation and dress and derived from books, literature, films, opera, business. In the field of politics women have some role models now – Indira Gandhi, Mrs Bandaranaike, Lady Thatcher. In the field of business there are too few and so I try to provide one model.

She was influenced years ago, however, by Phyllis Pearsall, of *Geographers' A–Z*, who she met two or three times.

> She struck me very much as an older version of me. She had taken her company into co-ownership and she gave me of her time and experience. I asked her the big question – 'Would you do it again?' and there was that terrible pause before she said, 'Yes, I would'. The cost to her was clear. It was very helpful to me.

Steve Shirley clearly sees the differences between her own generation of women as pioneers and the younger generation. Her generation became overqualified to allay arguments about being professionally equipped. With the battles won, the younger generation is much more relaxed in their approach to work and to life, displaying the flexibility that she sought in pioneering home based work.

> Women in their forties seem to have a much more selective approach and want to control their own lives. They are thrusting and have a different attitude about what they will and will not do.
> Young women are much less stereotyped in their aspirations and in their twenties and thirties are making life choices that accom-

modate both family and career – whether taking a franchise, helping their partners, travelling for six months. It is very nice and healthy.

Typical of all entrepreneurs, Steve Shirley has experienced many business failures and philosophically attributes these to experience.

After many years in business I am associated with success, but have had the most awful setbacks and failures. If you're going to be successful as a Chief Executive, you have to have many things on the go. Real innovation, from which growth stems, is risky and by definition, not all the opportunities are going to come to fruition. Some of them are going to fail and fail badly. Resilience comes from learning from errors to build on experience for the next task. Apart from that, forget the failures and concentrate on the successes.

Yet Steve Shirley continues to find failure difficult and considers herself risk-averse.

It is a fallacy to think that entrepreneurs take more risks or greater risks. I would never risk the organisation in its entirety. I measure and monitor risk carefully. Nevertheless, I take risks that other people wouldn't – this is one of the other differences between the entrepreneur and the professional manager in a mature organisation.

One of her most painful and visible failures was to lose a small fortune in the US in the 1970s, when for two and a half years she tried to develop a technical methodology for the computer industry. She was warned against the venture, was undercapitalised and 'too early'. 'I thought I knew better and was wrong. I was also wrong-footed by the sterling/dollar crisis. I wasn't even watching it and it changed. There was a lot to learn from that.'

She experienced at first hand what many others have observed (Liam Strong, Archie Norman, John Harvey-Jones) – Americans are much more forgiving of business failure, with a clear understanding of the risks incurred and lessons learned and that a foundation is often provided for future success. One can be down but not out. It is far more difficult to recover from business failure in the UK.

Interestingly, I gained in the respect of my American friends and colleagues – they thought that I had probably had it quite easy up until then! My British colleagues reacted very differently. There clearly is a feeling in the UK that someone is unsound if they have had a failure.

I certainly believe that certain types of negative behaviour, for instance, stealing, lying or manipulating, are a pretty good clue of how people will behave in the future. But if someone fails in their life in an honourable attempt in some way, it is a positive experience you can build on.

As a result of her setback in the US Shirley developed from a salesperson into a marketeer, learning to ask herself, 'If we can't sell this product or service what will people buy from this sort of centre of excellence.'

As a lifelong learner leading an information technology business, it is no surprise that international experience has been developmentally crucial.

The world is shrinking and expressions like the global village are really very meaningful in the information technology field. Innovation in computers comes from the States and Japan, so one is thinking internationally all the time. I am a Member of the British-North American Committee, which is a network of people interested in the strategic issues. We get an update on the US, Canada and the UK every six months, which is very invaluable.

Fundamentally, one learns lessons from one's own life but you can also learn vicariously from others. That is why one reads and listens and that is why the case study approach to learning is so impactful. Other countries experience can often be exploited. Without an international perspective, it is hardly possible to lead, except in the very smallest company. One has to be very conscious of what is happening to technology in your business sector and continually hone your skills so that you are using the best methodology available. In travelling, you learn about new ways, methods and approaches and this means we all have to be generous in sharing our experiences.

FAMILY AND PERSONAL LIFE

Happily married to a supportive husband, Steve Shirley has a profoundly mentally handicapped son, now in his thirties. The quest for balance has arguably had a more important impact on Steve Shirley's life than on that of anyone else in the study. As examined, FI in its conception was a vehicle to provide Shirley and other working women with children with the flexible alternative of home work.

> When my son was growing up, one of the reasons for working from home was to be able to combine an active professional life, a vigorous career with looking after him myself. There was no money for childcare so home working was one solution for us and in fact, we spent a lot of early time together. Social life and everything else was sacrificed. All I did was work.

Although her success at FI has been intensely rewarding, it has perhaps ironically also had tremendous costs, particularly for her personal life.

> One of the costs is the sheer dominance of professional life. It has taken over everything. When one feels passionate about something, there is a lot of energy and there is a creative drive when you are building a business. Artists work in a similar way. Work to me is not just something I do when I'd rather be doing something else. I lose myself in work. I also forget the problems of my family in work and that is the *only* time I forget them.
>
> Another cost is the isolation – the entrepreneur is doubly lonely because one doesn't have the money and therefore ability to buy help to make time. Especially when one survives successfully, people tend to forget the sheer financial commitment, having to take out a second mortgage on the family home. It was an incredible risk to take and one of the few that my husband and I actually took jointly. I had to spell out to him that there was no guarantee that FI would succeed.
>
> For many years it was also very difficult to find creative time for myself. In speaking to students about leadership, I stress that business leaders must be selfless, otherwise you are just making money, but you also have to be selfish, otherwise you get submerged.

Although the costs are clear, so are the rewards and she has no regrets about the balance struck.

> The burden of responsibility is heavy and for many years you never really switch off and that's very unhealthy. However, the rewards

are commensurate. The feeling of achievement when you actually
do succeed is enormous. I even use words like 'I feel fulfilled'. I
have done what I needed to do and how few people actually feel as
positive about themselves as that? Certainly I would do it all again
in hindsight.

The toll physically and mentally through the years of being a
superwoman should not be underestimated. At one stage in the
1970s, juggling the demands of a growing business and a severely
mentally handicapped son, Steve Shirley experienced a full-fledged
nervous breakdown, being hospitalised for a month and taking a
further eight months to recover enough to start work again.

Having day-to-day responsibility for FI and its over one thousand
staff was not only time-consuming but relentlessly pressured. Relinquishing first the running of the company, then the chairmanship,
then the control and finally retiring in September 1993 and seeing the
company continue to succeed has been a relief 'I feel so marvellous
simply because the sheer tension is gone'. Steve Shirley now has more
time to herself. Saturdays with her son are sacrosanct. 'I am lucky to
be able to spend this amount of time with a child of thirty.'

'Relaxing' in her life is not an issue. She renews herself by changing
course, doing something different and by travelling.

Steve Shirley describes her personal belief system as humanism: 'I
have been actively searching for God for over fifty years, but have
never found him, so remain a humanist or an agnostic. People ask
whether I am a feminist but no I am not. I am a humanist.'

LEADERSHIP AND SUCCESS FACTORS

Senior people outside of FI who have worked with her in different
contexts invariably attest to Steve Shirley's vision, commitment and
single-minded ambition to contribute tangibly to the computer
industry, to raising standards of vocational training and to realising
individual potential.

Peter Morgan, former Director-General of the Institute of Directors, speaks of Steve Shirley's impressive commitment to 'straighten
out' the institutions of the computer industry. As the First Master of
the Worshipful Company of Information Technologists, her goal was
to put the 'company on the map'; pulling the company together to

identify its own distinctive contribution, just as she had earlier accomplished as President of the Computer Society.

Sir Geoffrey Holland, Vice Chancellor of the University of Exeter, with whom she has worked on Department of Employment initiatives on vocational training, notes that her serious sense of direction, enthusiasm and commitment to the development of individuals have led not only to her pioneering flexible work practices at FI, but also to a commitment to elevate the level of vocational training and skills in the UK which fall far below standards internationally.

Sir Edwin Nixon, Chairman of Amersham, Deputy Chairman of National Westminster Bank Plc and former Chairman and Chief Executive of IBM in the UK, goes to the heart of her leadership in speaking of Steve Shirley's integrity.

> In the early days of F International, IBM and FI put together a joint proposal for a contract with a Government agency. The Government leaned on Steve to put in a proposal with ICL because it was UK-based. But she wouldn't hear of it. She had committed herself to going with IBM and stuck with it. That showed her *complete* integrity.

In examining her own success and leadership qualities, Steve Shirley clearly distinguishes between her strengths as an entrepreneur and those of the professional manager. The differences to her are clear as she neither enjoys nor excels at day-to-day management, unlike FI's Chief Executive, Hilary Cropper.

> In some ways, the skills are complementary and in some ways, chalk and cheese. The entrepreneur seems to have a much more strategic orientation, a real vision and a time span that is much longer, almost by an order of magnitude. I accept personal responsibility as distinct from corporate responsibility. I tend to match jobs to people, so I create opportunities for what individuals want to do or what they might be ready for.
>
> I focus very much on opportunity whereas Hilary focuses on setting standards and reviewing performance in a formal way. I always ask 'Why not, why can't we do this?' and she asks 'How can I do it?'. Running FI for so many years, I had to learn to manage like a professional manager. You can't get by without the toolkit of certain skills – I'm just glad I do not have to do it any more.
>
> Also I tend to expect total commitment and worry when it's not there. Most managers are just expecting a particular role to be

fulfilled and don't expect that total commitment. Also professional managers are accustomed to working within prescribed limits and I am just not. If someone sets a limit I immediately jump over the wall.

Her orientation did not prevent Steve Shirley from being an effective chief executive of a growing company for 25 years. She attributes her success to recruiting people who are 'far, far better' than she is, to setting the direction and persuading people to follow and to give of their best. 'You can't do anything on your own, you have to have a team.'

She also consciously developed herself, working on her weaknesses. 'Leadership requires excellent communication skills. For a long time I was really only happy talking to people on a one to one basis. I had to learn the skills of talking to people in groups because it is by talking to groups that one can bring about change and get people buying in.'

In preparing for a talk to the Commonwealth Studies Conference, she was impressed by the definition of a leader provided by Jack Weber of the London Business School – leaders challenge the status quo, take a chance to bring about the unprecedented, inspire others to share the challenge and personally exemplify the qualities they seek to instill. 'I buy into that. That is what I reckon to do. I believe that all we have in Britain is human capital, skills, people.'

She certainly seeks opportunities to develop her middle and senior managers, including looking for and creating non-executive director-ships. (When I approached her regarding a non-executive director-ship, she gave me the name of a senior woman manager at FI.)

In identifying and evaluating future leaders at FI, six-monthly appraisals of staff examine leadership potential based on track record 'you have to reward success', and more subjective criteria. 'There is a certain amount of gut feel about leadership qualities – good genes, health record, high energy, sound value system.'

Her belief in the importance of genes, and understanding family history in hiring people was mentioned nowhere else in the study.

We recently had a member of staff go through a nervous break-down and when we discovered her condition, her family record of instability was there staring us in the face. Knowing this record would not have prevented us employing her but we should have known that she was very vulnerable.

With flatter organisations and the rapidity of change, she sees the CEO of the future as requiring better communication skills, an understanding of global environmental issues and of changing relationships, for instance, between customer and supplier. Conceptual mastery of information technology, 'an appreciation of how computer networking and telecommunication can allow them to accomplish things' too will be vital.

For those aspiring to reach the top of a major organisation, Steve Shirley advises:

- Start with a broad basis, a general education.
- Then gain specialist knowledge, particularly in marketing, information technology (this is the decade of networking) and modern languages.
- Having specialised, it is necessary to broaden your perspective and experience to become Chief Executive. 'Grasp each opportunity and make the most of it as it comes along. I remember not wanting to take one opportunity at the moment it presented itself but it wouldn't have come the time I was ready, so you really have to grab it when it comes.'
- Don't be afraid to move under appropriate circumstances. 'If something goes wrong stick it out for six months. If you are blocked by a difficult boss, then get out – there is no reason to waste oneself when one is not learning or extending oneself. For women particularly, why remain stuck in unhelpful cultures?'
- Never stop learning. 'Lifelong training is so important. Our high flyers have to be in general management positions in their forties, maybe younger. If they haven't made it by their forties, they are never going to make it. Partly, it is a question of driving energy. Suddenly in your fifties, you find yourself playing the guru roles. It happens very quickly.'

16

Sir Graham Day

Former Chairman of Cadbury Schweppes Plc
PowerGen, British Aerospace Plc

Date of birth:	1933
Place of birth:	Halifax, Nova Scotia
Nationality:	Dual – Canadian/British
Marital status:	Married
Family:	Two daughters, one son
Languages:	French

Education:	Queen Elizabeth High School
	Nova Scotia
1956	Dalhousie University
	LLB

Career:

1956–1964	Private law practice
1964–1971	Canadian Pacific Ltd
	Regional Counsel, Assistant General Solicitor
1971–1975	Cammell Laird Shipbuilding Ltd
	Chief Executive
1975–1976	British Shipbuilders
	Chief Executive Designate
1977–1981	Dalhousie University
	Head of Canadian Marine Transportation Centre
	Professor – Business School
1981–83	Dome Petroleum Limited
	Vice-President, Marine Development
1983–86	British Shipbuilders
	Chairman and Chief Executive
1986–1991	The Rover Group Plc
	Chairman and Chief Executive
1991–1992	British Aerospace Plc
	Interim Chairman

Outside Appointments:

The Laird Group Plc, Non-executive Director
Crombie Insurance Company (UK), Non-executive Chairman
Thorn EMI, Non-executive Director
Altracraig Shipping, Non-executive Director
Jebsuns Thun Shipping (Luxembourg) SA, Non-executive Director
Bank of Nova Scotia, Non-executive Director
Crownx Inc.
Non-executive Director
Empire Company Limited
Non-executive Director
John Labatt Ltd, Non-executive Director
Nova Corporation, Non-executive Director
Nova Scotia Power, Inc., Non-executive Director
The Shaw Group Limited, Non-executive Director
Ashurst Morris Crisp (London solicitors), Consultant
Boston Consulting Group, Adviser
Stewart McKelvey Stirling Scales, Counsel
Dalhousie University, Chancellor

| 1990–1993 | PowerGen, Chairman |
| 1989–1992 | Cadbury Schweppes Plc, Chairman |

| Awards: | Honorary doctorates from Dalhousie University, the City University, the Council for National Academic Awards (UK), Cranfield Institute of Technology, Aston University and Warwick University, Humberside University, South Bank University. Fellow of University College (Cardiff), The University of Wales. |

| Interests: | Education and training, military history, Governments' economic policies |

INTRODUCTION

Sir Graham Day in 1992 was not only Chairman of three of Britain's largest companies, Cadbury Schweppes, PowerGen and British Aerospace, but also a non-executive of eight other major companies in the UK as well as several in his native Canada. With more non-executive directorships than any other chief executive in Britain, he had achieved almost legendary status for his turnaround of Cammell Laird Shipbuilders and British Leyland (renamed Rover) and for his penetrating strategic mind and his ability to render the complex simple and to master new industries through hard work and unerringly asking the right questions. He was equally well-known for his integrity and honesty, legendarily telling the unions at Cammell Laird 'I never lie and I never bluff', and also for being Prime Minister Thatcher's 'favourite industrialist'.

Graham Day's achievements are even more extraordinary considering his background. Not only did he live in Canada until he was 38, but he was given his first line management position at this age as Chief Executive of Cammell Laird in the UK.

The son of an English immigrant to Nova Scotia, his background was working-class, highly aspirational and rich in learning opportunities both at home and school. His high school and early university years were however academically arid, and he evinced early an independent and non-conformist rebellion against the mediocrity he experienced, with a history of expulsion from class. However, the choice of law at university set him on a road of high professional motivation and excellence that determined the course of his successful career.

He has never had a career goal and career decision making has been based on the selective acceptance of opportunities offered by others based on his reputation. This approach was successful but not problem free and resulted in two career mistakes that he regrets – his first experience with British Shipbuilders and his two years with Dome Petroleum.

Otherwise, his highly unusual career was both successful and rewarding. The private practice of law honed his problem solving and analytical capacity, while seven years at Canadian Pacific in legal and commercial advisory roles was the 'best school' he could have had. He was deeply influenced by two mentors in these years who taught him about the importance of people and the qualities of compassion, humility, courtesy and honesty which he still believes to be at the heart of leadership.

The leap from Canadian Pacific to Cammell Laird set Graham Day on his path as corporate doctor and recovery expert that was to govern most of the next twenty-two years. The Chief Executiveship was offered by the Heath government because of his previous involvement as a client with Cammell Laird, and accepted because of the classic discomfort with an autocratic new boss at CP.

At 38, with no line management experience but with broad and international exposure across a multi-faceted business, Graham Day headed his first of four turnarounds (Cammell Laird, British Shipbuilders, The Rover Group, British Aerospace) and began fifteen years of Chief Executiveship across three different industries (and Non-executive Chairmanship of two more).

Very happily married, Graham Day none the less acknowledges the primacy of work throughout his career. An exceedingly hard worker, he is committed to life-long study which accounts for his ability to master new industries so quickly and so thoroughly. Now 'retired' from executive life and living in Canada, he has a full portfolio of Non-executive Directorships and other commitments in Canada and Europe.

What has been important to the development of this leading member of the older generation of business leaders who arrived in the UK from Canada at age 38 with no line management experience to head up one of the most troubled companies in the country and twenty years later was one of the most respected Chairmen in the country?

EARLY INFLUENCES

Judson Graham Day was born in Halifax, Canada in 1933, the only child of an English immigrant. Although the family lived modestly, a rich learning environment was provided. His lifelong love of reading began when his father taught him to read and write before he went to school. His father also introduced him at age seven or eight not only to social history, reading aloud Charles Dickens but also fed his imagination on stories of adventure, tales of underwater exploration and Arctic/Antarctic exploration such as Byrd at the South Pole and breaking into the strong room of the Egypt, which he still vividly remembers today.

His stimulating home environment was perpetuated in his first school, which he attended for eight years, providing a firm foundation for later learning in spite of intervening, less positive experiences.

> It was an aspirational school in the sense that the school and the teachers were very committed to performance. The idea that anyone would not pass was unthinkable. The Principal Earl Winthrow taught grade eight, and he announced the first day that not only would everyone pass, we would have the highest aggregate in the City of Halifax for grade eight that year and we did. This aspiration was not focused on individuals but on the class. You will, you can perform.

After a bridge year Graham Day moved on to Queen Elizabeth High School for three unhappy years – 'the teachers were good, bad and appalling'. By this time he not only had high expectations, but was confident about his abilities and his perceptions, and not willing to accept mediocrity.

> By the time I had finished grade twelve I was only permitted to attend two classes. I was expelled from all the others. I had arguments with teachers. For instance, I was asked to write a business letter applying for a job and my father that day had got his annual bill from the Sun Life Assurance Company of Canada. Mrs Karl Clarke had said it couldn't be 'assurance' but 'insurance'. So I explained the difference between the two and was expelled from class.
>
> I remember with great clarity saying to her 'well, why are you teaching English when you can't even speak the language!' I learned to shut up later on. I just hated school. I remember every single verse of the *Rubáiyát of Omar Khayyám* because that was the penalty for being late.

Revealing an early courage of his convictions and non-conformist individuality, the experience was both disillusioning and no doubt strengthening.

Another legacy of his childhood is a profound belief in the work ethic. He was exposed to social ideals early, his father not only reading Dickens out loud but telling him stories about working in London as a young man.

> In growing up in very modest circumstances in Nova Scotia, one was conscious of the general social condition, but that didn't

produce in me a socialist because my observation has always been that socialism was misguided and ineffective. I'm fundamentally a believer in providing circumstances in which self-help can apply.

I am quite happy to contribute through my tax pounds or dollars to the aged, the infirm, the fatherless, but if someone is hale and hearty get him out to work. I believe in 'workfair' for example, because it preserves self-respect. I watched my mother's relatives in a small fishing village work off part of their municipal taxes by time and labour on the highways and that was a respectable thing to do. I don't believe in handouts with people not having to give anything back to society. Society's obligations are reciprocal with the recipients obligations to society.

I also find myself getting very short with talks on freedom of education because I had to save my money and work for years long before I went to university and even when I was doing my final exams in law school I was still working in Simpsons (a large department store chain in Canada). People say, 'Oh, well you can't get jobs'. Jobs were very hard to get in the fifties as well. But I always had a job. In fact, frequently I had two or three jobs.

Moving on to Dalhousie University, Nova Scotia's best university, was not a conscious decision – in an aspirational environment 'that's what you did'. The first two years, with no guidance about what course to take, were an 'unhappy continuation of high school'. He hated everything but history and political science, and in his second year was again threatened with expulsion because of an argument with a French professor, ultimately being expelled from class but allowed to write the exam.

Graham Day had a very good voice and his only pleasure at this stage was spending more and more time singing professionally, 'I got paid five dollars to sing and that was a lot of money then'.

At the end of his second year, in desperation 'My God, this is going nowhere', he investigated his options for the first time in the university catalogue and was rewarded with the discovery of a 'wee loophole'. In Canadian universities at this time, law was a postgraduate course but buried in the catalogue was a provision that with ten credits, the right mix of courses and a certain average grade, you could apply for admission to law school. With strength in history, political science and English and survival of the mandatory maths 1, he 'just squeaked in'.

By this time Graham Day knew that he was not interested in sciences, arts or social sciences for formal study. 'It had to be some cutting edge and law seemed to provide this.'

His initiative paid off handsomely, providing a complete turn-around in his university experience.

> God bless them all. They let me in. In many ways it was nirvana. The calibre of instruction was high with a lot of downtown practitioners giving special courses. Your peer group were more mature, brighter, more committed. Progressively I became a better and better student. The key in those days was to finish in the top ten and I finished in the top ten. So I almost drifted into law school because of my little loophole but by God, was very fortunate to have done so.

Although the loophole was lucky, it was his initiative and self-understanding that created the opportunity. It is clearly not true that successful people have no 'unsuccessful' or unfulfilling periods in their lives. In Graham Day's case, the solid foundation and expectations of his early formative years provided the confidence and insight not to accept conforming to experience that was not right for him. After five years of disillusionment, he was again on a path that drew on his strengths and engaged his mind and heart, but only after he had actively reached out for it.

He was also at this time seriously involved in amateur and subsequently semi-professional theatre, indeed so involved that by his second year, he had an opportunity to become a professional singer. It was the only time that his father intervened in his decision-making, asking him to think hard about how gifted he was as a singer, given the instability of a singing career. Graham Day concluded that he was not good enough.

Fortunately, not only was law intellectually challenging, with the cutting edge he sought but it also provided the theatrics he loved ('You don't gesture with the downstage hand, that kind of thing').

CAREER DECISION-MAKING AND DEVELOPMENT

Graham Day has never had a focused professional objective. Attributing his career decisions in some measure to chance, he also clearly understands the importance of the individual seizing and maximising opportunities as they present themselves.

In my life, I need a shape, a plan and some cohesion. Law provided that shape. To a degree, everything after that has been either serendipity or happenstance. A lot of people are in the right place at the right time but lack the courage to take a decision or the willingness to take the risk. I prefer the Shakespearean notion of 'catching affairs at the flood'.

Other than looking for part-time work when I was at university (I always worked) I never had to look for a job. People have always offered me opportunities. I haven't always said yes, but I've been fortunate.

In making career decisions, his priorities have been straightforward:

I ask myself first, can I do the job? Second, will I get some satisfaction out of doing it, i.e. do I want to do it? Third, is it where we, my wife and my children when they were younger, want to be in terms of location? Money might come in the fourth slot. I'm well paid but I've never maximised my financial position. I have in the past not accepted jobs which would have paid me a lot of money because I didn't like the job or didn't like some of the connotations.

His first job exemplifies not only this serendipity but also the influence of key individuals on each career move. After finishing law school he was articled to Leonard Lawson Pace ('we called him Lum') who one day was on the telephone, and asked Day who was in his office, whether he would like to go to Windsor, a town outside of Halifax. Day said, 'sure', and ended up taking over the practice of a single practitioner who was homesick for Cape Breton. Here he also met his wife, Ann, who was back for her school reunion.

Eight years later, equally out of the blue, the future Chief Justice of Nova Scotia, Gordon Cowan, rang to ask whether he would like to join Canadian Pacific, one of Canada's leading companies, and feeling that he was stagnating in Windsor, Graham Day agreed to an opportunity that he could not have chosen better.

Canadian Pacific was as close as I came to religion. It was the be all and end all. I thought it was the most marvellous place in the world and I loved every moment of every day. I sometimes joke and say CP was the best school I ever attended because of what I describe as the Canadian Pacific imperative 'you can do it'. The idea that you are given an assignment and fail to reach its objective is virtually unthinkable.

As at grade school, at 31, he thrived in an unashamedly aspirational environment. He moved to Montreal. His job was initially 100 per cent law, gradually evolving into doing 90 per cent business. The scope of the work was broad and for the first time, international, involving travel to the Far East, Europe and extensively within Canada. Importantly for him, the environment was trusting and encouraged people to say what they thought. Graham Day was deeply and positively influenced by two men in those years. He learned by watching Lesley Raymond Smith, 'an extraordinarily good manager of people'.

> Les Smith was a role model because he was such a good all round manager. As a manager he probably didn't have any fundamental weaknesses. He didn't have all the quantitative skills but he was marvellous with customers. He was a railroader. He was very good on the operating side. He handled his people very well. He was always available. He was a motivator. He was just a great man. We called ourselves 'Les's boys'.

Norris 'Buck' Crump, the Chairman, also provided a model of gentlemanly grace.

> He was such a kind, polite, considerate man. I was always very interested in how effective that kindness and consideration were in getting things done. Whether it was a technique I never knew but I believe that the man was implicitly courteous. I learned from him that there's no excuse for being rude or discourteous.

Inevitably, he also learned how not to manage from 'some awful managers', notably from Ian Sinclair, who became Chief Executive in 1969. Indeed, Sinclair was instrumental in Day's decision to leave the company to which he was devoted and in which he had always expected to stay all his working life.

> Sinclair was brilliant, almost in many ways a polymath, but he was an autocrat, not a leader. He was not a motivator. He was a demander and that for me was a change, because although the CP culture was rigid and quite demanding, it demanded equally all up and down the line and Sinclair didn't fit into that. The second or third Chairman after him is still trying to put the company back to what it was. I thought 'I can't work for that man for another seventeen years until he retires.' After CP I've never planned my career. I've planned each job with the knowledge that if I did it half

well, I would be working myself out of a job so I've just gone along with what was thrown up.

Again fortuitously, John Gardiner, Chairman of the Laird Group in the UK, speaking on behalf of both the Group and the UK government, 50 per cent owners of Cammell Laird, rang to ask if he would like to run the shipbuilding group. Graham Day had spent April to July 1970 in London, helping to develop a scheme to rescue the company from bankruptcy, because CP had contracted Cammell Laird to build three ships at Birkenhead and stood to lose a great deal.

He knew something about shipbuilding and engineering, the UK appealed because of his English father, he was disillusioned with Canadian Pacific management and he took the job.

Graham Day is unique among the males in our sample in acquiring line management experience for the first time at age 38 – his positions up until then though broad in commercial scope, had been advisory.

I had been doing staff jobs most of my life until then. Canadian Pacific in those days had no career planning at all. I had always wanted to do a line job. By my standards, 38 is very old to move into a first line job especially at the top of the company. I asked Nicholas Ridley, the Minister at the time, 'Why me, Minister?' and he replied, 'It just occurs to us that it is easier to shoot the colonials than it is to shoot the natives.' I subsequently learned that it was very difficult to get someone to do that job and take that sort of risk. I had a young family and we moved to Birkenhead. But we had the money from the sale of our house in Montreal and thought the risk was acceptable.

His observation of good managers at Canadian Pacific provided a sound management model and his own inclination to compensate for weaknesses (as he had earlier to develop numeracy and a knowledge of economics) by concentrated study stood him in good stead.

Although he had travelled little until he joined Canadian Pacific at age 31, having an English father in Nova Scotia sensitised Graham Day to cultural differences. Certainly he always found the UK a very easy working environment, although he clearly also feels very Canadian.

I found the UK difficult in the seventies because I couldn't find a work ethic. When I went back to Canada in the late seventies, early eighties I couldn't find a work ethic in Canada. The work ethic is in the UK now. The only time I can see a living, breathing work ethic in Canada is when I go to Calgary. That doesn't mean that all Canadians are lazy, but they don't work the way they worked when I was a boy!

I've never worked in the United States, although I've been offered some interesting and high-paying jobs there. It sounds silly to say but if I'd gone to work in the States it would have been just a job whereas working in the UK is more than simply earning a living because it's part of my culture and background and the country actually matters to me. I would like to think that I'm making a broader contribution.

His major challenge at Cammell Laird was to inject commercial discipline and market focus into an essentially engineering driven organisation.

There were no systems, nothing else. You were writing on a clean sheet of paper. I took very hard decisions which caused a tremendous upheaval in people's lives. I could press these decisions because we had no bank credit, no one would loan us any money and the receiver was outside the gate. Although the decisions were brutal, the delivery wasn't necessarily so. I remembered Buck Crump's example of consideration at CP.

The general engineering activity was closed, the business refocused, customers persuaded not to cancel new orders, a believable accounting system introduced, money found for capital investment and soon, profits made.

In December 1975 he made the worst mistake of his career. For once 'going with the flow' without examination failed him. The government had changed, and he accepted the Secretary of State for Industry's offer to become the Chief Executive Designate of British Shipbuilders, which was to be the nationalised operation.

That was an appalling decision because I should have taken a little more time to understand the way relevant Ministers were going to function and to think also about the paper thin Parliamentary majority which later was lost. It was outside my control and the fatal mistake was not knowing the circumstances. It was emotionally damaging, because first of all you suspected that you were ineffective and then you knew you were ineffective. I stayed from 1

January 1976 when it became effective until the 27 November and then because the bill failed I was a free agent.

Declining to renew his contract and badly burned by the experience, he decided to take three months to think. Again, he was approached by Dalhousie University to run their new Marine Transportation Centre, and to accept a professorship at the Graduate Business School. Signing a two-year contract, he taught strategic planning and transportation as well as undertaking consulting work.

His second 'bad career decision' was made in 1981 when he next accepted a secondment for three years to one of his consulting clients, Dome Petroleum.

> I had actually done my homework this time. The company had severe difficulties. I cleared up the area that required help. I met some very good people and keep in touch with them to this day. But it was a stupid thing to do. It wasn't damaging, financially or otherwise, but other than the people it was a waste of time.
>
> You learn from your mistakes, but you know that you have taken a duff decision. It is important not to walk away from those decisions, to work your way through them, to honour the commitment you've given. Then analyse what you got right and what you go wrong.

Twenty-eight months into his contract with Dome and intending thereafter to return to Dalhousie he was again approached through John Gardiner, this time to head up the privatisation of British Shipbuilders. This time, the Minister, Norman Lamont was very explicit that Day's objectives would be to manage the government out of the shipbuilding business, a timetable was agreed and a very different contract from 1975 signed.

> I had a contract I describe as 'my way or the highway'. I would do it my way or go quietly. I said, 'here's an undated, signed resignation. You don't have to pay compensation if it doesn't work, but don't interfere.'

The agreement was delivered well on time and in December 1985 Graham Day was approached for the third time by Margaret Thatcher to join British Leyland. He accepted reluctantly and only out of loyalty and respect for the Prime Minister. Becoming Chairman of British Leyland in May 1986, he renamed it the Rover Group and after ten years of losses, made it profitable within a single year. Rover was then effectively privatised through a sale to British Aerospace.

His approach at British Leyland was classically strategic. He conducted an internal evaluation or 'operational audit' about organisational strengths and weaknesses and an external evaluation or 'environmental scan' to provide information about the marketplace and the competition before developing a strategy. He then changed top managers, sacking five, recruiting two and promoting others from within and dealt with financial issues and capital investment.

His reputation as a company doctor or troubleshooter is based on his track record in turning companies around and his clarity of strategic vision.

> I've been fortunate since leaving Canadian Pacific. I've almost invariably been at the apex of the firm and therefore have had the luxury or indeed the necessity of setting the agenda. Particularly in difficult situations I am inclined to say after analysis there are only two things that are going to make us or break us. I'm going to concentrate on those, anything else, please deal with. I want to know everything that falls between those two things, any hour of the day or night. If you actually address a couple of these issues, you might add one or two less critical ones to the bottom of the list. I always had clear cut priorities and generally everybody who works with me knows what my priorities are. I get very impatient if other people don't have business priorities for themselves.

While turning around British Leyland/Rover, Graham Day became Chairman of Cadbury Schweppes and Chairman of PowerGen and also accrued more non-executive directorships both in the UK and Canada than any other senior executive in the country. During this period he also served on the initial NHS Policy Board to help with the reforms and was the first Chairman of the School Teachers Review. Graham Day subscribes wholeheartedly to the importance of contributing to society and both positions were unpaid.

In 1991, with an unrivalled reputation for corporate turnarounds, Graham Day became Interim Chairman for British Aerospace, after a boardroom *coup* unseated Sir Roland Smith. In spite of pressure to accept the role on a permanent basis, Day was committed to retiring from executive life at age 60 and to return to Canada in 1993, which he duly did and now meets his transatlantic commitments by travelling in the other direction.

Although he appears to have had a crushing burden of commitments while chairing three of the UK's major corporations with eight
other non-executive directorships in the UK alone he was able to
fulfil his responsibilities without dropping a ball. Day is renowned for
his strategic brain, his ability to get to the heart of issues and, through
doing his homework, to understand a new industry sector as well as
executives who have spent their lives within it. In 'retirement' from
executive life, he now has a full portfolio of non-executive directorships and other community and university attachments.

FAMILY AND PERSONAL LIFE

As with several others of his management generation, Graham Day
regretfully acknowledges that in terms of priorities 'I have to tell you
that other than providing for the family, the job won. The family
understands that, but I resent it and that's one of the reasons that I
wanted to retire at 60'.

On the other hand, he attributes his success to the emotional
support of his wife and his ability to share professional issues with
her and to benefit from her wisdom and good sense. He is also close
to his three children, and the family, accepting his long hours, found
ways to keep in touch.

> When the kids were young, both when I was working with CP and
> at Birkenhead, whenever possible I would be home for the evening
> meal. It tended to fit my working pattern, not theirs. Now we're
> spaced out, but if we're together, the evening meal is still where the
> family's affairs get cleared and aired. That's very important.

Unmentioned by others, his high profile also impinged on his private
life in an unwelcome way.

> I try to keep my private life private and it is a battle because the
> media feel that if you do jobs which are high profile they have a
> right to know, which I don't accept of course.
>   My wife also resented the lack of privacy in some jobs. When I
> was at British Leyland which became Rover, I couldn't go to a
> supermarket without someone wanting to talk to me and that was
> difficult. Once we had skived off for about four days to Crete and
> were in a little taverna one evening for a meal. Right next to me

someone said, 'Ah, I know you'. It's got very much better since then, but not perfect.

Although he needs eight hours sleep a night, 'If I got it, I'd be a world beater', he normally gets four or five.

Reading relaxes him, allowing him to change mental gears. He reads early in the morning, late at night and on airplanes and he reads 'everything', paperback thrillers, history, particularly military history. He reads not only to relax but to learn. 'One's always trying to learn. If you are not in a lifelong learning situation then you are the person who has thirty-five years in business and one year's experience 35 times.'

Included therefore are business case studies, economics texts to compensate for his lack of formal economics background and because of his elder daughter, increasingly organisational behaviour texts and commentaries.

LEADERSHIP AND SUCCESS FACTORS

Although Graham Day identifies intelligence, compassion and breadth as critically important leadership qualities, he also understands the difficulty in providing a checklist for leadership.

I look first of all for a good level of intelligence. I worry the older I get that the level of intelligence isn't high enough, by that I mean straight IQ. One is offered in lieu specific skills.

I also want a good basic education, as broad as possible and including both qualitative and quantitative studies before anybody has done anything specific. Not least of the problems I have with the English system of education is its narrowness and how quickly you get into a professional school.

A friend of mine who teaches at INSEAD, Manfred Kets de Vries used to teach at Harvard with Abraham Zaleznik who taught organisational behaviour. Zaleznik used to say we're woefully short of 'substance, humanity and morality' and these are the attributes of leadership. It's not the gung-ho, follow-me, John Wayne kind of fix.

Jung says that some are predisposed to be more effective and if you're going to accept that proposition then one says that leaders are born, not made. I think there is a lot of truth in that because leaders come in all sorts of shapes, sizes, and in both sexes. But you can enhance leadership attributes. Some of these attributes are physical. The military looks for command presence.

There's a marvellous book called *Why Leaders Can't Lead*. As you move people up toward the apex of the pyramid, the one characteristic that you look for above all else is leadership. It is vital. As Viscount Wavell used to say, he could tell whether leadership was there or not but he couldn't necessarily define it. You can't go through a checklist and say 'if all the ticks are there, this equals leadership'. Not necessarily.

Zaleznik's view on leadership as based on substance, humanity and morality profoundly appealed to Day because it confirmed his early assessment of the power of Buck Crump's genuine courtesy at CP. He is absolutely intolerant of its absence:

> Courtesy is much less common these days, particularly among the young and that irritates me. It's the 'kow tow upward' and the 'kick ass downward'. I have personally smothered the careers of some quite capable younger people who I have watched exhibit those characteristics. I first of all try and sit them down and say 'look, do you realise what you are doing' and generally the response is 'well, of course I don't behave that way'.

Day's personal belief system is based on the absolute primacy of honesty and he is constantly astounded how difficult it is for people to accept his word.

> It sounds very trite to say but it is so absolutely, critically important to be honest. Not only does it avoid the necessity of trying to remember what lie you told last, it just simplifies your life greatly. The curse is, throughout my life people have said to me after an event 'I didn't really think you were serious'. So I've developed a habit of using the old army technique of instruction. 'I'm going to tell you what I'm going to tell you, then I'm going to tell you what I've told you.' Then I say, 'you do understand, this is the straight goods'. But people still say, 'Oh, I didn't really think that you mean that.' I say it over and over but people still think it's some kind of con.

In identifying high flyers when he was Chief Executive, Graham Day observed carefully not only what they achieved but how they behaved. He tested them all the time, including through psychological testing ('I am firmly convinced that it reduces the chances of getting square pegs in round holes') before moving them to the next job. He also consciously would put the best people in the most difficult circumstances.

If he were to advise his children about their professional lives, although he does not think in these terms ('they give me advice!') he would say;

Advice sounds sort of formal, but I like to feel that they have a commitment to something including to themselves. If you do something, do it well. Don't say 'well, what the hell. I'm only paid until five o'clock'. Give a little more value than you are actually paid for, because you have got to live with yourself at the end of the day. That's why the three of them are all doing what they want to do although they are very fortunate.

17

Lord Sheppard
Chairman, Grand Metropolitan Plc

Date of birth:	25 December 1932
Place of birth:	Forest Gate, London
Nationality:	British
Marital status:	Divorced and remarried
Family:	No children
Languages:	A very little French and German despite examination certificates thereon

Education:
<table>
<tr><td>1939–1942</td><td>Fairlop Junior School</td></tr>
<tr><td>1943–1950</td><td>Ilford County High School
'A' levels in Economics, Geography, Government, Economic History</td></tr>
<tr><td>1950–1953</td><td>London School of Economics
BSc (Economics) Upper Second
Chartered Institute of Cost and Management Accountants
Chartered Institute of Company Secretaries
Associate Institute of Taxation
Chartered Institute of Marketing, Fellow
Institute of Management, Companion</td></tr>
</table>

Career:
<table>
<tr><td></td><td>National Service</td></tr>
<tr><td>1958–1968</td><td>Ford of Europe
Junior Financial Analyst, Dagenham, UK
Marketing and Sales Controller, Warley, UK
Divisional Manager, Parts Operations (Aveley, UK)
Marketing Director for Europe, Parts Operations (Cologne, Germany)</td></tr>
<tr><td>1968–1971</td><td>Rootes (Chrysler)
Managing Director, Parts and Export Supply (Birmingham)</td></tr>
<tr><td>1971–1975</td><td>British Leyland
Marketing Director, Leyland International
Managing Director, Europe
Managing Director, Unipart
Managing Director, Parts and Manufacturing Components</td></tr>
<tr><td>1975 to date</td><td>Grand Metropolitan</td></tr>
<tr><td>1975–1982</td><td>Managing Director, Watneys</td></tr>
<tr><td>1982–1986</td><td>Managing Director, UK Operations</td></tr>
<tr><td>1986–1993</td><td>Group Chief Executive</td></tr>
<tr><td>1987 to date</td><td>Group Chairman</td></tr>
</table>

Outside appointments:
<table>
<tr><td>1994 to date</td><td>Bowater Plc, Non-executive Director</td></tr>
<tr><td>1994 to date</td><td>Brightreasons, Non-executive Deputy Chairman</td></tr>
<tr><td>1993 to date</td><td>McBride Limited, Non-executive Chairman</td></tr>
<tr><td>1992 to date</td><td>Pavilion Services Group, Non-executive Deputy Chairman</td></tr>
<tr><td>1992 to date</td><td>London First, Chairman</td></tr>
<tr><td>1990 to date</td><td>Business in the Community, Deputy Chairman and now Chairman</td></tr>
<tr><td>1990 to date</td><td>International Business Leaders Forum, Deputy Chairman</td></tr>
<tr><td>1990 to date</td><td>Standing Committee of the London School of Economics, Governor and Chairman Campaign Committee</td></tr>
<tr><td>1990–1994</td><td>Prince's Youth Business Trust, Chairman</td></tr>
<tr><td>1990–1993</td><td>National Training Task Force, Member</td></tr>
<tr><td>1990–1992</td><td>National Economics Development Unit, Member</td></tr>
</table>

Previous non-executive Directorships with UBM Plc, Mallinson-Denny Group Ltd, British Railways Board, Meyer International Plc

Awards: Several honorary Doctorates
                         Knighted, 1990
                         Life Peer, 1994

Other interests: Gardens, reading and red setter dogs

INTRODUCTION

Allen Sheppard was nominated in October 1993 by financial institutions in a *Sunday Times* survey as the 'toughest' boss in Britain for most fully exhibiting qualities of boldness, decisiveness and ruthlessness and for his demanding management style. Sheppard's reputation as an 'uncompromising, courageous and risk-taking executive' and his track record in completing highly risky strategic acquisitions at Grand Met, such as the $5.2 billion Pillsbury takeover, successfully focusing Grand Met as an £8 billion food and drinks business with strong international brands were decisive in making him a clear winner for the title.

Allen Sheppard comes from a close, supportive, and aspirational working-class family and his earliest ambition was to make enough money to give him independence. His measure at that time of this ambition was to earn £2500 per annum!

This early concern to make money led to economics at the LSE and then to business. Specific career moves were either serendipitous (Ford) or catalysed externally by job offers (Rootes, British Leyland, Grand Metropolitan). His successful move from almost twenty years in the motor industry to head up the brewing business at Grand Metropolitan was unforeseen and unsought but called for the same strengths that he had developed through broad functional experience in finance, marketing and sales and early general management experience. His international experience at Ford and Leyland were also fundamental in preparing him to lead multinational operations at Grand Met.

Allen Sheppard was not influenced by mentors. He is open about the hard times in his career, and sees a failure as a vital necessary ingredient for management development and success. A self-confessed workaholic with an understanding wife, balancing personal and professional lives has not been an important issue.

Allen Sheppard was awarded a baronetcy in 1994 for his tireless involvement in community organisations as Chairman or Board Member and is a committed believer in equality of opportunity and in business contributing to the communities within which they operate.

An early interest in politics, first Labour, then Conservative, has led to party approaches to become an MP and recently to rumours (unfounded he tells me) that he will become a future Chairman of the Conservative party.

What has been important to the development of one of the most driven and driving business leaders in Britain and how would he advise others about how to get to the top?

EARLY INFLUENCES

Allen Sheppard grew up in Ilford as the younger of two sons of an engine driver. He was most influenced in his early life by the ambition of his parents, particularly his mother who had gone to grammar school, had longed to become a schoolteacher, and because of her parents' financial position, ended up working in a bank. Her great dream was for her son to become a schoolteacher. If a general sense of wanting to achieve was passed on, that specific objective was not 'I had a very strong determination from an early age that I would never be a schoolteacher whatever I did!' He describes his father as being ambitious 'in his own way', working 'terribly hard and loyally' for 51 years and buying his own house in 1938, when home ownership was much less common.

As with several other people Allen Sheppard was the second son. In his case, he was less emulating or competing with his older brother by four years since he was fulfilling a role in which his brother was not interested. 'My brother was and is a nice guy and he helped me a lot when I was a kid. He had my father's ambitions – he was also an engine driver, has bought his own house and sent two great children to college.'

Because of the London blitz, he started school formally at eight, until then being taught by schoolteachers attending home groups in different people's houses. He recalls that when he came to take his eleven-plus, many thought he was wasting his time because, with a December birthday, he was almost a year younger than most of his peers. His teacher, Miss Osbourne, and his parents were determined that he be given a chance to pass and in the event, he came thirty-second in the whole of Ilford. 'I still have the book presented to me by Miss Osbourne when I passed the scholarship – *His Big Opportunity*!'

Sheppard was an excellent student, and his parents, helped by his older brother, supported his staying on at Ilford County High through the sixth form, although they could offer little guidance about the next step. 'It seems funny nowadays. Neither I nor my family had any idea about what going to university meant. We had never met anybody who had gone to university. So I guess I became quite self-reliant from an early age.'

As with several others with working-class origins, his earliest ambition was to make enough money to give him the independence he sought. He has a lingering regret that he began life poor.

He decided that he wanted to become an accountant after his father told him that a friend of a friend was an accountant and had made a lot of money. At this time, in the late forties, his ambition was to make fifty pounds a week. His aunt and uncle were 'on the stage' ('comedy runs in the family') and they each earned fifty pounds a week in the summer shows and Christmas pantomimes. This set the benchmark at a time when his father's weekly earnings were just over five pounds.

Sheppard at the same time wanted to become a Member of Parliament.

> I would have been somewhere between a Labour party supporter and a Liberal Democrat, but I lost my party halfway through because I fell progressively out of love with the Labour party. My allegiance began to crumble at the edges at university – I can hear my LSE tutor now saying to me: 'Have you ever considered that the size of the cake is as important as how you divide it!' Finally I ceased to be a member. In the Heath elections in 1974 I voted Conservative and have done so ever since.

He ascribes his interest in politics partly to ego and partly to a passionate belief in equal opportunity.

> I was very fond of history and I remember saying to my parents as a young guy that my ambition in life was to be one line in the history book. I don't think I'll make that but I'm working on it! So my interest in politics was partly driven by ego, if you call that ego.
>
> But it was also driven by a quite passionate belief in equality of opportunity, and fighting on behalf of the downtrodden classes, which included myself. I fell out with the Labour party because I began to discover that equality of opportunity is quite different from so called equality as they have since found in Eastern Europe.

Sheppard was approached fifteen years ago by the Conservative Party to stand for nomination and actually went through the initial nomination process at Smith Square but has never taken it further.

His desire to go into politics and to merit one line in a history book suggests that he was attracted by power and by fame. This interpretation may be too simplistic however.

All my life I have feared most of all saying as I was dying 'I wish I had . . .'. Wanting to be a line in a history book means that recognition must have been important to me, but the sentence might have said I was Hitler or something negative like that. Without sounding too serious, the desire to make history was more to do with not wasting the life that had been given to me, rather than necessarily winning acclaim or a popularity poll. As I got older, recognition of peers was probably important to me but early on it was not, although you obviously need to win the support and respect of people working with you.

In spite of his headmaster's ambition that everybody go to Oxford or Cambridge, Allen Sheppard chose the London School of Economics because he saw it as being more connected with industry and business. He notes that his degree in economics specialising in 'industry and trade' would be akin to business administration today. 'The advantage was that it gave one a professional qualification and general knowledge of everything from accounting through to law and office procedures, so one became a generalist.'

After university, Sheppard went into National Service for two years reaching the rank of Acting Corporal.

It was quite a good experience because although I had a working-class background I discovered that there were rougher types than me who, if you caught them at the wrong time, would try and knife you! So I learned to move fast! It also knocked all the ego out of me. Having gone to college I felt that the world was waiting for me and after a few weeks in the army I realised that it wasn't true. It also gave me an intense hatred of authority which I have kept for the whole of my life.

Being reduced to one of a number also left him with a burning ambition not to experience this anonymity again.

While in the army, he began to write intensively and to lecture part-time at Nottingham Technical College in history, economic history and economics. With a friend he wrote a book called *Your Business Matters*, about how to go into business as a small trader and the lessons to be learned. It sold 10,000 copies. 'Quite how we felt we were qualified to write it I do not know!' He also wrote articles on economics and accounting. 'I also did things I wouldn't have the courage to do nowadays. I stood up in front of professional bodies and for instance, lectured on the Budget on the evening of Budget Day.'

CAREER DECISION-MAKING AND DEVELOPMENT

Beyond early ambitions to make money, become Prime Minister and occupy a line in the history books, he has never had any 'clear, positive ambitions about getting on'. He acknowledges an objective at Ford of Britain to become Finance Director but believes this was conceived after the fact. He displays above all the intrinsic motivation to meet challenges rather than get to the top as an end in itself.

> I've never planned to become Chairman of Grand Met. I thought that it was a pretty unlikely scenario. Not because people were better than me but it was always tomorrow's job. I have always been most concerned to do today's job well.

The catalyst for his first career move was serendipitous. His mother cut out an advertisement from the local paper for a Financial Analyst at Ford, thinking it was right for him – a good company, and a role he would enjoy. It wasn't an obvious match to him and he went to meet John Barber, the Finance Director who later became Managing Director and Oscar Deville, the Personnel Director to gain experience in job interviews. 'Despite not having any experience I went along with six copies of my book which had just been published. Decades later both of them told me they were quite amused by this apparently egotistical guy starting to distribute copies of his book, saying that his arrival could be great for Ford!'

Sheppard joined Ford at an exciting time with many other talented people with a wide variety of backgrounds, accountants, historians, classicists ('"Barber's babes" we called ourselves'). These high flyers changed jobs every three months, were deeply committed to Ford's success and fuelled each other's enthusiasm and ambition. 'It was the spirit of the group that drove us on.' He identifies his early years at Ford as one of the two most rewarding of his career. 'One was on a steep learning curve, it was very exciting because the moment you showed any signs of knowing what you were doing, you were promoted.' He also met his first wife, a Senior Financial Analyst at Ford during this period.

Although Sheppard does not consider that he has ever had a mentor, John Barber was a strong influence in these years. Sheppard spent just over ten years at Ford, acquiring broad functional experience and very early line management responsibility. He moved from Finance, to become Sales and Marketing Controller, then into line management on the after sales service side, and for the last year gained international experience in Germany. Throughout this period, he established a pattern of working fourteen hours a day.

His first experience as a line manager in charge of after sales service at Ford was a typical sink-or-swim opportunity. He notes that he and Terry Beckett were at that time the youngest division managers ever at Ford. 'They probably go in much younger now!' Ford used their after sales activity as a management development opportunity and at 33, he was given freedom to run a complete profit centre, responsible for sales and marketing, purchasing and supply, a labour force and above all, the bottom line.

The move from two years of complete profit responsibility back to a staff role in Germany as Marketing Director for Europe at a functional level but on a larger scale was terribly frustrating. Disturbingly, he was at the same time rung by the soon-to-be Chairman of Ford, Sir Leonard Crossland, who asked him not to accept the marketing position as he wanted to appoint him as Ford of Britain's Finance Director when he became Chairman.

> During my whole career at Ford, my unconscious dream had been to become Finance Director for Ford of Britain but it was only when I was offered the position and turned it down that I realised that it had been my ambition! That was quite a painful decision that my then wife and I had to take overnight and I felt absolutely adrift because I had turned down my life ambition at 33 because I didn't want to return to finance. Having taken the decision I was told by my new American boss next day that the marketing job was in Cologne, not Essex. I grew up a bit during those few days!

Leaving Ford was like 'leaving home' and was finally precipitated by a demoralising incident that crystallised his dissatisfaction and by a simultaneous approach by head-hunters.

> Ford of Britain had been very profit conscious. I was temporarily living at the Dom Hotel in Cologne, and spent one whole weekend working out how Ford should deal with the just announced Sterling devaluation. It involved how to improve after sales

revenues across Europe and was quite complex. On the Sunday evening I told my boss, also staying at the hotel, that if we moved quickly, Ford could add several million pounds to our profits over the coming months. The response was 'How dare you disturb me about work on a Sunday evening'!

He had always thought he would make his whole career with Ford but for the first time was 'completely open' to the approach of a head-hunting firm. Even now, some ambivalence remains about his decision to leave Ford and in advising his own graduate engineer nephew about how to make career decisions at a crossroads, he shares what he has learned:

> In taking career decisions, it is important to understand clearly what one is doing and why, to have thought it through, not to knee jerk. Choose positively to join the new company, rather than move only in order to leave the other company. I left Ford for negative reasons. It was a desperately tight decision and could easily have gone the other way because I had done amazingly well at Ford. Ultimately, you look rationally at the costs and benefits and then you must let your heart win.

On the advice of head-hunters, Sheppard met with Gilbert Hunt, Chairman of Rootes (soon to become Chrysler), and joined as Head of the After Sales and Parts operation in Birmingham, which proved to be 'a complete and utter shambles'. Disconcertingly, his first task was to part company with the Director he was replacing, although Sheppard bemusedly observes that 'he was quite pleased in the end'. Moving from a highly structured business, with safety nets, 'if you did made a mistake at Ford there was somebody else doing your job anyway' to an 'entrepreneurial but pretty badly run family business' was initially very difficult. However, the experience taught him to think for himself rather than to rely on the system. 'People would chat and ask me questions. I would give off the cuff views about everything. I then found that they immediately began to implement what I said, which I found frightening for the first three days, and then began rather to enjoy!'

After three and a half years, Sheppard was running the export side as well as after sales service, spending a great deal of time in Iran, and acquiring negotiating skills. He had always had doubts about the viability of Rootes, by now bought by Chrysler, and although recently appointed to the Rootes Executive Board, he became increasingly concerned about the company's future. John Barber, by this time Joint Managing Director of British Leyland, had been encouraging Sheppard to join Leyland since he left Ford. About the '44th time of asking', Sheppard agreed to join Leyland International as Marketing Director. By the end of six weeks he had accrued the roles of Managing Director of Europe, Marketing Director, Parts Director and eventually Finance Director 'because there was nobody else'. Within a few months, he was running Leyland's continental activities, including manufacturing, 'I was virtually killing myself visiting about four countries a week, trying to give them all the kiss of life, although we had nothing to sell because of supply problems ex-UK!'.

The international experience at Leyland has been fundamentally important in equipping Sheppard to run a large multinational.

He asked to be transferred back to the UK and Lord Stokes put him in charge of Unipart, their after sales business, and a self-contained profit centre. Although Unipart was making substantial profits of £100 million, British Leyland was going under, 'John Egan and I prided ourselves that we kept Leyland afloat more than three weeks longer than it would have been'!

Although he survived the Ryder Investigation (ironically, he observes, 'Ryder came round and gave me twenty minutes of his time and spent an hour and a half with my shop stewards. Maybe he had his priorities right!'), Sheppard was by this time fed up with the motor industry.

To his irritation, the call from head-hunters came during a meeting at which he was trying to persuade his workers to keep working. By the time he had the opportunity to meet with the head-hunters six weeks later they had filled the job in question but had another opportunity they considered 'absolutely right' for him. In spite of never having heard of Grand Met, he was approached to run Watney's Brewery. 'I fell off the seat laughing. Eighteen years in the motor industry was strange training to run breweries!'

Although he had changed companies three times within the motor industry, it was a difficult decision to change industries. He agonised over whether his skills were transferable for some days before joining Grand Met. Mary, his new wife, was the determining influence:

Mary said to me, 'You are too busy to notice, but you are unhappy at Leyland. I am certain you will succeed at Grand Met but if it doesn't work out it is not a death sentence!' It was this common sense that prevailed. I found the transition very much easier than I felt it would be and that a lot of the skills were transferable. People skills and customer orientation were of course entirely relevant.

He had also been give a useful piece of advice about changing companies from the Managing Director of Leyland, Alex Park, when he resigned: 'Don't carry across your terminology, carry across your ideas. Very quickly you should adopt the new company's language. If they talk about budgets, talk about budgets. If they talk about plans, talk about plans'.

He began at Grand Met by running brewing and within a few months took over the tenanted (franchised) pubs plus 'other bits like soft drinks and overseas brewing'. After five years he took over the rest of the UK operations, initially the Chef and Brewer managed pubs and then food (Express Dairies) and later leisure (Mecca).

By 1982/83, three joint Managing Directors were running operations at Grand Met; Sheppard the UK, Anthony Tennant International (wines/spirits and hotels) and Walter Scott, an American, the US business. Sheppard became Chief Executive in 1986, while Tennant (now Sir Anthony Tennant) left to head Guinness and Scott is a university professor in the US.

The period of indecision when Sir Stanley Grinstead, then Chairman and Chief Executive, was deciding how to split his role and was choosing between Sheppard and Tennant as Chief Executive was the most frustrating period of Sheppard's career at Grand Met.

> Anthony and I got on very well and still do, but one of us had to be made Group Chief Executive. We said we were quite willing to throw a dice for it. The important thing from Grand Met's point of view was that somebody should become Chief Executive. We were worried about ourselves but we were also worried about Grand Met. Of course, in the end, we both did very well as did Grand Met and Guinness.

Together with his early learning days at Ford his period as boss of Grand Met has been the most rewarding of his career.

> As a team we have taken a very successful company, developed our vision and changed it quite dramatically, ready for what it must be in the next century. We succeeded in making this transformation without losing momentum. Although it was very exciting we didn't get any praise for it externally. People wrote that we were

hyperactive and on ego trips, but one didn't expect much praise from outside. Our reward is that Grand Met today has the skills and businesses necessary to compete in tomorrow's global markets.

Grand Met's strategy was to focus what had been a diversified 'typically entrepreneurial business with a bit of everything/everywhere' to become a world player in branded food and drink. It moved out of hotels, betting and gaming, brewery and unrelated retailing. Despite these disposals Grand Met's size more than doubled with the purchase of Heublein/Pillsbury/Burger King and successful organic growth.

> In the mid 1980s, Grand Met was in twenty-eight different businesses – we had to decide what value we added to each and then decide in what sectors we could become world players. We focused the company on consumer marketing and married professionalism with the entrepreneurial culture that already existed in Grand Met. The challenge was to grow the business, implement our vision and spread our combined culture of enterprise and professionalism throughout the Group.

The commitment to an international marketing focus was confirmed with the appointment in December 1993 of George Bull as Group Chief Executive, Grand Met's 'marketing supremo', former head of Grand Met Food business and the driving force behind the development of IDV, Grand Met's worldwide drinks business.

Allen Sheppard is due to leave Grand Met early in 1996: 'it is very important that one doesn't block the whole pipeline and there is a need for a constant regeneration of drive'. He plans then, in Charles Handy's terms, to 'manage a portfolio' of non-executive appointments 'if anyone thought that I had anything to add' and 'to slow down from a ten day week to a six day week'! He cites as an example fellow Grand Met Board member John Harvey-Jones who is 'probably busier today than he was when Chairman of ICI and enjoying life greatly'.

Until George Bull's appointment, Grand Met had chosen not to split the roles of Chairman and Chief Executive as recommended by the Cadbury Report, trying instead to meet the spirit of having a countervailing force on the Board by having one of the most powerful non-executive representation of any Board in the country in Richard Giordano, Sir John Harvey-Jones, Sir Colin Marshall and

David Simon (BP) and more recently Professor Gertrude Hohler from Germany.

Although he describes his career as immensely rewarding, Allen Sheppard is open about the hard times and the toll taken.

> I don't think I could do it all over again. From time to time I advise my nephew, a graduate engineer now in his thirties. He recently asked me about how I had tackled various decisions I had made in my own life. Afterwards, my wife said to me, 'I could see you reliving a lot of pain'. I said, 'I hope nothing came through. I don't want to put him off.' And she said, 'No, it all came through as enthusiasm, but I know you very well and could see that some of the memories were painful.'

He believes that he is tolerant of failure and he understands the inevitability and learning value of adversity. 'Most of our executives have failed at some time or other in their career and making mistakes is a very important experience to have gone through, provided that they don't make too many of them at Grand Met!'

In his own career, he identifies his experience with Ford in Germany as highly frustrating. At Leyland, at age 40, the sheer physical stress of running Continental Europe was enormous, contributed to by the breakdown of his marriage at the same time. 'I was in danger of folding under physical strain.'

The Ryder period at Leyland he describes as a 'torment, because we were failing and it was beyond our ability to control the failure, as we didn't have the authority actually to do anything to correct the situation'. He regards this period as a dismal professional failure, in spite of his own division remaining highly profitable. He learned a lot about people skills at that time: 'Uncertainty is a killer and I promised myself that I would never torture anybody to death because they didn't know what was happening to them.'

He believes his greatest mistake to have been staying too long in the motor industry.

> I imagine it was rather like leaving the beaches of Dunkirk – although you should have left pretty fast, there were a lot of people who stayed and kept fighting. The biggest mistake people make is to fall in love with their business and not look at it clearly and objectively. I don't mean coldly. You can be quite emotional about it but you shouldn't be blinded by the fact that you're doing something for pure emotion.

FAMILY AND PERSONAL LIFE

Allen Sheppard is a self-confessed workaholic and was divorced from his first wife in the 1970s. He remarried soon after. He is the only male in the sample who has never had children. His single-minded devotion to work has rarely been challenged by personal priorities, although he feels personal priorities would come first.

> I have never been in a position where my priorities have really been tested. Recently I surprised (and delighted) everybody when one of our dogs was taken ill, by cancelling everything and going home immediately. When a personal issue arises, it very rapidly becomes the priority, and I am capable of dropping everything when the going gets really tough. I think I've got my priorities right in that sense! Without a happy and relaxed home life I could not survive in business.

Although he relaxes completely on holiday, he rarely sets time aside otherwise to relax, for instance to watch the sport he enjoys. His time outside of Grand Met is largely devoted to a large portfolio of community and other voluntary organisations and he is deeply committed to the involvement of business in the community. He was Chairman of the Prince of Wales Business Youth Trust for four years and is currently Chairman of Business in the Community and of London First.

Although he has never been conventionally religious in the sense of attending church, he would like to believe in God. His belief system is inherently moral rather than religious.

> I would never knowingly cheat, not because I would go to prison or be punished, but because it would just unhook everything I had done in my life. If I could win by cheating, what the bloody hell did I do all that work for? So I guess I've got a strong code of ethics.

LEADERSHIP AND SUCCESS FACTORS

For Allen Sheppard, leadership consists straightforwardly of three ingredients – an interest in people, a vision of what one is trying to do and the application of common sense. His own success he attributes to common sense and hard work.

Fundamentally, his greatest satisfaction comes from 'the ability to influence and actually make things happen' and also to draw the best out of people. He has always enjoyed his work in a single-minded way. 'Single-mindedness is a strength in that it helps you to get on with things, but it doesn't make you particularly lovable or even balanced.'

At the heart of Allen Sheppard's effectiveness is the clear vision he himself identifies as necessary for leadership as well as courageous decision-making, high motivation and an extraordinary work ethic. His selection in 1993 by financial institutions as the 'toughest' boss in Britain carries the ambivalence of part admiration, part fear and reinforces an interesting apparent contradiction in Allen Sheppard's management style. For instance, he believes in the pre-eminence of interpersonal skills, but has described his management approach as a 'loose grip by the throat'. He appears quite emotional with an easy, self-deprecating sense of humour but his decision-making about businesses and individuals is unsentimental in the extreme.

A close colleague believes that there is no contradiction – the key lies in distinguishing between the businessman and the man himself.

As a man Allen Sheppard is amazingly modest and very kind. He talks to Princes and Prime Ministers in the same way he talks to the most junior member of the staff – he is completely unchanging in this respect – no pomposity, grandeur or pretension. He has the most wonderful sense of humour, that every now and again is his undoing! He is also the master of the magic phrase, able to capture the essence of the situation in a few words and to motivate people with these words. Not many people know the extent to which he helps all those who approach him without work. He is whole-heartedly committed to help people who are unable to help themselves, and feels passionately that those who need a leg up should be given one. His involvement in the community is motivated by this conviction.

As a businessman Allen Sheppard *is* tough and very demanding. He is totally uncompromising in the pursuit of his objectives and expects people to operate at the same phenomenal pace as he does. He imposes extraordinarily high standards on himself and sets massively ambitious – but achievable – objectives for his people (what he calls 'magic numbers'). He has the most exceptional mental energy and vigour. (He is also one of the world's great interrupters because he must share his ideas as he has them.)

Allen Sheppard is no-nonsense and direct and is incapable of implying anything (or wrapping things up) to be acceptable. In deals, he is an unbelievably tough negotiator, beginning with an extreme position that he then toughs out. He will use whatever tactics are appropriate within the bounds of ethics and the law and single-mindedly gets on with the deal without, like most people, considering for a moment how he appears in negotiation. He also has a tremendous memory, keeping almost no paper but filing things in his mind. He is a risk taker and having locked on his objectives is like a heat-seeking missile in achieving them. Whenever he serves at match point, he goes for the ace. A good example of this is that when Grand Met bought Pillsbury, InterContinental Hotels had to be sold the same day!

If someone knows him only partially it is impossible to begin to understand him. He believes that friction is energy and often says that he can't bear a 'well-swept graveyard'. He therefore deliberately provokes controversy, and manages in a way that he calls orchestrating anarchy, so that while the organisation is always under control it is only just under control – just the way a Formula One driver achieves maximum performance in a Grand Prix. He understands that in continuous change lies Grand Met's advantage. In a world where change requires courage and apathy is more natural, Grand Met has an enormous advantage in its appetite for change. If you want the quiet life don't work with Allen Sheppard!

In considering the qualities required of a CEO in the year 2000, Sheppard believes that interpersonal skills will remain paramount with, perhaps predictably given his own managerial priorities, skills in consumer inspired marketing and an awareness of and involvement in the community becoming increasingly important.

Volunteerism is increasingly an important part of people's activities outside the company. We encourage participation in the community and in charities because they provide opportunities for management development. Our people can cut their teeth on another, and completely different, organisation. Involvement in community work is an important part of the profile of the manager of the future.

In identifying high flyers at Grand Met, Sheppard examines their track record for evidence of an ability to inspire change, people skills and professional competence. By this stage, the nature and quality of their degree is irrelevant.

> Once a person is into the system, whether they're an anthropologist, engineer or accountant or went to Oxford, Cambridge or Harvard or nowhere doesn't matter. It does not mean that being a graduate is not important. In some cases you wouldn't have got into the system unless you had succeeded academically. But people learn from life and acquire new skills.

In advising ambitious young people about how to get to the top in a large company, Allen Sheppard advises:

- Qualify within a function, whether as an accountant, engineer or whatever. The field does not matter very much.
- Develop people skills as quickly as possible.
- By the early thirties move away from your narrow functional specialisation and particularly develop sales and marketing skills if you have not already done so. Do not become too far advanced along a functional line such as finance without breadth unless your career objective is to become a top finance professional.
- Changing companies and experiencing different corporate cultures can be valuable (changing from Ford to Rootes taught me self-reliance) but it depends on the circumstances and it is impossible to generalise about the value of changing companies. If your career is blocked and you are no longer gaining valuable experience, then a move is likely to be worthwhile.
- International experience is essential if one aspires to run a large multinational.
- Think through quite seriously whether getting to the top is what you want in life – you might think you want to be boss but do you want to work a fourteen day week and have the buck stop with you? If you are only 75 per cent serious about it, don't do it. Accept that it is exciting but also sheer bloody hard work and that you are choosing a life style for your whole life.
- 'The best thing then is to do what I did which is to forget to think about it.' Put your head down and work.
- You must be resilient and flexible, able to cope with the need to change personally and to manage change with others. 'If you want a steady life with no frustrations, then you ought to change your ambition.'

- 'You will fail at different times – I don't mean fail to get a promotion but you will dismally fail to achieve your objectives. Provided you actually come through, that fire is beneficial.'

18

Sir Neil Shaw
Executive Chairman of Tate & Lyle Plc

Date of birth:	31 May 1929
Place of birth:	Montreal, Canada
Nationality:	Canadian
Marital status:	Divorced, remarried
Family:	Two sons, three daughters
Languages:	French

Education:	Lower Canada College, Montreal
	Knowlton High School Many night schools and correspondence schools

Career:

1946–1947	Royal Bank of Canada, Montreal Clerk
1947–1954	Crown Trust Company, Montreal Trust Officer
1954–1972	Canada and Dominion Sugar Company (later Redpath Industries Ltd)
1954–1963	Merchandising Manager, Montreal
1963–1966	Export Sales Manager, Tate & Lyle, London
1967–1969	Vice President, Sales, Redpath Sugar
1969–1972	President, Daymond Co Ltd (Plastics and Aluminium)
1972–1980	President, Redpath Industries Ltd, Montreal
1980–to date	Tate & Lyle, London
1980–1986	Group Managing Director
1986–1992	Chairman and Chief Executive
1992 to date	Executive Chairman

Outside appointments:	United Biscuits Holdings, Non-executive Director Canadian Imperial Bank of Commerce, Non-executive Director Princes Youth Business Trust, Advisory Council Business in the Community, Former Chairman Association of Lloyd's Names, Chairman Foundation and Friends of Royal Botanic Gardens, Kew, Chairman

Leisure interests:	Tennis, sailing, skiing

INTRODUCTION

Neil Shaw at 65 has been in the sweeteners industry for more than forty years, and has headed up Tate & Lyle for almost fifteen. His stature as one of the UK's most respected business leaders is the more extraordinary because he spent almost two thirds of his working life in Canada. Highly regarded as both professional manager and corporate strategist, he has transformed a family dominated company valued at sixty million pounds into the world's leading sweeteners company with market value of over two billion pounds. His goal is to continue the transformation of Tate & Lyle into a truly global company. It is well on its way with operations in every continent.

Neil Shaw has been described as one of the 'nice guys' of the business world, with overwhelming enthusiasm for his business, and the energy, optimism and sincerity to take people with him. His management style has been described as very much hands-on. As the leading international statesman in the sugar industry, with outstanding people skills, the range and depth of his contacts both in the UK and internationally are invariably described as outstanding.

Neil Shaw learned early independence and self-reliance when his father became ill when he was twelve, and the family fortunes were reversed. Strongly influenced by a community-minded mother, he continues to value community involvement both for developmental and philanthropic reasons and is a former Chairman of Business in the Community.

Although competitive and ambitious in a general way, Neil Shaw never had a specific career goal and after high school graduation at seventeen went to work in a bank in Montreal, then moved to a trust office before joining Canada and Dominion Sugar Company. During this period he took a multiplicity of 'night school' and correspondence courses at various universities (McGill, Queens, etc.) on financial and legal subjects.

Since then he has had virtually a one company career (Canada & Dominion Sugar Co Ltd became Redpath Industries which was taken over by Tate & Lyle), gaining cross-functional experience in finance, marketing, government affairs and manufacturing and assuming his first general management post at 40. He has never planned his career but has relied on hard work, continued further education and performance to succeed.

Growing up in bilingual, bicultural Quebec, Shaw speaks fluent French and is now passionately international, at ease doing business on all continents.

Influenced in his early years by mentors, he would advise young people to work hard, perform, learn and not to become a 'know it all'. He is a great believer above all in the value of 'track record' and relatively sceptical of evaluating individuals based on their degrees or formal training.

What has been important developmentally to a Canadian who has headed up one of Britain's leading companies for almost fifteen years, and how would he advise others about how to get to the top?

EARLY INFLUENCES

Neil Shaw was born the youngest of two sons of a middle-class family in Montreal, Canada. The first ten years of his life were privileged. He attended Lower Canada College, the most highly regarded private boys school in Montreal, and spent summers at the exclusive Hermitage Club in the Quebec countryside.

Suddenly, and no doubt rather traumatically, at age 12 his life changed. His father, at age 63, became very ill, was told he had six months to live and was forced to retire. The family sold both the family house and a country home and moved to a much smaller house in Knowlton, a small town in the Eastern Townships outside of Montreal.

> I was very disappointed to leave Lower Canada College because it was a superb school. (They have just started an LCC 'Old Boys' association in London!) I went first to grade school in Knowlton and then to Knowlton High School. We moved to a small country town into a much smaller home. There wasn't much money around. As I grew up, I worked in the summer and Easter holidays in this small community. These were all major changes in my life. How did it affect me? I've always been an optimistic person and I'm not sure that I thought about it that much at the time. I just knew my life had changed. I don't remember these as bad years. They were good years.

This experience of loss, not only of a way of life but also in a sense, of a father figure would have engendered early self-reliance and resilience, and also perhaps, a high level of motivation to succeed, to restore a lost way of life or at least not to have to worry about money.

Certainly Neil Shaw's mother and her deep involvement in the community has profoundly influenced Shaw's own conviction about the importance of community work, a cornerstone of his approach both to management development and corporate responsibility.

> My mother was a great Christian and a wonderful woman. She did a lot of work in the community and was very gregarious and involved. We had a big garage in our home which was full of secondhand clothes for children in need. It was a small town and if somebody needed help, whether it was food or education or clothing, it just happened. There was a core of seven or eight people who took responsibility, the Catholic Minister, the Protestant Minister and a few other people like my mother. Everyone knew what was going on in that town. As our towns grow bigger we tend to lose that sense of 'community'.
>
> I was Chairman of Business in the Community in the UK for several years and I saw the same loss of community involvement in big urban areas of London and other cities. We have 2000 employees in a big plant in the East End of London. There was a time when all those employees (and more) lived within a few hundred yards of the plant. The company owned the houses, our employees all lived in them and everybody knew what was going on. Sixty years later, they all drive in, work all day and drive home again and the local community is suffering. But it's still a very strong community, with long standing values. I love it. The challenge is to encourage employees to become involved with their business community.
>
> Being involved with people is the greatest manpower developer you can have. If we encourage a young employee to take on a community project in the East End of London, give him strong company support and he succeeds in resolving a community problem through motivating people I'll promote that person in Tate & Lyle much faster than someone who has received three degrees but who has not exhibited leadership or interpersonal skills.

Neil Shaw was brought up to go to church and he remembers that 'at one stage in my life it was thought I should become a minister'. Though not a churchgoer now, Christian values remain a touchstone. His years in a French/English community in Quebec, brought up by a bilingual French Canadian/Irish mother (who was Catholic with Catholic friends and Protestant with Protestant friends) provided not only language skills but also an early understanding of two cultures which would later make the flexibility of international life an easier transition.

> I was not deliberately brought up to speak French but it all sank in.
> I was very fortunate, because so many of my friends who grew up
> in Westmount (the privileged English speaking part of Montreal)
> didn't speak French. It has been one of my greatest assets.
> Particularly in Europe, I get great value out of my French!

His father died when he was 17, but the impact of this loss was attenuated by the deeper shock at age 12.

> Did his death affect me a lot at that stage? No, I don't think it did.
> I wasn't close to my father because he had been so ill. He also had
> children late in life, at 52 or 53, and he was 69 when he died. We
> didn't have a father – son relationship based on participation – we
> never played ball or that sort of thing – he was too ill.

CAREER DECISION-MAKING AND DEVELOPMENT

None the less, his father had an indirect influence on his first career decision. Emerging from high school, he decided to join the Royal Bank, as a result of too little money to go to university and the advice of a friend of his father, Morris Wilson, who was both President of the Royal Bank of Canada and Chancellor of McGill University.

> It was 1946 and Morris Wilson's view was that McGill wouldn't be
> a worthwhile experience at the time, with all the vets returning
> from the war and not enough teachers. He said to me, 'I think,
> young man, you should join the Bank and at night take all the
> courses on offer in the banking system – you'll do just as well'. So
> that's what I did.

Neil Shaw had no clear idea where he wanted to go at this stage. Although many of his friends went off to university and he 'felt sort of out of it', he does not remember envying them. In fact, he enjoyed work and it gave him a professional head-start over his contemporaries.

> I had no clear idea where I was going. I just wanted to do my job
> well and learn all I could. That was really all. I've always been
> competitive by nature, I've always worked hard. From the time I
> was 13, I worked all my spare time, week-ends, summers. I bought

my own car with my own money the day I was 17. By the time my friends left university and went to work I was definitely ahead of them. Even at 17 I had made a significant contribution and was recognised. I had had two promotions and my superiors told me I would go far. My love of numbers, mathematics, taxation gave me a good base on which to grow.

In spite of his success at the bank, he moved after a year to the Crown Trust Company, following a friend who had also left and had recommended him to the President, who coincidentally again had been a friend of his father's during the war. At this stage, Shaw gave no thought to where he would be in twenty years, 'I hadn't the knowledge or the luxury.' He left simply for the satisfaction of working with his friend and mentor, Gordon Shemilt, eight years older and a former Spitfire pilot in the war. Shemilt proved to be an early dominating influence on his career decisions. After seven years with Crown Trust, Shaw left again to join Shemilt at the Canada and Dominion Sugar Company, where Shemilt had been for two years. Ironically, although Shemilt subsequently left the Canada and Dominion Sugar Company, they worked together again with Tate & Lyle in London, after the Canadian company had been taken over.

Another mentor at the time was a board member and prominent lawyer, Honourable G. B. Foster, who not only supported him but took an interest in his career progress. Again, Foster was a friend of his father.

At no stage in his career did Neil Shaw plan where he wanted to go or what he wanted to be. Only once did he interfere with natural career progression within the company because of dissatisfaction.

I worked hard and did a good job, as well or better than anybody had before. I also enjoyed the work and kept learning more and more about the industry I was in. So natural progression worked as far as I was concerned. I never stayed in one job more than a couple of years. Later on I did get fed up and wanted to move and that's when I came over to England. I was temporarily 'stalled' in Canada so I went to see the Managing Director, asked to change jobs and he agreed. I didn't expect the change to be that dramatic!

His first job at Dominion Sugar was as an Executive Assistant to an able but autocratic Chairman which over five years not only brought breadth and an understanding of how to deal effectively with the government over sensitive sugar-related issues but also travel to Europe for the first time.

His next role was in marketing, thrown into the deep end without training or advice, opening up new marketing areas both on the east coast and the midwest. When Tate & Lyle acquired a controlling interest in the company, Chief Executive of Redpath Industries, Saxon Tate diversified operations into non-sugar activities and made Neil Shaw, at age 40, President of a plastics and aluminium company, his first general management position.

Although he succeeded in turning around this new business in a completely new industry, he believes that it is inherently dangerous to put someone in charge of a business without previous experience and indepth knowledge of the industry. He would not himself take such a risk but echoes the advice that is often given in management circles – the biggest challenge in a new industry is learning the language, the people and the culture of the industry.

In 1972 he became President of Redpath Industries (the new name for Canada & Dominion Sugar), running both the core sugar business as well as the diversified businesses. Management was becoming more professional and he further developed Saxon Tate's formal planning system to give the company a clear understanding of its market position, the competitive environment and where the company should be heading. An opportunity was identified to move into the US, with the acquisition of a sugar company in 1976, which proved successful.

Although Redpath was going from strength to strength in North America Tate & Lyle was suffering in the 1970s with UK entry into the EEC and competition from sugar beet. Logically but unexpectedly, Shaw was asked to become Managing Director of Tate & Lyle in 1980, which he describes as the highest moment of his career. Although there was some scepticism about importing a colonial, he followed his earlier strategic approach, reducing issues to their basics and setting a clear direction. He got rid of the swarming management consultants, acquired companies in their core sugar refining business internationally and in successful non-core businesses.

Lord Haslam, former Chairman of Tate & Lyle notes:

Neil Shaw's appointment in 1979 as Chief Executive by the Board then under my predecessor, Lord Jellicoe, was absolutely the right timely move for Tate & Lyle. The company had gone through a bad patch, and he brought a strong sense of leadership to the organisation and an unmatched wealth of experience of the sugar industry. Although at that time he understandably lacked a deep knowledge of the UK, our government procedures and national culture, he learned very quickly. I took over as Chairman in 1983 and we immediately enjoyed one of the most rewarding and congenial relationships of my whole career.

Neil was very pro-active in every way, and if I had to provide any balance, it was to restrain him from making acquisitions we could not then afford! But his judgement was absolutely spot on and we went on to make our first significant acquisition of Western Sugar in the US from the Hunt Brothers, followed by the purchase of Alcantara in Portugal. When he became Chairman in 1986 this was followed by a rapid sequence of major acquisitions of US sweetener companies such as A E Staley and the Domino Sugar Corporation.

Neil Shaw has dramatically reshaped Tate & Lyle, initially in North America and thereafter internationally in an ever-increasing diversity of countries and, as a result, it is now the world's leading sweetener company. He has pursued a strenuous and classic policy of 'going back to basics', concentrating on the core sweetener businesses and by diversifying territorially rather than on a product basis. Over the years, he has been a great achiever and has hardly put a foot wrong, which is quite extraordinary given how vigorous he has been!

In 1986 Neil Shaw became Chairman and Chief Executive. In 1992, an outside executive was appointed as Chief Executive of Tate & Lyle; in the event, it was recognised that an insider, fully in tune with the corporate culture, would be more effective in leading Tate & Lyle into the future. Neil Shaw became Executive Chairman in April 1993, devolving responsibility for running the business to the four division heads. He notes that his greatest satisfaction has been growing the business and developing fifteen or so very confident executives to run the businesses successfully worldwide. Rewarding too is providing strategic direction to the company as Executive Chairman.

It's satisfying to know that you have a good team in place running the operation, that you are recognised and respected by them and they really want you there when discussions about the strategic development of the company take place. Likewise I know that any one of them could run the company if I fell under a bus.

Although Neil Shaw has never had a clear career objective, he has had a powerful underlying motivation to be successful. Beginning with very little, money also was an early motivation.

> Money had to be important. When I had very little money and without anyone to help me out significantly I had to put my five children through private schools. It was not important for its own sake but as a means to be able to educate my children and buy a house and do a few other things.

Consistent with most chief executives in the study, his primary motivation has been to do a good job. In answer to a question about the importance to him of recognition, Neil Shaw notes:

> I don't think recognition as such is that important to me. If I've been recognised, it is because I have done a reasonably good job and I've never stopped learning.
>
> If your performance record becomes outstanding, especially in a financial community and you grow your company to significant size, you are asked to speak, to give seminars, all that sort of thing. But the point is you don't say afterwards, 'I planned it all. I sat there ten years ago and said this is what I'm going to do'. That's rubbish.
>
> I was asked to be Chairman of the Association of Lloyd's Members, which I needed like a hole in the head, but I was fed up with the way it was being run. So I decided to do something about it – to make a contribution to change.
>
> Three years ago I took on the job of running 'Business in the Community' which was also a big job. It was a lot of work, speeches, dinners, travelling to many different places trying to motivate people. My work as Chairman of the East London partnership was more rewarding because it was more 'hands-on'.
>
> In neither case did I accept because of recognition – I just wanted to see some changes and to make a contribution.

Although he travelled little early in his life and career, and knew little outside of Quebec, Neil Shaw's knowledge of French and his understanding of Quebec's two cultures were a good foundation for international life.

None the less when he first moved to London he experienced a transition to thinking outside of the parochial world of Quebec and Canada and valuing different ways of seeing and doing things.

For the first three or four months I would laugh at my colleagues and say, 'In Montreal, we do it this way' and in fact I was showing my ignorance and *naïveté* by talking that way. Obviously you get through this, and start to realise how different people are and you try to mix in well and respect other points of view. Western Europeans are far more sophisticated internationally than we are in Canada.

Shaw transfers talented people at Tate & Lyle internationally for developmental purposes, and witnesses the same transition to internationalism.

At first some people are reluctant to move. 'Zambia! Oh, I don't think I want to go to Zambia. Zambia!' Three years later they return and say 'That was good! I'd love another posting. The children went to boarding school and they saw a lot of Africa!' So they became broader and better people. We have many people like that, some of them never want to come back. They run a company in an African or European country, and become part of a very close-knit community. Ultimately, they will choose what makes them happy; if they want to stay where they are, they can; if they want to keep going up the corporate ladder, they will return and move upward.

Certainly the global nature of Tate & Lyle's business has been a major strategic challenge, and necessarily developed a keen interest in and understanding of international economics and politics.

I talk incessantly with my managers about how we can get involved in Central Europe, Mexico, South East Asia. Given our market share and size now in Western Europe and North America and the very low population growth in these two areas, growth means going international.

This international network is a source of great satisfaction. 'I am very fortunate to have quite a few friends in different parts of the globe. If I get off a plane in Portugal, Mexico or Australia I know a friend or colleague will welcome me. I know him, his family, what he likes doing and I will welcome him when he comes to London.'

In fact, the only change he would have made in his career would be to move internationally sooner.

Neil Shaw is philosophical about the inevitability of some failure in business life and the importance of tenacity:

I can't think of any massive failures, such as a bankruptcy. There are times when I know I could have done better, either through my failure to relate to my immediate superior or getting fed up with my job. It's part of the normal career pattern when chemistry doesn't work between two people. You might both be very bright but not be able to mix.

If you are in the food business, there can be external causes – changes in climate or world prices in various commodities that can cause a serious drop in profits. I wouldn't like two or three of them in a row, though; then you might start to lose a bit of confidence! You can have a couple of failures lasting a few years and still be convinced that you are going to come out of that failure and be successful. You have got to have some staying power and not just escape.

He is also forgiving of certain kinds of business failure and equally sceptical of certain kinds of business success.

For instance, although Olympia & York is bankrupt the Reichmans are still recognised in the property market worldwide as being the best equipped property developers in the world. The Canary Wharf failure was due to a lot of external factors which unless you walked on water you could never predict.

On the other hand, you see a lot of short-term successes where people have rolled the dice and won. They have been lucky, borrowed 90 per cent of their capital but eventually they will probably collapse. Success can go to your head very easily. They take another big risk and win and by that time they are sure they do walk on water. You can usually tell who is living in the fast lane because it happens very quickly. You could not say that these people are really successful.

FAMILY AND PERSONAL LIFE

As with most chief executives of his generation, Neil Shaw has put work first before family most of his professional life. He would unabashedly do it again. Although his first marriage ended, and he regards this as a personal failure, he does not attribute this only to overwork.

> There's no question that having a divorce is a personal failure but people change, and grow apart, with neither one at fault. Your objectives and how you want to live become different because you have been exposed to different things. It's a failure in terms of your children because it hurts them very badly. In my case it didn't happen until they were all through university so it was not quite the same as for six-year-olds but nevertheless it was a failure.

It is his opinion that over time his priorities did not adversely affect his children.

> I have five very fine, very successful children. They are all nice people, married to nice people, and are producing wonderful children. I have thirteen grandchildren. I have sometimes worked too hard to the disadvantage of my family, at least in the short term, but all of my children work very hard and they always say that they watched my example. But they also talk about the need to keep enough time for their families, which I never thought about as clearly as they do today.

Shaw relaxes through tennis, sailing, skiing and spending time at his home in Ascot. He reads a minimum of fifteen minutes every night and on planes – usually spy novels or 'turn-off' fiction. He reads *The Economist* routinely but no business magazines regularly.

In terms of a personal belief system, he acknowledges that although he is not a keen churchgoer, he believes in God and Christian values, 'the golden rule, a way of living your life. At the end you have the satisfaction of having done what you can do'.

LEADERSHIP AND SUCCESS FACTORS

In future leaders Neil Shaw looks for: 'Track record, personality, an ability to get along with people and the big picture outlook.' Consistently these are the very attributes that close colleagues attribute to his leadership.

With more than forty years in the sweeteners industry and a 'powerful intellect', Neil Shaw has a strategic understanding of the industry and his business that is second to none. Integral to this understanding and to his effectiveness in an industry with heavy government involvement has been gaining a deep insight into the 'interplay between government and the marketplace' and Neil Shaw's contacts and networks both in the UK and internationally are recognised as outstanding.

Invariably, colleagues affirm Shaw's genuine interest in and excellent relationships with people, whether colleagues, family or in the community. He is a 'people manager', a 'terrific guy' with a 'pleasant and outgoing personality, great friendliness of manner and approachability'. He is also known as a clear and cogent communicator with an 'instinctive feel for media relations'. At the heart of his ability to lead effectively, is the trust that he inspires. He is said to 'manage through first hand contact', with a good feel for his company and his approach is described as practical rather than intellectual. Neil Shaw is also a dynamic, natural achiever, full of enthusiasm and energy, who 'takes the risks a good Chairman must – he thinks deeply but decides quickly'.

A former close colleague notes that Neil Shaw, unlike almost everyone he knows, has 'no skeletons in the closet'.

> He is a very strong leader in every sense of the word. You would have to be hypercritical to identify a weakness. It has sometimes been said that he can be a bit autocratic but at times of change such as experienced by Tate & Lyle in the last ten years, too much emphasis on consensus can be damaging. He is certainly not domineering and is very willing to listen. At the end of the day, he has a clear view of what he wants to achieve.

Neil Shaw himself is keenly aware of the dangers of leadership and believes above all, like his compatriot Graham Day, in the importance of humility.

> Leadership is very difficult but I believe that the key ingredient is your own style. You lead by example. It is so important not to get out of touch. There was a wonderful ad that said, 'Every once in a while, ride the subway or go to a baseball game or walk home. Get down there and see what's happening'. Although I have no trouble doing that, I also know that I could do it more often.
>
> I was recently at a function in one of the great guildhalls. Along with the Mayor of Hackney and the Mayor of Tower Hamlets was

a delightful old black cockney Eastender, totally out of his surroundings. He was really not comfortable until I asked him about his City Challenge Project. 'City Challenge' is a government competition to successfully compete for £15m for your community by illustrating in some detail how you would use the money to improve your community. These East End people, many are socialists, now work hand in hand with local businesses and community groups to prepare a detailed business case on their proposal for presentation to the government. This fellow brightened up and we had a wonderful conversation. And they succeeded! An illustration of business and the local community working together for their mutual benefit.

Leadership is partly about making the other person feel at home. I see Prince Charles occasionally, he is the President of Business in the Community and he is outstanding at making people feel at home and finding out their interests in a very short space of time. I don't know if he realises this strength but he needs to be told he does it very well.

Although there is no single leader Neil Shaw particularly admires, he has had a general admiration for the chief executives he has known in his own company. 'I always admire the fellow at the top of the pile. There's no question that they all command dignity, respect and are decisive.'

On the other hand, he is disappointed in the quality of some chief executives of other large companies.

I know many business leaders, but I don't actually like some of them. I don't understand how a lot of them were selected which probably means they are brighter and better in ways that I just don't see. Some people at the top of big companies are there for a reason, often related to what 'the financial community wants' not because of industry knowledge.

Having worked with a superior where the chemistry was wrong, he is sensitive not only to selecting individuals for positions but also as members of a team.

In placing people throughout an organisation it's just as important to find out who they are going to be working with as it is to understand their own qualities. You learn very quickly in the development of a corporation of our size that if you put the right two people together in a subsidiary, the company hums and alternately, if you put two people together who should theoretically work very well, but the chemistry doesn't work, you know you have to make changes.

He is wary of people who have, in a sense 'had it too easy', and expect to succeed in a programmed way, as long as they work reasonably hard. He encourages such people to get to the coal-face.

People who have too precise a career ideal become upset if asked to do something that does not follow this prescribed path. If someone is a real egg-head, we might want to make him a salesman in the East End for six months. That's often the end of this person's world. I say to them, 'You need to understand what the real world is all about'. They think they do understand. You can't programme your career. It doesn't work that way.

His advice to aspiring senior managers is straightforwardly to 'work hard and learn hard. It is so important to develop a truly inquiring mind. You should also analyse what it is you are trying to accomplish then go for it'. Certainly energy devoted to organisational politics is energy wasted.

19

Sir John Harvey-Jones MBE

Former Chairman, ICI Plc

Born:	16 April 1924
Place of birth:	London
Nationality:	British
Marital status:	Married
Family:	One daughter
Languages:	German, Russian

Education: Tormore School, Deal, Kent
                        Royal Naval College, Dartmouth
Career:
  1937–1956   Royal Navy
                        Served in submarines during the War and after the War
                        in Intelligence appointments as well as a period on
                        secondment to the Cabinet Office. Resigned with the
                        rank of Lieutenant Commander
  1956–1987   ICI
    1956–1958   Work Study Officer, Wilton
    1958–1964   Deputy Supply Manager then Supply Manager, Wilton
                        Council
    1964–1967   Sales Control Manager, Heavy Organic Chemicals
                          (HOC) Division
    1967   Technical Commercial Director, Heavy Organic
                          Chemicals Division
    1967–1968   Personnel Director, HOC Division
    1968–1970   Deputy Chairman, HOC Division
    1970–1973   Chairman, HOC Division
    1973–1975   Main Board, responsible for Petrochemicals and
                          Organisation and Services
    1975–1976   ICI Fibres, Product Director
    1976–1978   Organisational Director and Territorial Director for
                          Continental Western Europe
    1978–1982   Deputy Chairman
    1982–1987   Chairman

Outside appointments:
  1983–1994   Grand Metropolitan, Non-executive Director
                        (Non-executive Deputy Chairman, 1987–1991)
  1987–1994   The Economist Newspaper Ltd, Non-executive Director
                        (Non-executive Chairman, 1989–1994)

                        Past appointments with some 36 other charitable,
                        academic and business-related organisations as well as
                        some 16 current such appointments

Awards: Numerous honorary doctorates and fellowships and
                        Industry and Management awards

Interests: Ocean sailing, swimming, countryside, cooking,
                        contemporary literature, pony driving,
                        author of six best selling books on Management and
                        Presenter of the successful 'Troubleshooter' series on the
                        BBC

INTRODUCTION

Sir John Harvey-Jones, former Chairman of ICI is the closest the UK comes to having a management guru. His career decision making and development have been well documented in his number one best-selling autobiography *Getting It Together* and his views about management and leadership outlined in the celebrated 'Trouble-shooter' television series and resulting books, as well as the best-selling *Making It Happen, Reflections on Leadership, Managing to Survive, A Guide to Management through the 1990s*, and in *All Together Now*, his most recent book about how to get the best out of people in the 1990s.

Sir John Harvey-Jones began his career in the Navy before joining ICI at 32 because his daughter Gaby contracted polio. He was Chairman of ICI from 1982 to 1987, in which capacity he topped the *Sunday Times* poll of captains of industry five years in a row. Although his career is well-known and readily accessible through his own books, we outline here some of the key influences on his career development and decision making, as well as his life in the 'third age' and his views on leadership.

EARLY INFLUENCES

John Harvey-Jones's childhood offers a case study of the unhappiness, sense of inadequacy and feeling of being unloved that is said so often to drive leaders to succeed as they seek the approbation they lacked as children.

He grew up in India until age six, quite pampered and well-loved by his mother but in many ways ignored, rejected and even humiliated by his insensitive father, the guardian of an Indian Prince who had himself received little love in childhood.

> I left India with hardly any memories of my father which cause me pleasure. I never felt, or if I did I cannot remember, any warmth or love, or moments when I felt at one with him. Worse I felt little concern or interest from him. One thing is certain, I was to spend a great deal of my life trying to earn my father's approbation both consciously and subconsciously. If I received it I was never to know. (Harvey-Jones, 1992, p. 21)

At age 6, like his parents before him, John Harvey-Jones was sent to board at prep school, not to see his mother again for three years. Leaving his parents and all that was familiar to him for rigid institutionalised life proved to be deeply traumatic. He felt abandoned, lonely and miserably inadequate in the strange surroundings.

> My detestation of the other boys was matched only by their loathing and total contempt for my small, foreign being. Tolerance is a rare virtue amongst the young. The objective of British institutions and schools in those days seemed to be to ruthlessly stamp out any signs of individuality or difference in order to produce a sort of homogeneous, clean cut, stiff-upper-lipped clone with the same clear and unquestioning view of duty and honour which my father exemplified so well. I felt and indeed was, totally on my own, as a misfit of massive proportions. (Harvey-Jones, 1992, p. 48)

Friendless and cruelly bullied, desperate for approval and sympathy, to the extent of lying about deaths in the family to win compassion, he was severely marked by the loneliness of his prep school experience. As a legacy, he believes that his ability for friendship was irreparably damaged, as well as his ability to share his feelings. On the other hand, this isolation may have given him the emotional resilience and self-sufficiency required of leadership and he was certainly to develop a generous ability to share his experience and emotions with a wide audience through his books.

One of the compensations for his loneliness at school was that he became a voracious reader, spending more and more time in his imagination. He also learned to 'laugh at troubles and crises, a facility which has often proved to be a life-belt of preservation'. To his childhood and delayed physical and emotional development, he also attributes a lifelong openness and love of learning.

CAREER DECISION-MAKING AND DEVELOPMENT

In 1937, at the age of 13, John Harvey-Jones was accepted as a cadet into the Royal Navy. He longed for escape, for self-sufficiency and uniquely, the Navy 'allowed boys to be men'.

> I made the decision to join the navy when I was ten, so it wasn't the world's most sophisticated decision. There's no doubt that my

decision at the time was compounded of a wish to do something which was 'adventurous' and which was in a line of service which my family saw as the true calling of a gentleman. It was a happy choice and a marvellous upbringing and it turned out that I would have ended up in the Navy anyway. But the decision at the time was pure romanticism.

He thrived on the predictability and fairness of life at Dartmouth, learning practical skills, gaining the equivalent of an engineering apprenticeship, self-confidence, the pursuit of 'officer-like qualities' and high standards.

His naval career from 1937 to 1956 is well documented, as is his personal reason for leaving the Navy.

I wouldn't have left the Navy except that my daughter, Gaby, got polio. Once it became clear that I had to leave, I again wanted to do something which I felt had some element of social 'worth-whileness' to it. That led me pretty inexorably into industry. I thought at the time that the country was likely to face economic troubles so I wanted to do something solid and basic rather than something frothy. To that extent the choice of ICI was deliberate. As I think I made clear in my book *Getting It Together* ICI didn't at that time seem to represent a career. It merely represented a way of earning a living and hopefully being home and helping with my daughter every evening.

He began his career at ICI at the age of 32, as a work study officer at Wilton, a job that required rigorous analysis and questioning of operations. In his view this was the first of a series of positions that equipped him as though by design for future responsibilities.

Looking back, I can't help but feel that perhaps the hand of fate was already at play because the particular jobs I did during that period gave me insights and understandings into the workings of Wilton which were absolutely invaluable in later life. (Harvey-Jones, 1992, p. 231)

Two years in work study provided close relationships with and insights into the people on the shop floor and a good understanding of the infrastructure of the site, the largest petrochemical plant in Europe. These years provided him with a lifelong understanding of how much more people know and are capable of than they are usually given credit for.

His promotion to Deputy Supply Manager was not only the most fun of any role he ever held, but also the most rewarding period of his life – reflecting neatly that is not always the top job that provides the greatest satisfaction. Here he was exposed to the imperative of what is fashionably known as continuous improvement, which was to deeply influence his business philosophy thereafter.

Promotion to Manager of the Supply Department led to the setting up of the precursor of quality circles and to the recognition of how under-utilised people were, how much more they generally had to offer.

The addition of new responsibilities as Sales Manager for the hydrocarbon business in 1965 marked the nadir of his professional life. He was personally involved in major sales to international customers and in this heady atmosphere, at age 40, he experienced the closest thing to a mid-life crisis that he ever would. For the first time he realised that promotion to Commercial Director was feasible, if he could out-perform an experienced, knowledgeable and deserving colleague. He grew apart from his family, in his preoccupation to get ahead, playing an ever smaller part in their lives. His experience eloquently supports the view that over-attention to politics and climbing the corporate ladder is ultimately counter-productive.

> For the first and luckily the last time in my industrial career, I found myself in the grip of personal ambition. I became more and more engrossed, not just in the achievement of my selling and profitability goals but also in constantly seeking to demonstrate my corporate superiority over my competitor. I do not think, even in retrospect, that I did anything that was dishonourable but I know that I diverted too much of my energy from doing my job into pursuing my own personal professional interests. I also neglected my family and my home in ways I was later to regret. I found myself departing from my own standards of integrity, concealing unfavourable news and proselytising unduly and immodestly about achievements. I failed to give credit to my subordinates as generously as they were entitled to and instead sought the lime-light for myself. I became less and less involved with my family and more and more involved with my external appearance. I was forty years old and I have often wondered whether that had any bearing on my abandonment of so much I had cherished before and was to cherish again. If there is such a thing as male menopause I guess I had mine at about that time. The saddest thing was that those years

were wasted unnecessarily. If I had stuck to my belief in doing the best job I could and letting the chips fall where they may, I am pretty sure I would have reached the same end point without compromising myself on the way. More importantly I would have retained my position with my wife and daughter which meant so much to me. (Harvey-Jones, 1992, p. 289)

This experience has left him with a mistrust of personal ambition and a desire to help those in its grip.

In 1967 he was appointed to the Division Board as Technical Commercial Director, involving the buying and selling of know-how and development of patents. As the Board member with fewest responsibilities, he also came to function as unofficial personal assistant to the Chairman, filling any gaps in other Board members' responsibilities. From the Chairman he developed a keen interest in the process by which decisions are taken.

His next promotion to Personnel Director, facing severe union problems, was again improbable. Again he found himself prepared:

In a curious way, it was as if my whole life, on a personal level, had been a preparation for this improbable job. My early naval experience, my time with the shop floor on work study, my attempts to involve my staff in the world of supply together with my knowledge of the wider world scene of our industry which again stressed the need for us to change all contributed to giving me a perspective – and a chance. (Harvey-Jones, 1992, p. 291)

Given the vital importance of people to an organisation's success, it is perhaps surprising that Harvey-Jones is virtually the only chief executive in our sample who held a personnel role. Within a year, having integrated a management team that was to gain the credibility of employees, he became Deputy Chairman of the Division, with responsibility for the site and Chairman of the Wilton coordinating committee.

At 47, he became Divisional Chairman of Petrochemicals, the closest role in ICI to captain of the ship, in hindsight, he believes prematurely, when two others were more deserving. 'I had plenty of time ahead and could have taken my turn. Indeed I still think it would have been better use of my talent than the way my career was to develop' (Harvey-Jones, 1992, p. 291).

The three years in this role he sees as growing up, redirecting himself and forming his own philosophy of management. He believes the leader's role to lie in three overlapping areas; vision, delegation and projecting the organisation's values. The values he sought in people were openness, informality, high achievement, a restless dissatisfaction with the status quo and humour. During these years he also began to play a wider role in international operations.

This development coincided with a recognition of the importance of his family, an attempt to firmly separate his professional and personal lives, and an insight that putting work into perspective actually helped rather than inhibited professional progress.

> My attempt with Betty to create a new balance in our lives had the greatest effect on me and was of the greatest importance. For a start, it punctured my belief in the vast importance of what I was doing at work. This feeling freed me to take risks and to stick to my beliefs in ways which I now realise actually made me more likely to move ahead rather than the reverse. (Harvey-Jones, 1992, p. 305)

It was with unusually mixed feelings that he accepted his appointment to the ICI Main Board in 1973, to this day believing that one needs five years, not the three he had had to really establish change. He refers to the next five years as 'the bored years' in his autobiography. Under-loaded, convinced about the need for change in the company, with a newly balanced personal life and reduced ambition, he felt that he had peaked at ICI. Fortuitously he was appointed to the boards of Carrington Viyella and Reed International which brought home to him the importance of broadening his business experience, something which he has ever since valued and pursued.

In 1982 he became Chairman of ICI beginning five years of 'one of the hardest and least enjoyable periods of my life' (Harvey-Jones, 1992, p. 356) due in part to his discomfort with being 'on parade' and the difficulty of responding to multiple audiences, when his natural style was to be as forthright and authentic as possible. He was also acutely aware of the dangers of his position to his fundamental character.

> The area which caused me most concern on a personal basis was the whole business of the effect of power on the individual. I do believe that power corrupts and I can think of very few powerful people who have been improved by it as individuals. Positions of power are, by definition, ephemeral, while one's personal characteristics remain with one until death.

Despite this, the pressures on the individual to change the attributes he or she has fought for all their lives is unremitting. If you appear to be successful it is all too easy to believe that it is due to your own cleverness, rather than due to the host of others who have actually done the work. As power grows, so does the chorus of flattery. Some is obvious and sickening, but much is insidious. In common with many people I am vain and would like to like myself. I also struggle continuously to improve my own moral courage and willingness to take the unpopular ground. There are few tests for such weaknesses more profound than to be the Chairman of a large international company enjoying a period of relative success. (Harvey-Jones, 1992, pp. 358–9)

The highest moment of his career was a purely private one, not discernible to anyone else as a milestone. For one intrinsically motivated, it is achievement itself rather than public recognition that satisfies.

There was a moment in ICI after about fourteen months as Chairman when it was obvious that the ideas I had held for fourteen years or more at last were having the effects that I had hoped they would. I was always very conscious that it was going to be a big risk despite all my apparent confidence when I first started. But it was a purely personal moment. There were no fireworks and we didn't suddenly make an enormous profit. It was the moment when I knew that the problem was being shared and my vision was actually taking root.

Although John Harvey-Jones's two major career decisions were based first on the romanticism of a 13-year-old boy in joining the Navy and second on the necessity of leaving the Navy to spend more time with his polio-stricken four-year-old daughter, he has taken a more structured and planned approach to his retirement. His experience in 'retirement' introduces another important truth or truism – no matter how carefully you plan, you cannot predict the success of the outcome. In his seventies, he still cannot predict what will give him satisfaction because (a) the environment frustrates our expectations and (b) we do not always understand how we will respond to experience. In his words:

In some ways the life which I have led since retiring is a more interesting case study than my formal career, because when I retired I had thought out roughly how I wanted to apportion my time in a very careful and logical way.

I decided I wanted to spend a quarter of my time on education, because I think education is the future of the country; I wanted to spend another quarter with companies but no more, and those companies were to be quite different from ICI and I didn't want an executive job. I wanted a quarter on unpaid good work which was a gross miscalculation and a real pain too. The other quarter I wanted to try and write. In the event, I manage to keep the quarters roughly balanced by being pretty ruthless and once one of them starts to spread, cutting it back. But the satisfaction I get out of the quarters has been quite different from that which I envisaged.

I always thought I would get much more satisfaction out of the unpaid good work and it is really very frustrating for a business-man. The correlation between effort and result is poor. You put about five times the amount of time and effort into something to achieve about a quarter of the result and an awful lot of massaging of people's egos. I'm accustomed to just getting our heads down and pushing. An awful lot of these places are talking shops and don't even seem to be very keen on going anywhere – mere survival is the name of the game. So I found that much less rewarding than I had expected.

Curiously enough, the most rewarding, both personally and financially, has been the writing that led to the television and paid public speaking. It is personally rewarding because I'm having to learn a whole new range of new skills. I'm not one of those idiots who think that anyone can write. You have to work at writing to consciously try and make it better. So it's an interesting new skill to try and develop.

Writing was not his idea. Although he had wanted to write as a boy, it was the encouragement of his literary agent, June Hall, that gave him the 'nerve' to try. Given his overall objectives, he sets aside only five hours a week for his writing, from six to eleven every Sunday morning. 'By eleven o'clock I really feel great. I have a real lift. I don't feel too bad at six either!'

Frequent speculation in the press about John Harvey-Jones joining the Labour Party, most recently rumoured to be the offer of the post of Trade and Industry Secretary in a future Labour Government, has ended with the recognition that his priorities lie in leaving a large legacy to his daughter Gaby, who has suffered from polio since aged four. Forgoing his current two million pounds in earnings from public appearances, board directorships and other lucrative activities for a £60,000 ministerial salary would defeat this objective.

FAMILY AND PERSONAL LIFE

John Harvey-Jones unhappily identifies and regrets periods in his life when professional concerns clearly took priority over personal ones. Although as Chairman he continued to work gruellingly long hours, consciously his family came first.

> Generally speaking I used to start about six and end about midnight when I was in ICI. But that was Monday to Friday, and Friday night I would get home and I have never worked at home, until I retired sadly. (I've always worked long hours. I'm lucky that I have an infinitely elastic sleep pattern, really deriving from the Navy. I can make do with two or three hours a night or if I go to bed and nobody bothers to wake me up, I can sleep for 24 hours.)
>
> Ultimately personal life must have priority. If you extend to the ridiculous extremes of your wife being involved in a car accident while you are in a Board meeting, what do you do? You drop the Board like a ton of bricks and shove off as fast as your legs will take you. So ultimately personal life has to take priority.
>
> The trouble is that one of two things happen; you either allow your personal life to be squeezed or to be subsumed which is almost worst.
>
> Your personal life becomes your professional life. Your poor wife has to go to dreary parties every single evening and she becomes a sort of appendage for the company. That's absolutely monstrous. It is degrading to one's wife and as far as I'm concerned my wife is far too precious to be bought by a company.

Although John Harvey-Jones is not conventionally religious, he does believe overall in a just universe where good is rewarded.

> I have a faith of a sort, a rather paradoxical faith in something, I suppose, in ultimate goodness. I really don't believe that evil men win all the way or (although there is not much evidence to support this) that the world goes to the shits. But by and large there is a

curious sort of justice. I certainly don't believe that the end justifies
the means. I go to church and I do pray, but I've not so far felt that
ability to take one's feet off the pedals and leave it to some divine
driving force.

LEADERSHIP AND SUCCESS FACTORS

Based on his personal experience and on observation, John Harvey-
Jones accepts the 'grit in the oyster' theory – that many leaders are
driven by early suffering and the need for approbation they lacked in
childhood.

> You can't ignore the fact that if you look at many leaders, a
> disproportionate number of them come from broken family back-
> grounds or some sort of family tragedy. It is a sad fact that a
> certain amount of adversity at a minimum seems to be an essential
> part of the make-up of most leaders. I don't believe in golden boy
> scenarios.

Yet his favoured view of the leader is that put forward by University
of Southern California Professor Warren Bennis with whom he has
worked and shared ideas and experiences over the years. Leaders are
people who most fully express themselves and their gifts, and who
'master the context', that is, go beyond the scripts and expectations of
others to become fully independent.

> If your own standards don't happen to suit other people, too bad.
> Again there is a paradox in that, isn't there? The extraordinary
> thing is that you need a certain level of sensitivity but it is hard to
> get the balance right. If you're too sensitive, you're all marsh-
> mallow and ineffective, yet if you're not sensitive enough you can't
> do a thing.

He also believes that being driven primarily by extrinsic concerns,
such as status or recognition does not succeed over time.

> There appear to be some leaders who are primarily motivated by
> the need for recognition but they don't generally speaking last very
> long. The danger is that recognition is a sort of Frankenstein
> monster. It can easily persuade you that you are something special
> and the moment that you think you are something special, you've
> had it.

In speaking again of the period in his own professional life when personal ambition exceeded the pursuit of professional goals, he reinforces the importance of devoting one's energies single-mindedly to the job while acknowledging that playing politics does work for some.

> Frankly the period when personal ambition took over was the period when I did the least good work. I don't mean that I did anything criminal or wrong, but I just know that I could have done better if I hadn't been trimming against what I perceived to be the political requirements.
>
> I'm fairly critical of myself but I try not to dislike myself and I did not like myself during this period. The difficulty is that playing politics is quite successful professionally for quite a lot of people and it depends to some degree on what you want. If I had a nightmare it would be getting a job which I couldn't do. If you actually play politics to get jobs, you are likely to find just that.

Throughout the rest of his life, he has been guided by a personal vision that is consistent with Bennis's view of the leader, expressed at the end of *Getting It Together*.

> From my early boyhood, when I spent so much time living in my imagination and the world of great adventure books of the 1920s, I have had a picture in my mind of the sort of person I wanted to be. A sort of *Boy's Own Paper* composite, archetypal British gentleman – simultaneously strong and compassionate, stiff-lipped yet emotional, courageous both physically and morally, doing incessantly to others as you would be done to yourself. The nice thing if you start from this viewpoint is that there is always more to aim for, so life is never without purpose. The problem is that no matter how much you do 'get it together', there are always other bits to be gathered in.
>
> I do not believe that the purpose of my life was to lead ICI, nor to help to try to arrest Britain's industrial decline. All those years ago I believed that life was about continuously trying to grow – to develop one's talents, such as they are, and to try every day to do a little better. Maybe that recurrent belief is actually what 'getting it together' is really about. (Harvey-Jones, 1992, pp. 375–6)

If he believes fundamentally with Warren Bennis that leaders are those who fully express themselves, he in no way romanticises leaders.

One of the things that was of benefit to me was seeing great world leaders close-up as a young man and realising they were only really just the same mixed up muck as you or I. They all have their own problems. The differences between humans are really very marginal. Particularly in Britain and America, there's a great wish to believe somewhere there is a race of supermen and women who can do everything. Of course, Margaret Thatcher was one who not only believed that but believed that she was one of them. It's fatal.

He attributes his own success primarily to extraordinary luck, but also to self-examination and being as true to himself as he is able.

I try not to become a different person to the person I think I am. I am very willing and constantly do, point out my own weaknesses. I am very willing to admit my own mistakes and constantly do. Trying to be true to yourself is ultimately what it's all about.

In *Managing to Survive, A Guide to Management through the 1990s*, Harvey-Jones concludes that the rapidly changing environment will require different management qualities and above all the ability to manage change (p. 21).

We have tended to have a high regard for the aggressive 'ramrod' type of manager, who forces action through a reluctant system – the man who fights his corner and brooks no opposition. The qualities we must seek for the nineties are the more controlled and collaborative, forward thinking and creative person; the individual who possesses 'helicopter vision', thinks his way through the opportunities and difficulties ahead and has planned his reaction to them. Moreover, and unusually, he has to be able to visualise the consequences and costs of his actions in a financial sense. The mind that is needed is one that can perceive trends and forecast the range of likely developments. (p. 56)

The winners will be those who think radically, embrace change and create adaptable organisations that switch people on and release energy. (p. 14)

Successful managers in the nineties will be those who have the flexibility to adapt their organisations and behaviour to the needs of their people rather than the reverse. (p. 15)

Given the changing nature of demands, he advises looking for the following experience and competences in selecting people for the 1990s.

> The people you want in your team for the future are those with a continuous track record of being in businesses that have changed and improved and have always been ambitious in their aims. You want people who can work with others. Some people are the human equivalent of catalysts. Their involvement is crucial in terms of creating change within the team and a new freshness of approach and attack. You need people who will forgo apparent personal advantage for the sake of the group as a whole, and people with originality of view, who are their own men. Inevitably, these individuals cause waves and are not always valued when the going is easy. The temptation is to let them go (and they will be more than ready to do so) and keep the 'reliable' team men, who will always agree. The difficulty with this approach is that you are losing the prime movers. (p. 67)

He is also slightly uncomfortable with his role as management guru, to the extent that he is seen to provide solutions rather than ways of examining problems.

> I have relevant experience that I can tell people about, but I don't think the experience is *directly* relevant to them. One of the unfortunate things about the 'Troubleshooter' series is that it has given me a reputation for being a know-all about everything and I don't think I am. What I try to do is to look at somebody else's problems and say 'Look, in my experience, this is what I would do but I'm not telling you to do this. I am merely suggesting that there are these ways that you might look at it'. That's very different from saying 'Oh, well, of course, if you don't do so and so, you are absolutely knackered'.

As with several others, he has been influenced by and learned from people (usually low-profile people with different personality types from his own), without having a mentor or a role model.

> I've never had a model man. I have a mythical man but I've never had a real live breathing man that I wanted to be. On the other hand, I have learnt immense amounts usually from people who, rather sadly, were not as highly considered by others as by me.

There are an awful lot of unsung heroes and I've learnt tremendous amounts from them. You are filling lacunae in your own make-up. You find somebody whose approach to things is so diametrically opposite to yours and you come to admire him. Then you attempt to do a sort of lobotomy or a brain graft of what you see. And of course, that still happens.

John Harvey-Jones's strong motivation to grow and to realise his gifts necessarily entails commitment to life-long learning, and his early life in India, his early professional association with Germany 'a life-long affair' and Russia provided the beginning of an international perspective that goes hand in hand with an interest in best practice.

Along with other management writers, Tom Peters, Rosabeth Moss Kanter, Charles Handy, he examines at length the consequences of the turbulence, rate and unpredictability of change in the 1990s and beyond in his book *Managing to Survive*.

Success comes more easily to those who study the world around them, and are continually updating their craft, than to those who try to repeat a formula that worked once in the past. The world is littered with failed heroes, who were too intoxicated with success that they failed to adapt to new circumstances and new demands. (p. 6)

20

Backgrounds and Motivation

In coming to grips with their own leadership potential people necessarily seek to understand the extent to which their own history and life-circumstances are similar to or differ from those of proven leaders. As the youngest child in my family, am I less likely to succeed? Am I limited by my working-class or my middle-class background? Does it matter that I have no degree?

Psychologists often suggest that the high levels of motivation required to succeed are caused by some early insecurity or unhappiness that provides what has been called a 'grit in the oyster', driving people to compensate for the lack of love or approval experienced in childhood. Is an unhappy childhood necessary to provide the drive one needs to succeed? Are the childhood experiences of business leaders in fact relevant at all to their later success as leaders?

BIRTH ORDER

My early assumption that birth order would be relevant and that oldest children would predominate because they were used to leading and responsibility was proved wrong. Youngest children were the largest single group. Two were only children; three were eldest; four middle and nine were the youngest. Other studies of larger samples have suggested that position in the family is relevant, with the youngest and eldest being more assertive than those in between (Cox and Cooper, 1988, p. 9).

SOCIAL ORIGINS AND EARLY EDUCATION

Although in the past most business leaders in the UK had middle-class backgrounds, no one today will be surprised that those in our sample were equally likely to come from working-class as middle-class families, again with no sex or intergenerational differences.

Eight straightforwardly came from working-class backgrounds as
self-described. Steve Shirley, as a refugee at four, was fostered by a
working-class couple, although her parents were middle-class intelligentsia in Germany. The other nine business leaders, although by no
means all wealthy had middle-class origins.

Just as class was not predictive of success, nor was early schooling.
Eight people in the sample went to public or fee-paying schools.
Three people, including two women, attended grammar schools and
one person attended a Catholic Seminary to enter the priesthood
(Gerry Robinson). The six individuals born and educated outside of
the UK, all attended state-run schools.

HIGHER EDUCATION

Of the fourteen graduates, only four were Oxbridge (Christopher
Hogg, Archie Norman, Martin Taylor and Charles Mackay) with
Richard Giordano attending Harvard, the American equivalent. Two
attended the London School of Economics (Jean Denton, Allen
Sheppard).

Nor does undergraduate honours or concentration seem relevant
to predicting success – although three studied economics, no more
than two people studied any other single subject as an undergraduate.
Three studied law (Graham Day, Charles Mackay with Richard
Giordano studying law, as required in the US, as a graduate at
Columbia after studying political science as an undergraduate). Two
have accountancy degrees and one each studied engineering, literature, chemistry, philosophy, mathematics and Chinese.

It is noted that all three women with degrees chose social sciences
and sciences, rather than traditional humanities subjects.

The way degree subjects were chosen and the impact on their
careers is dealt with in the next chapter on decision-making, as is
experience and advice relating to the MBA.

EARLY FORMATIVE EXPERIENCE

Most business leaders were able to identify a dominant influence in
their early life, without supporting the psychoanalytic conclusion that
leaders are driven by a need for recognition based on feeling unloved
in childhood. Certainly there was some trauma recalled, but this was

not the common experience. This is consistent with Jennings, Cox and Cooper's (1994) conclusion that both the intrapreneurs and entrepreneurs in their study described their childhoods as normal and happy, even though a high proportion of the entrepreneurs experienced the death or prolonged absence of one or both parents before the age of 16 (p. 56). Of course, the childhood of these in the current study may have been more traumatic than expressed, either because of difficulty in talking about it or because unhappy experiences are often locked in the subconscious. Nevertheless, most people identified circumstances which drove them to excel and to take early charge of their lives.

Adversity

When I began my research into leadership, two psychologist colleagues shared with me the psychoanalytic understanding of the foundation of leadership drive. People are driven to succeed because of the 'basic fault', a powerful underlying feeling of not being loved in childhood and an unquenchable search for appreciation and recognition. I was interested in exploring this profile further as it coincides with a quite common view in the UK that people who get to the top are often motivated primarily by power, status (and money).

Both John Harvey-Jones and Gerry Robinson agree with the premise that adversity and lack of feeling loved is what motivates most leaders in the first instance to succeed, in order to gain the approval they did not receive as children.

Adversity appeared to play a part in a small minority of our business leaders' lives. John Harvey-Jones's story is almost a case study of the experience of feeling abandoned and unloved. Steve Shirley was a child refugee from Nazi Germany. Martin Taylor and Ann Iverson lost their fathers as young children. Martin Taylor regards a 'profound requirement for security' as a legacy of his father's death and John Egan identifies the self-reliance developed from the hardships of a very tough Catholic boarding school as important.

Aspirational parents or school

A higher proportion of business leaders volunteered that the positive aspirations of parents or school were instrumental in motivating them to succeed (Liam Strong, Neville Bain, Richard Giordano, Graham Day, Jean Denton, Penny Hughes, Ann Iverson) and in engendering an early belief in themselves and self-reliance.

Three of the four women also mentioned aspirational parents and school environments as most influential early forces. A much larger sample of high-flying women, studied by White, Cox and Cooper found that 75 per cent of parents were ambitious for their daughters to succeed and concluded that in most cases 'the parent/child relationship facilitated the development of an early sense of independence and self-sufficiency' (White, Cox and Cooper, 1992, p. 28).

Working-class background/poverty

Early poverty and the resulting drive to be financially independent also was an explicitly powerful early motivator for a group with working-class origins (Liam Strong, Allen Sheppard). Again, from an early age it was clear that they were on their own in achieving financial security.

Graham Day, though speaking more about the aspirational nature of his environment as influential, none the less worked his way through school and university, often juggling several jobs at once. For Steve Shirley, money is only part of a more general story of insecurity and survival guilt.

Competitive family

What then provides the 'grit in the oyster' for those from well-off, secure families, if anything? Both Christopher Hogg and Archie Norman mentioned sibling relationships as most important. The second son of four children, Christopher Hogg in his early years was driven to emulate his older brother, who was a brilliant athlete. Archie Norman, again the second son of four, mentions above all the self-reliance engendered in the rough and tumble of a large family where he was expected to fend for himself. Although he acknowledges that insecurity drives him, he does not believe that conceiving of this as a 'need to prove' himself is particularly helpful: ' "The need to prove yourself" is a very fashionable way of putting it. Obviously I really want to succeed but whether I have a need to is another matter. I am a very motivated person. To me it's just natural to be motivated.'

Gerry Robinson as the ninth of ten children also sees his family position as relevant; without mentioning sibling rivalry, it is clear that his share of parental attention was necessarily small. Neville Bain mentions sibling rivalry among four boys as a positive force, essentially a supportive team 'when one hurts, we all hurt'.

Childhood experiences engendering early self-reliance may help to provide the autonomy later necessary in positions of leadership. A significant problem, however, in identifying common formative influences is that these very same influences often operate apparently as powerfully in the lives of unsuccessful people as in those of leaders. Perhaps the 'grit in the oyster' is necessary, but it is certainly not sufficient. Early adversity, environmental and parental aspiration, competition, poverty do not always lead to success or leadership.

MOTIVATION

Understanding their early lives, even in a superficial way, and from their perspective, leads us to the question of what fundamentally motivates people who achieve success in corporate life. What drives them to excellence, to work so hard and does their motivation change over time? We have seen that an early 'grit in the oyster', whether feeling unloved, poverty, family competition or a deeply aspirational environment, provided a spur to self-reliance and perhaps a desire to prove oneself or to excel. What do the people say themselves about what fundamentally motivates them?

Overwhelmingly, most people said they were fundamentally motivated by what psychologists term 'intrinsic' factors, that is, the challenge or interest of the job and doing the job well. Although cynics may scoff, believing leaders to be primarily motivated by wealth, status and power, there is persuasive evidence that most high achievers in business are motivated by genuine interest in their work and a commitment to perform and to achieve outstanding results.

John Egan, in reflecting on some research into the psychology of happiness concludes:

Happiness was found to come from doing things that are goal-oriented, doing things where you get feedback, where your skills are commensurate with the task. Yet most people think that doing very little is relaxing. I certainly get my greatest satisfaction out of working hard and doing a good job and I am obviously not alone.

Martin Taylor exemplifies this pursuit of interest and learning, above all else:

> I am influenced by curiosity and fear of boredom more than anything else and just horror of not having enough interesting things to do. That makes one ambitious but only in the negative sense that the interesting jobs are the most senior jobs usually.

Several people (Allen Sheppard, Charles Mackay, Jean Denton) kept as a guiding principle that they should have no regrets, no 'I wish I hads' on their death-beds. Archie Norman believes he is motivated by a sense of duty, by providing a valuable service to other people.

Although research shows that most leaders are motivated by 'intrinsic' considerations related to their ability and interest in the job, the psychoanalytic interpretation of the basic fault, lack of love in childhood, and the ensuing need for approbation would lead to individuals seeking 'extrinsic rewards' such as recognition or status in their leadership roles. The study of personality types suggests that this would be more true of extraverts than introverts and the study of life stages that it would be more prevalent in those under 45 than those over. As 'extrinsic' motivation is often considered to be less strong and admirable than 'intrinsic' motivation, there may be a reluctance to admit that one wants fame or recognition based on a need to prove oneself.

Most people acknowledged that recognition from others as being successful was welcome and pleasant, but not sought as an end in itself. Self-acknowledged introverts such as Christopher Hogg, Graham Day, and Martin Taylor were persuasive that validation from others was not a primary motivation. In Graham Day's words, 'It's not that approval isn't important but I don't need it in order to function. That's why leadership is so lonesome. If you believe you're right, but others aren't with you, introverts have an easier time going out on their own'.

It is probably true that most of those saying that they valued recognition were extraverts but again, in virtually all cases, it was a question of emphasis. While they seem to place greater importance on appreciation from others than introverts, they are also motivated by challenge and a job well done.

Also, as examined, several people recognise that their motivation has changed over time. Liam Strong expresses neatly the moving up the Maslovian hierarchy.

> Recognition is important but it's not a be all and end all. I'd rather have respect than undying affection. To be respected and seen as somebody who is consistent and straight is important. To put too high a value on what people think of you can distort your actions. Recognition is a little bit like possessions. It seems important to you before you get it, but once you have had a fill of it, the point of difference disappears.

Archie Norman, nine years younger, has a different perspective. As he sees himself as motivated above all to turn around Asda, his eye is completely on the ball and personal recognition is irrelevant. He believes that this is true of most young chief executives and that it is only in one's fifties, the job done, that one lifts one's head and starts looking for recognition, primarily in the UK in the form of honours. Thus in early middle age, he sees chief executives as intrinsically motivated to do the job well, and in later middle age as extrinsically motivated, seeking status and prestige. Although this is the reverse of Levinson and Erikson's findings in the US, it may be that the honours system in the UK is an important influence, engendering a powerful expectation of public recognition in later life.

Predictably, money was an early motivator to those brought up in homes with little money. No one any longer was primarily motivated by making money although some acknowledged that it remained a motivation. As John Egan notes, 'It's the lingua franca of business – the better you do, the more money you get.' In addition, both Steve Shirley and John Harvey-Jones have as an important goal to leave enough money to their only children (Harvey-Jones's daughter had polio as a child and Steve Shirley's son is mentally handicapped).

21

Career Decision-making

What can be learned from the way business leaders have made decisions about their careers? Have they in fact approached their careers as advised by career counsellors, analysing carefully their strengths, weaknesses and interests, developing career goals and systematically exploring opportunities?

Is it actually *necessary* to have clear goals to reach the top? Is it in fact *better* to have them?

Are there generational differences between the experience of new business leaders and those of the older generation? How did they make career decisions and how would they advise others?

PLANNING AND CAREER GOALS

In spite of commonly held views such as 'if you don't plan to get to the top, you'll never get there' or 'heads of companies were single-mindedly devoted throughout their careers to one thing – to reach the top', not a single business leader articulated an early goal to be chief executive of a large company. In fact, very few individuals had a clear and specific goal for their working lives, particularly as regards to level or position reached. Although they invariably had clear goals and strategies for their companies, this paradoxically rarely extended to their own working lives.

No one had planned their career in a detailed way; most have planned, if at all, only in the most general sense, with an underlying driving ambition to succeed but without a clear idea of where this would take them. Archie Norman was an exception in conceiving a broad early goal to run an organisation but this was not at first confined to business and he attributes most career moves to chance.

This is fundamentally different from the approach of entrepreneurs who invariably have a clear personal vision (but which is of course inextricably linked to that of the business). Indeed, Steve Shirley, the founder of computer software house, the F.I. GROUP, and the only entrepreneur in the sample, is the exception, at any one time having a clear (but changing) personal goal.

On the other hand, a large group had a general idea about important elements sought in their careers, without a specific goal, career path or end-point in mind and over time, made active career choices to acquire skills and experience that would move them in the desired direction. In fact, many of the new generation of chief executives were in this category of more actively shaping their careers. When the reasons for joining their first employer are examined, it is clear that in almost all cases they did not 'fall into' the job but applied after some thought and were selected.

Typical of this group was Bill Castell at Amersham who had a general goal to be a successful businessman in the world of science and over time consciously sought the knowledge and skills required. Iverson sought 'winning cultures' where she would grow and be challenged professionally. Archie Norman acknowledges the importance of chance while also positioning himself for opportunity – 'you create your own luck'.

Of the older generation, Christopher Hogg is more rare in acknowledging that he had a clear though general career goal conceived at Harvard Business School, unspecific as to level, company or industry that he was then to pursue single-mindedly – to be in general management in an international organisation and to 'use my abilities fully and in a wide perspective but how high that took me remained to be seen'. He neatly describes a process of conscious selection that no doubt was operating in the career decision-making of most, if not all, our business leaders.

> You could say that most of my career moves have in a sense been calculated. There is a serendipitous element, but what happens is that opportunities come at you all the time and you select some and discard others. I don't know whether you call that calculated or not but there was a conscious process of selection going on in my case.

Many of the older generation attributed career decisions to chance and serendipity, without emphasising to the same extent the role of choice involved in the selection of opportunities. They were more likely to refer to external influences such as mentors, head-hunters, circumstances and luck than to rational moves actively chosen and first employer choices often reflected this.

Accompanying the experience of relying on chance for career moves was the belief that luck and hard work, doing the job well were most important to success and in some cases that excessive planning was not only Machiavellian but unnecessary, indeed counter-productive.

Of the newer chief executives, only three attribute most choices to serendipity or chance and all three mistrust the effectiveness of too much career planning. Penny Hughes, while quite active herself in choosing to leave two positions for rational reasons, none the less reflects the experience of most business leaders of being pulled along in their careers. 'You will find me quite unusual because I have never planned my career. Things have always happened more quickly than I was thinking of moving on!'

Reliance on serendipity or chance was often accompanied by a sense/recognition that their experience often prepared them, sometimes unpredictably, for their next career move.

Personal reasons for career moves were instrumental for all the women interviewed, Jean Denton and Penny Hughes moving location to be with boyfriends, Ann Iverson accepting jobs that fit with her husband's work, Steve Shirley setting up her own business to spend time with children, becoming a forerunner of what is the increasingly common practice of going out on one's own to achieve flexibility.

Steve Shirley also notes that many of her career decisions were influenced by health issues: 'Why did it happen? Because my son was ill. Why did it happen? Because I was pregnant. Why did it happen? Because I had a miscarriage.'

If personal reasons were instrumental in men's careers, it usually related to an illness of a family member or a death in the family. Thus John Harvey-Jones left the Navy because of his daughter's polio, Charles Mackay left Pakhoed and Holland because of the death of his 17-year-old son and the need of the family to escape old memories and start again. Such personal reasons provide stark examples of the limitations of planning.

Indeed, if there was consensus about anything it was the importance of luck to success, with some conceiving of luck as not just chance but the product of hard work (and no doubt following your interests and using your strengths) encapsulated by 'the harder I work, the luckier I get'. It is not just modesty operating but a reflection of reality – many talented people do not get to the top.

A certain amount of ambivalence was evident on the issue of career planning. Neville Bain was one of very few who unambiguously advised people to plan and prepare themselves for the next step. He also believes that senior managers plan their careers much more carefully than most admit. His chairman, Sir David Alliance, a classic entrepreneur, goes further – he does not believe that it is possible to succeed without a clear goal. Ironically, the instance Bain gives of preparing for the next step, resulted in the only time in his career where he felt unhappy and in the wrong slot. He was in the role for only nine months.

Only in retirement has John Harvey-Jones planned rationally how he would spend his time and ironically has found the source of satisfaction to be unpredictable.

This finding is consistent with other studies on the career decision-making of senior managers both in the UK and the US which reflect that systematic career planning is rare (McCall, Lombardo and Morrison, 1988, p. 103) and that careers are usually 'a set of improvisations based on loose assumptions about the future, rather than a coherent match between personal values and skills and corporate needs and goals' (Golzen and Garner, 1990, p. 1).

Based on the experience of our business leaders and on their advice, the following conclusions are drawn.

Know Thyself and to Thine Own Self Be True

When asked what advice they would give their children about how to make career decisions, hardly anyone spoke about the need for clear goals and plans. Almost all, however, spoke about the need to 'know thyself', to carefully examine one's own strengths, interests, motivation and to choose a career path based on this understanding, rather than on what others or society thought was statusful and worthwhile.

Certainly this advice is at the heart of most career counsel, whether put forward in books, by professional career counsellors or out-placement agencies.

Understanding one's personality type is another insightful means to 'know thyself' and helpful in the choice of occupation. As a great deal of research supports the matching of type and occupation, the Myers Briggs Type Indicator is useful in understanding occupations that will exploit one's strengths and preferred ways of looking at the world.

Ann Iverson advises young people to 'try different summer jobs, find a good career counsellor and look for role models in professional fields to talk to about your interests and experiences so that you can start to formulate career objectives that match your likes and dislikes at an early age'.

Articulate a career objective, based on your deepest interests and strengths and plan primarily to develop the skills necessary to fulfil that objective. Do not concern yourself with management level as an end in itself. Plan no more than five years ahead and be flexible in responding to opportunity.

Career counsellors go beyond advising one to understand oneself and to base career decisions on one's interests and strengths to concluding that it is necessary to examine the environment systematically and to *plan* one's career moves. Few people interviewed considered detailed career planning useful or necessary.

Certainly no one supported the value of having a career goal to reach the top. Martin Taylor considered such an ambition inappropriate and Gerry Robinson expressed cynicism about someone deliberately seeking a route to the top, believing that success in business is more about 'getting on with it than career planning.'

Although few advised their children to set goals, those who did put this in the context of the need to know themselves. As Bill Castell advises:

What do I say to them? Be true to yourself number one. Set goals that are achievable but that will stretch you and try to match your skills realistically to whatever walk of life you wish to pursue. And don't feel that greatness necessarily gives happiness.

Allen Sheppard has no children but quite frequently advises his nephew. 'I advise him that you should always be strategic in knowing where you are going but not so strategic that you don't enjoy what you do. . . . Think it through logically and then let your heart win. If you don't follow your heart, you will end up frustrated.'

Martin Taylor does not believe in career planning and advises people to choose to do things where they are learning, and that they are fundamentally interested in. It is also important to understand where a career step is taking you, not in a hierarchical sense but whether it is broadening or narrowing you developmentally. Liam Strong makes decisions in the same way, trying to understand whether they increase or narrow options.

Jean Denton not only advises ambitious women to think ahead and plan the next step but to tell people that they want a fresh challenge – it is less necessary so to advise men as she believes that they more naturally approach their careers strategically.

Select corporate environments that suit your personality type, approach and values, where you will enjoy your work and be good at it.

Several people emphasised the importance of matching one's type and values to the corporate culture of the organisation and Ann Iverson, for instance, consciously made career moves based on a recognition that she would grow and contribute more in a different organisational culture.

Take Time to Decide

A few people, particularly of the younger generation, notably Liam Strong and Archie Norman, advised people not to be in too great a rush to make career decisions and to take time, even time off before entering the workforce.

Liam Strong, while advising like most people that one should do what one most enjoys and is best at, understands that realistically one often does not know without first trying.

> You must be prepared to adjust if you don't hit it right first time. For most strong-minded, competent people there is an appropriate path out there but you can take a lot more time in your twenties than a lot of people think. I have always been in too much of a hurry. Above all, as you look for your line, take advice. The first step in getting ahead is to listen.

Levinson in *The Seasons of a Man's Life* agrees, wondering at the paradox in human development that necessitates making crucial choices before we have the knowledge, judgement and self-under-standing to choose wisely. He suggests that it is only at 30 that one need make a strong occupational commitment and enduring choice.

It was at just this age that Martin Taylor first conceived of a career in business, having spent all of his working life until then as a financial journalist.

Work Hard and Be Committed – The Harder I Work the Luckier I Get

Closely associated with advice about understanding yourself and being true to yourself was the importance of fully exploiting one's gifts and working hard. Graham Day advises his children: 'I like to feel they have a commitment to something, including themselves. If you do something, do it well and try to do just a little more than you are paid for, because you have got to live with yourself at the end of the day.'

Working hard, doing a good job, was viewed as far more important than planning to career success. In Charles Mackay's words:

> Concentrate on doing the job well and the opportunities will come. It really is a question of 'the harder I work the luckier I get'. Don't sit there planning each career step. You'll come unstuck if you do. You've got to give absolutely everything to what you are doing now and then be prepared to be opportunistic if something should come up.

In Mackay's experience those people who were too highly organised about career planning and promotions rarely made it to the top because they were too mechanistic and not flexible enough.

CHOOSING A DEGREE SUBJECT AND A SPECIALTY

Whether studying literature, philosophy, chemistry, Chinese or law, economics or accounting, not one of the 14 graduates had regretted their choice of degree subject. The experience was seen primarily as teaching one to think, rather than as vocational training. Most of those not attending university expressed no serious regrets. Although Neil Shaw acknowledges missing the full-time university experience of his friends, working gave him a professional head-start.

In advising their children, several people would encourage them to pursue a formal education. For Bill Castell, education represents freedom to choose. Jean Denton similarly emphasised the importance of gaining a 'ticket' to get on board. Allen Sheppard stressed the need to qualify within a function – but the field didn't matter much. The message overwhelmingly was to choose to study what interests you most.

Nor did our business leaders favour any discipline above others as a route to the top or as developmentally most useful. As we will examine, other considerations, such as breadth of functional experience, were considered much more important.

In considering what experience would be required of chief executives in the future, most believed there would be little change. A few considered that international experience would be more important, as well as computing skills and the ability to handle large amounts of information. In 1989 Korn/Ferry and Columbia University undertook a study of over 1500 top executives in twenty countries to gain an understanding of what they considered would be important to leadership in the year 2000. This revealed little change in the areas of expertise considered necessary for future CEOs (the 1988 order of top four most important areas were strategy formulation, marketing/ sales, human resource management and negotiation/conflict resolution), although human resource management supplanted marketing/ sales in number two place, reflecting a slight shift from understanding customers, the people outside the company to developing and retaining personnel within the company.

A short analysis follows of views on the value of specific chosen degree subjects and disciplines.

Finance and accounting/economics

The choice of an accounting degree by Neville Bain and Bill Castell was in each case a carefully thought-through vocational choice to equip them for a career in business. As Bill Castell notes:

> I think it was a very lucky move when I decided that I was going to do finance because that gave me the long pants. It made me a professional. If you are a lawyer or an accountant then you can go and deal with a 45 or a 55-year-old and they will accept you because you are a professional. If you go in with a marketing degree, they won't accept you.

Accountancy traditionally has been a favourite professional route into business in the UK. As Charles Handy notes in *Making Managers* (1988, p. 8), 'if 10 per cent of all British undergraduates aspire to be accountants it is not because they want to be auditors, but because they want to be businessmen and women'.

Allen Sheppard, Jean Denton and Archie Norman all chose economics at university, Sheppard because of an interest in business, Denton and Norman because they were interested and good at it. Sheppard's career took an early financial route. Norman became Group Finance Director at Kingfisher without an accounting qualification, as had Sir Geoffrey Mulcahy before him, and both succeeded with good strategic brains and breadth of understanding. Denton still describes herself as a pragmatic economist, a background that has been useful both in business and government.

Law

Richard Giordano, Graham Day and Charles Mackay all valued the study of law for developing analytical skills. Richard Giordano, however, considered that the study of law was no more useful for business than any graduate degree (it is a graduate degree in the USA) although the practice of law was good training for business as it essentially required problem-solving. On the other hand, Graham Day did not view law as particularly good training for a senior role in heavy industry:

> My background has been a little risky because I've been managing heavy engineering companies for a lot of my life. Had I been an engineer, perhaps I could have done some things better and gone faster. Perhaps I'd have been less reliant in a difficult situation on someone whose judgement I didn't know if I could trust.

Engineering

On the other hand, John Egan as the only engineer in the group, believes most engineers to be poor managers and undertook an MBA to overcome the limitations of his own training and experience to become a good manager.

The powerful combination of engineering and business qualifications for a senior management role in manufacturing has been recognised by the Sainsbury MBA designed specifically for engineering graduates.

Other Subjects

The choice of other degree subjects was usually made because of interest and aptitude. Martin Taylor with Chinese and Steve Shirley with mathematics provide support to following your heart in choosing a degree subject. Although Christopher Hogg is an exception in going against the grain in studying English when a more natural choice would have been engineering or accounting, he believes that he is 'marginally more civilised' as a result.

Penny Hughes values her chemistry degree as providing discipline and a useful background for product development with Procter & Gamble leading into marketing and one of the traditionally most highly regarded backgrounds for senior management. Liam Strong, studying philosophy at Dublin University, also chose marketing with Procter & Gamble.

If marketing as a background was not mentioned alone as valuable, it was because it was viewed as one of several critical skills necessary for general management, not because understanding of the customer was not vitally important. As we will examine, breadth of functional experience was seen as crucial, with no real preference about initial specialist training or background which also accounts for the perceived value of the MBA.

THE MBA

Significantly, five of the graduates went on to do Masters of Business Administration. (At almost one third of the total sample, this is again much higher than the 5 per cent of UK Chairmen/ Chief Executives over 50 and the 10 per cent under 50 found to have MBAs in the Boards of Directors study in 1994 published by Korn/Ferry Carré/ Orban.)

The MBA graduates all value the experience highly as providing a rigorous analytical framework, and a theoretical knowledge of all key management disciplines with the caveat that it is no substitute for practical experience. It also provided in most cases a lifelong appetite for keeping at the cutting edge of management thinking and best practice. Archie Norman particularly values the confidence a good MBA provides.

All MBA graduates would recommend undertaking this course for aspiring senior managers but the following provisos are also given:

- There are MBAs and MBAs. Especially in the US, with 60,000 MBA graduates a year, the currency has become devalued. Make sure that the business school has a sound reputation.
- It is important to work for a few years before undertaking the MBA. Only Christopher Hogg went straight from Oxford to

Harvard Business School and while acknowledging the MBA as vital to his later success, he has expressed reservations about not first having had business experience.

- Do not return from an MBA to join the same speciality – use the MBA to broaden your experience, the width you will need for senior management.
- Do not be arrogant or expect special privileges. MBAs have been given a bad name because they promise more than they deliver. The evidence is clear that starting salaries for MBAs are higher but there is no evidence that MBAs are more successful professionally over time than their counterparts. After a few years, the MBA as a qualification is largely irrelevant – it is your performance on the job and track record that is the key.
- If your goal is top management, after business school think carefully before joining a consultancy firm or management services firm, where the salaries are most attractive. Although it worked for Christopher Hogg in banking and Archie Norman in consultancy in McKinsey, neither is a short cut nor even an easy or logical route to senior management in business.

CONSULTING – SHORT-CUT TO THE TOP?

In the 1980s, high proportions of the most talented business school graduates trotted off to merchant banks and consultancies, where they were much better paid than in industry and much more highly valued. In the US at least, in the 1980s, management consultancy was often viewed as a short-cut to the top. Lester Korn in *The Success Profile* concluded this categorically in 1988. Although there have been some notable success stories in the US (Gerstner at IBM), there is little evidence yet that consulting is a short-cut to the top in the UK.

Archie Norman, Chief Executive of Asda and Charles Mackay, Chief Executive of Inchcape are the two most prominent exceptions. Even Charles Mackay's experience however does not support the 'short cut' theory as he began his career at McKinsey with twelve years at BP, at least six of them in responsible line management positions. The value of his McKinsey experience is indisputable in terms of his ability to think strategically across a variety of companies and industries, but he has no illusions about how consulting experience is viewed in industry.

Consulting experience will not help you to find a line job, because there is still nervousness about putting someone straight into a line job from consultancy. An outstanding consultant will not necessarily be an effective line manager or chief executive. Consultants are very good at analysing problems, but not necessarily effective at making things happen in practice.

Just as there are now companies that value a good MBA from well-known business schools, there are a few companies that value consulting experience (particularly if there happens to be a McKinsey, BCG, Bain, Booz Allen alumnus/alumna within the organisation). Generally, however, consultants first enter a large company, if at all, through a corporate planning or business development role.

Archie Norman at 41 is an exception. Although he made the transition from consultant to senior manager with client Kingfisher successfully, he also believes that the profiles of chief executive or senior line manager and effective consultant are different.

CHANGING COMPANIES

Young people in the exploratory first stage of their career often are concerned about the acceptability of either moving too often or alternatively staying too long with one employer. One is frequently asked such questions as how many job moves can I make and still be considered to have a 'stable track record'? How little is the minimum one can acceptably stay in a job? If I stay too long with my current employer, will I be unemployable/undesirable elsewhere? If so, how long is too long?

Our results suggest that many successful professional managers have quite frequent moves, with several different companies and often in different industries. On average, the business leaders made four career moves, or had been with five organisations so far in their working lives. (As almost half are in their early fifties or younger, there is of course opportunity for this average to increase.)

A study by Kakabadse and Margerison of CEOs in the US and UK revealed that on average in the US they had been with 3.6 separate organisations and in the UK with 2.9 separate organisations. (Cox and Cooper, 1988, p. 39)

Rather surprisingly an analysis of company moves by age in our sample revealed that people were only slightly more likely to move before 30 than between 30 and 40, and after 40.

Within this average, there were of course extremes at either end, with Jean Denton having 10 career moves, and Richard Giordano effectively one. Only two people ever left a company within a year of joining. Although early job moves were often made after two years, this was very much the exception after the late twenties. Most people felt at this stage that it was imperative to stay at least five to six years to achieve something identifiably one's own. Christopher Hogg believed that ten years minimum heading up a big company was required to determine whether success was attributable to one's own actions rather than those of another.

In this context, several people regretted leaving jobs too soon, with the sense of 'unfinished business', not having completed the task set for oneself. It is in this spirit that Graham Day regrets leaving Cammell Laird too early. Similarly, John Harvey-Jones believes that he was promoted too soon into the Divisional Chairman role, before he had fully developed in and contributed to his current role.

Allen Sheppard, with experience of leaving Ford for essentially negative reasons of frustration, advises people not to knee jerk, not to leave the company for negative reasons.

Career counsellors almost invariably advise people not to leave their current employer without a job to go to, because this often puts one in a difficult and defensive position. Charles Mackay's career history reinforces that there are no iron-clad rules, in that he four times resigned without a job, each time landing on his feet because of his track record, the support of key individuals (including his wife) and his own confidence that he was doing the right thing. Although it worked for him, he would not recommend this course for others.

If most business leaders have moved companies several times, is it 'dangerous' to stay too long in one company, in terms of both internal and external opportunities? There is no doubt that changing companies, and particularly changing industries, can provide valuable breadth. Changing companies, even within the same industry, provides a steep learning curve. As Bill Castell notes in moving from Wellcome to Amersham. 'It's very difficult walking into a firm as a complete stranger – you don't know anything about the business. I just didn't know where to start.'

Lester Korn in 1988 wrote that most successful careers in American companies are built by staying put, not moving. His sample had spent an average of 17 years with the same company and had had two employers on average. Of the eighteen in our sample, Christopher Hogg, Neil Shaw, Allen Sheppard, Richard Giordano, Steve Shirley and John Harvey-Jones had been with their companies for longer than fifteen years. Not often, but occasionally, people regretted staying too long in a company or role. Jean Denton considers this a particularly female predisposition.

There is no formula relating to number of moves, other than not to have so many, so frequently that your career looks unstable and you cannot reliably point to your own achievements. Korn suggests that three to four moves in ten years is too many: the experience of our business leaders suggests that one can get away with moves every few years in one's twenties, but not thereafter.

Most of the business leaders in our sample acquired their reputations and spent most of their careers with large companies. It is true that large companies, when looking externally for people, often prefer people from similar large corporate environments. Most of the moves made were from large companies to large companies, although with exceptions early in careers.

CHANGING INDUSTRIES

Lending support to the conclusion that in the early stages of a career one must usually experiment or 'suck it and see' before settling down, almost all people are not now in industries in which they started their careers. In some cases, such as Christopher Hogg and Archie Norman, there was no intention to stay in their first chosen industry, banking – it was a place to learn necessary skills for a later career in industry.

In many cases the transition from one industry to another was made in their twenties. However, quite a few people changed industries close to or at the top of the organisation (Gerry Robinson, Neville Bain, Martin Taylor, Allen Sheppard, John Egan).

Those who have changed industries, while deferential about the value of industry knowledge, also see the value of a new perspective. They coped by asking foolish questions, adopting as quickly as possible the language of the company and industry and concentrating on basics.

In addition, there was often a recognition by individuals that they would not risk changing into any industry – the new industry would need to exploit their skills and be of intrinsic interest to enable them to succeed. Thus Martin Taylor felt comfortable moving into banking from textiles because of his interest in and knowledge of financial markets from eight years as a financial journalist but would not consider changing at the top into computing or motor cars where he had no interest in the products.

LINEAR MOVES NOT ALWAYS BEST

There are times when the best career move is not a linear one. Sometimes our business leaders took opportunities that could appear irrational to outsiders, that proved instrumental to their success. For instance, Charles Mackay chose to head a division of Inchcape, his third divisional chairmanship, instead of running a large public company.

Jean Denton gives strong support to not thinking in a strictly linear way about one's career. 'You should not worry about the odd diversion because you will always learn from it. This includes taking time off to have a family.' Penny Hughes agrees with Charles Handy and Rosabeth Moss Kanter that it is most important to develop transferable skills that will provide employability rather than conceive progress in hierarchical terms.

22

Career Development and Career Paths

Is there a model career path to the top, or experiences that one must have or skills that one should acquire? Do the career paths of chief executives and managing directors have elements in common that distinguish them from less successful colleagues? What can be learned from their own experiences and what do they view as important? What should be avoided?

There is virtual consensus that there is no 'model' route to the top. There do, however, appear to be common elements in the experience of many, if not most, business leaders.

EARLY LINE MANAGEMENT RESPONSIBILITY / EARLY SUCCESS

Almost everyone had very significant early responsibility (before their early thirties), often being thrown into the deep end to sink or swim and conspicuously succeeding. By the age of 45, most of the sample were already chief executives of major PLCs or in the case of women business leaders running a business or business unit. This was as likely to be true for the older generation as for new business leaders in spite of a general view that chief executives are getting younger.

There are always exceptions for exceptional people. A powerful exception to this pattern was Graham Day's taking over Cammell Laird shipbuilders as Chief Executive at the age of 38 without any previous line management experience. His excellent strategic brain, ability to focus on what was important and to bring people with him, and his knowledge of the industry enabled him to be successful.

Jean Denton at 44 was given the opportunity to run Herondrive because of the credibility afforded by an eclectic background which included marketing and racing car driving!

Gaining early general management experience was regarded as critical by the majority of people. In Charles Mackay's words:

There is no substitute for learning the hard way and making your
own mistakes, finding what works and what doesn't, starting out
small and then moving on to something bigger. General management forces you to think of all aspects of the business. The actual
size of the unit doesn't matter – developing the ability to think
about a number of functions simultaneously and their impact on
profit is what's important.

At 32, two years after joining Courtaulds, Martin Taylor became
Managing Director of part of the clothing business, which has been
the most developmentally important experience of his career thus far.
Unconventionally, he does not believe it necessary to 'start small'.
'Although I was managing a business unit of a couple of thousand
people, you never really manage more than twenty wherever you are.
I think people get very hung up on numbers. It's irrelevant whether
you are managing twenty or two thousand.'

Gerry Robinson valued the early opportunity general management
provided to see the business in the round and to demystify other parts
of the business which he had not understood. Jean Denton points out
that it is easier to measure one's performance in line management – 'if
you are in a function, everyone has a different opinion of how you are
performing'.

Success in early roles of significant responsibility not only provides
a track record and reputation, a 'stepping-stone' for rapid promotion
to senior management but most importantly develops the skills and
approaches required in senior roles. The more difficult the management challenge, the better. As concluded by McCall, Lombardo and
Morrison, 'comfortable circumstances are hardly the road to the top'
(1988, p. 58).

BROAD FUNCTIONAL EXPERIENCE

Almost all of the sample had broad experience across a number of
different business functions and businesses, most, if not all in finance,
marketing and sales and operations and attributed their success to
this breadth.

Bill Castell's story was a common one:

I was extremely lucky that a career path was determined for me
within Wellcome that gave me a breadth of experience. I had

finance, marketing, production, R&D and general management and not many people get that, you are usually single function. That experience gave me a vocabulary that allows me to be a more capable generalist.

Other people who like Castell began and were successful in finance such as Allen Sheppard, Neville Bain and Gerry Robinson, moved into sales and marketing, then general management. Allen Sheppard advises:

> By the early thirties move away from your narrow functional specialisation and particularly develop sales and marketing skills if you haven't already done so. Don't become too far advanced along a functional line such as finance without breadth unless your career objective is to become a top finance professional.

Ann Iverson spent most of her retailing career in the buying function but the unusual move into operations provided her with almost unique breath for her move into general management. Breadth was not always achieved by being directly responsible for different functions. At CP, Graham Day began as a lawyer, but increasingly advised on commercial issues across a wide variety of CP's activities. Archie Norman, Chief Executive of Asda at 38 after five years as Finance Director at Kingfisher and seven years at McKinsey, had advised on corporate strategy across a wide range of companies and industries. Martin Taylor as a financial journalist gained similarly broad knowledge of industry and finance.

Another means of achieving breadth of perspective is to work in a small company, where no one can afford to be too specialised. Neville Bain speaks of the benefit of beginning his career with Cadbury Schweppes in New Zealand, a market of four million people. 'New Zealand business is small, compact and easier to see the big picture. One is involved in the whole business system, not a specialist experiencing a very narrow part. There is the ability to move across frontiers.'

In their study of 'derailed' executives, high flyers who never fulfilled their promise, McCall and Lombardo (1983) concluded that what distinguished their experience from those who succeeded was a series of successes in similar situations, where the challenges and learning opportunities were the same.

INTERNATIONAL EXPERIENCE

The value of international experience was stressed again and again throughout the interviews and aspiring senior managers almost invariably advised to gain it. Given that I was particularly interested in international experience and chose the sample partly on this basis, it is no surprise that only three people had not lived outside of the UK for at least a year.

In the past, working abroad in large companies was often seen as risky, taking oneself from the corporate centre to the sidelines where one might be forgotten. Increasingly it is seen as essential for senior managers in large multinational companies. In Korn/Ferry Carré/ Orban International's 1994 Board of Directors Study, 37 per cent of Chairmen and CEOs over 50 in the UK had spent more than six months overseas and only slightly more (40 per cent) of those under 50.

The experience of living or working in another culture, the direct understanding that there is more than one way of looking at the world, approaching problems, doing things, is of course an important contributor to a characteristic of leadership to be examined later – the search for best practice and 'life-long learning'.

Working for a company headquartered in a country not your own also provides the cultural jolt of international experience. Thus Allen Sheppard working for Ford and John Egan for General Motors experienced unexpected cultural differences while working in the UK for American companies.

Although international experience was highly valued, it was surprising that many business leaders in both generations were not fluent in another language.

Charles Mackay, one of the most deeply international chief executives in the UK, was among the exceptions, learning French in Algeria, Dutch in Holland and German. In the 1994 study mentioned above, there was a significant difference between those chairmen and CEOs over 50 who spoke more than one foreign language (19 per cent) and those under 50 (38 per cent).

LIFE-LONG LEARNING AND CONTINUOUS IMPROVEMENT

Early line responsibility, breadth of functional experience and international experience may be useful but they are not alone sufficient to provide the development necessary – it is obviously critical what the individual does with his or her opportunities.

It was clear that our business leaders are life-long learners, continuing to grow and develop throughout life. As Neville Bain notes, 'Continuous learning and development is a must, "one must continue to journey and never arrive"'. Fundamental to learning, particularly learning from mistakes, is seeking to understand and 'improve' oneself. In the pursuit of self-knowledge or as a result of that knowledge, many business leaders are intensely self-critical. For instance, Christopher Hogg considers himself too orderly in his thinking.

> I keep coming back to the fact that I am probably my own sternest critic and ten times a day I laugh at myself for doing something because I say, 'There you go again. It's just because you have an orderly mind, you shouldn't be doing this, you should be doing that'. I just know myself quite well by now.

Bill Castell is very deferential about his own abilities; although many consider him to be a risk-taker he is critical of his innate conservatism, which he consciously struggles against.

It was in this context that Steve Shirley underwent psychoanalysis to come to terms with her early trauma as a child refugee, which provided her with the strength, confidence and self-understanding to develop professionally and personally.

Learning from experience was valued above all although several business leaders mentioned that they were avid readers of management books and a few that they valued training courses. John Egan is disciplined about training:

> I always make sure that there are a couple of days each year where I am basically learning – from peers, from educational places, where ever! I would advise people to ensure that their personal training programme keeps them up to the cutting edge of skills they need.

LEARNING FROM HARDSHIPS, MISTAKES AND OBSTACLES

There is no doubt that mistakes and failures are one of the most powerful sources of development and learning for most business leaders. It is not the mistakes themselves (or absence of them) that distinguishes leaders but how they deal with and learn from them. As is clear to psychologists, good mental health becomes clearest when the going gets tough and mental toughness and resilience are critically important to leadership.

Many of the business leaders identified mistakes from which they had learned. Often, however, no single mistake stood out and it was frequently acknowledged that there were mistakes from which one could not recover, either because they would be psychologically disabling or because of loss of external credibility.

The failures/setbacks mentioned by the business leaders fell into three major categories.

- Business mistakes and failures.
- Career mistakes.
- Mistakes, traumas in personal life.

Business mistakes

Richard Giordano provides a clear example of a business misjudgement resulting in multi-million dollar losses, acceptance of responsibility, learning from the mistake and moving on. He recognises too the value of mistakes as necessary to development, to the extent that someone with a flawless track record is regarded as unproved.

> This sounds like a cliché but I think mistakes do form character. Whenever I interview a guy for a senior position I ask him about his mistakes. I am very suspicious of someone who has never made any. If he has never made any, I wonder how he would behave if he made a great big mistake. We either have an untested character or he has made mistakes and he's not telling the truth.

Many business leaders cite mistakes in choosing, promoting or dealing with people as important. For Gerry Robinson the circumstances of the departure of David Plowright, the Head of Television at Granada was a failure he regrets. Liam Strong also considers his greatest mistakes to have been people decisions – increasingly, he needs less evidence, less time to make up his mind.

In witnessing the optimism about people necessary to bring out the best in them, it is inevitable that mistakes will be made. As expressed by Christopher Hogg:

I am guilty of constant failures of judgement in handling people, particularly in matching people to jobs or levels of responsibility. But I believe that in this respect in business you have got to keep taking risks. You have got to keep pushing people out of their depth or beyond their reach. Incidentally the success ratio is comfortably more than 50 per cent but that means that a third or more decisions are 'failures' to a greater or lesser extent and with those one can kick oneself for not seeing this or that.

Career mistakes

In speaking of his two career mistakes, agreeing in 1975 to plan the nationalisation of shipbuilders, and in the early 1980s to accept a secondment from Dalhousie University to Dome Petroleum, Graham Day outlines not only the self-analysis required to learn from mistakes but also the staying with them, living out the consequences fully.

> You learn from mistakes, but you know that you have taken a duff decision. It is important also not to walk away from those decisions, to work your way through them, to honour the commitment you've given. That's very important. Analyse what you got right and what you got wrong.

Neil Shaw speaks not of any specific failure, but of the times in his career when his performance/learning/experience were suboptimised, often because of personal chemistry and the lesson he drew from this.

> I can't think of any massive failures – a calamity of going bankrupt or something of that kind. There are the inevitable times when you realise you didn't do so well, perhaps getting fed up with the job or a failure to relate to my immediate boss. It's part of a normal career pattern when the chemistry doesn't work between two people. You might both be very bright but not be able to mix. So when I place people throughout the organisation, it's important to find out who they are working with.

Personal mistakes

Jean Denton's remembered mistakes are personal academic disappointment and the failure of her marriage. For Neville Bain and Neil

Shaw, the failure of their marriage is also regarded as a mistake for which they are responsible.

> There's no question that having a divorce is a personal failure. People can grow into different people as they get older and can grow apart, with neither one at fault. Your objectives and how you want to live became different because you have been exposed to different things. It's a failure in terms of your kids because it hurt them very badly. In my case, the divorce didn't happen until they were all through university so it was not quite the same as being married with six-year-olds – none the less it is a failure. (Neil Shaw)

In Shaw's view the harshest failure would relate to 'parents/children. The rest you can beat'.

Nor has unbroken academic success been a feature in all business leaders' lives. Several people experienced early academic failure. Like Jean Denton, who took three tries before winning a scholarship, Bill Castell took his 'O' levels several times before passing.

Although Graham Day was a good student he was very unhappy at high school, and his first two years at university, frequently challenging teachers and being expelled from classes.

Recovery from failure

Not only is response to failure critical but there was a general recognition that there are failures from which one would not recover, because of either the impact on reputation or one's self-confidence. Neil Shaw emphasises the importance of tenacity: 'You can have a couple of failures over a couple of years if you are convinced that you are going to come out of that failure and be successful. You have got to have some staying power, not just to pack up and leave.'

Had I been researching this book a few years ago, I might have approached people who have since 'fallen from grace'. Are these people no longer successful? It is also of course possible that one or more of the people included in this book will suffer the same fate. What is it to be a success?

Many people considered that the UK business environment judges certain kinds of failure too harshly, without distinguishing between unethical behaviour, misfortune arising from calculated risk and external, environmental changes. Many felt that the the environment in the US is far more forgiving of honest but misjudged risk-taking. Liam Strong believes that not only in the US but worldwide there is greater tolerance of mistakes – it is up to the individual to learn and to recover.

> Frankly, rehabilitation from failure depends on the individual. Recovery is to do with your ability to rethink yourself and go out and do it again. One knows a number of people who come a cropper and you can see one person who has got a chance of doing it again and another who has basically lost self-confidence. In the US people who have failed still have value. I wonder whether you analyse the reasons for your success as closely as you analyse the reasons why you have failed.

Gerry Robinson believes that recovery from failure is usually dependent on a track record of success.

> If you get a few things wrong at the wrong time, you've just had it, I suspect. You can probably have failures and still reach the top after you've had some successes. Like most things, a great deal depends on finding yourself in the right situation.

Christopher Hogg, acknowledging that he makes 'endless mistakes', also distinguishes between the mistakes he can accept and those that would dispirit him.

> I agree that an important part of the art of being successful is to learn from your failures but not to let them get you down. I can live with a wrong decision which has been properly thought through. But if I make a big and risky decision carelessly and that's my fault, then I not only kick myself for falling short of standards but I also brood about it as well. Someone who is kicking themselves and losing confidence is just no good to anybody else so I avoid getting myself into those sort of situations or else I try always to go through a process that lets me off the hook. I go through a process of consulting others. But what other people might call failures wouldn't necessarily worry me at all provided I thought that I had handled them in a sensible way.

THE ROLE OF MENTORS

It is commonly assumed that business leaders have benefited from a mentor, in Levinson's terms, an older, senior person who has served as sponsor, teacher, guide, exemplar, counsel and moral support (p. 98). Levinson (1978) in *The Seasons of a Man's Life* notes that the mentor is usually older by half a generation (eight to fifteen years) and experienced as a responsible, admired older sibling with the relationship usually lasting two to three years and eight to ten at most. (In his study few had received mentoring.)

Most people of the older generation identified mentors as important to decision-making and their careers, in some cases following the pattern of a somewhat older superior, in others with older bosses who served as exemplars and supporters. John Harvey-Jones, Steve Shirley and Jean Denton were alone in this generation in identifying no single mentor, but a number of people who had supported them.

Most books advising women on how to succeed stress the importance of a mentor relationship – in practice Penny Hughes is an exception in identifying two mentors in the fullest sense of the term. Such books also emphasise the value of networking for women, and both Jean Denton and Steve Shirley have been conscientious networkers.

Of the 'new' chief executives, just over half were influenced by mentors. Perhaps this also reflects the relatively active role that many younger chief executives have played in their own career moves.

NON-EXECUTIVE DIRECTORSHIPS AND OUTSIDE INTERESTS

All the business leaders sit on the boards of other companies or non-profit organisations and frequent mention was made of the value of such involvement. For instance, Archie Norman notes: 'If you don't have that broader vision and outside interests, the small things that happen in your own company become disproportionately important and you get upset and worked up about them and then it starts to get to you.'

Frequent mention was also made of the value of a different perspective on the business issues of one's own company, the recognition that there is more than one way of doing business.

WHAT TO AVOID

The flip side of 'what to do to get to the top' is of course what not to do. How do promising business leaders become 'derailed' and what should be avoided?

Politics and excessive ambition

Although there are as many books advising people to cultivate image and to spend energy marketing themselves, being seen in the right places as there are those advising people to attend to performance, there was little or no support among business leaders for such an approach. Both in reflecting on their own careers and much more commonly, observing the behaviour of colleagues, they concluded overwhelmingly that excessive attention to rewards, image, personal ambition was counterproductive. Such an approach was seen to work some of the time, but very rarely in the long term. In fact, excessive ambition, thinking of the next job, playing politics was found in one American study to be one of the key causes of derailment of successful executives (McCall and Lombardo, 1983).

John Harvey-Jones provides a persuasive anecdote about the dangers and inefficacy of excessive personal ambition. He portrays his own experience at 40 when constantly seeking to demonstrate his corporate superiority over his competitor at ICI he diverted too much energy from doing his job to pursuing personal professional interests. He also feels it is the time he did his least good work – wasted years. Characteristically, however, he learned from this experience.

There was virtual consensus that one does not get away with political, self-interested behaviour as it is both transparent and ineffective:

> If you are excessively ambitious, then it distorts everything you do. I have seen people who, as they make a recommendation, think 'well, that's the business issue. Now how is it going to suit me.' Over time it becomes quite transparent, so there are limits to the extent to which one can trust their judgement. (Liam Strong)

It is also true that Machiavellian strategies may take people one level above their natural level of competence, which is not only uncomfortable but dangerous. As John Harvey-Jones notes:

> Playing politics is quite successful professionally for quite a lot of people and it depends to some degree on what you want. If I had a nightmare it would be getting a job which I couldn't do. And if you actually play politics to get jobs, you are likely to find just that.

The walk-on-water syndrome

Many business leaders showed great sensitivity to the intrinsic danger of leadership and of power referred to by Liam Strong as 'the walk-on-water syndrome'.

> The walk-on-water syndrome is very dangerous because the more senior you get, the more people tend to agree rather than disagree with you and you can understand why. One of the critical things is to give people permission to disagree with you and to create an atmosphere where people speak their minds. It sounds silly to say that but the number of people who are prepared to go to the trouble to disagree with you is very few.

Bill Castell actively seeks feedback from people he knows will tell him the truth and welcomes positive criticism. Neville Bain recognises the dangers of power, of believing one is infallible and stopping listening and counteracts this in the same way as Liam Strong and Bill Castell – through strong, independent-minded colleagues. 'I say to my people that I don't want people who are going to agree with me necessarily. I want irritants in the best sense of the word – people who make me think of something that I haven't thought of before.'

McCall and Lombardo confirmed the ineffectiveness of narcissistic behaviour over time in finding that, along with specific performance problems, the most frequent cause of derailment of senior executives was insensitivity to others and an abrasive, intimidating, bullying style. Coldness, aloofness and arrogance also was an important factor (as cited in McCall, Lombardo and Morrison, 1988, pp. 168–9).

Women's career development

As a group, the careers of the women differ in some ways from those of the men, and offer an interesting representation of possible career paths for successful women in business, and different ways of integrating family and occupational roles (the latter will be dealt with at greater length in the next chapter).

There are of course hardly any women in the UK running major public companies, and the obvious exception, Anita Roddick, is not only the Chief Executive but also the Founder of The Body Shop. Only Ann Iverson in the sample, now running a billion dollar company in the US, has been Chief Executive of a major company and there is necessarily greater diversity among our women business leaders.

The two 'new' business leaders, Penny Hughes and Ann Iverson, thus far have pursued relatively linear careers, to an observer indistinguishable from the careers of men in their industries. On closer examination, however, Ann Iverson has probably had more lateral moves on her way to the top because of her family circumstances and Penny Hughes, with a new child, withdraws for a few years from this linear path when she leaves Coca-Cola in October 1995 to pursue a portfolio of interests.

The two women no longer actively leading businesses, Steve Shirley and Jean Denton, had far from conventional linear careers in companies. Steve Shirley as an entrepreneur who founded her own business 30 years ago represents an alternative increasingly pursued by women who seek flexibility and more control over their working lives, while Jean Denton's career path for the first fourteen years was characterised by frequent, usually lateral changes driven by interest rather than obvious career logic. (Driver has labelled such an unstructured pattern as 'transitory', and White, Cox and Cooper have identified it as quite common for the successful women in their study (1992, p. 108).) However, following her natural interests resulted in an eclectic mix of skills, including marketing and, improbably, racing car driving, which equipped her for a more stable period in her career and general management. Although Denton shares a few career regrets, both she and Steve Shirley have been generally fulfilled professionally, not least in their current roles respectively as a working peer and as a 'third age' manager of a portfolio of directorships and other interests.

Most importantly, all four women have adopted the same learning approach to their experience.

Most business leaders volunteered no special or separate advice for women. The women in the study advised women to be themselves, 'not to clone', in Denton's words. Ann Iverson advises women 'to forget gender' and notes that she was herself completely and unambiguously not approachable as a women at work. If ever she sensed obvious discrimination, she would 'shut the door' and straightforwardly express what she was observing.

None of the women mentioned discrimination as an ultimately debilitating factor in their careers (even though Steve Shirley changed her name to 'Steve' from Stephanie to get through the door with her early business development efforts at FI). It was less her position as a women than as a creative thinker that prompted Shirley to start her own company. 'I originally went into business because of being blocked in the corporate world. In talking to business leaders, I always stress the need to retain the mavericks and innovators as "intrapreneurs".' Penny Hughes, at least 15 years younger than the others, saw discrimination as a non-issue and performance as key:

> I believe that women are their own worst enemies – they expect to be treated differently and therefore discern a difference. In my experience, organisations value performance.

Both Jean Denton and Steve Shirley, members of a group of top women over 50 referred to by Shirley as 'pioneers', did, however, have separate advice for ambitious women.

Steve Shirley refers to research that shows that one of the biggest obstacles to women's progress is lack of confidence which results in low career aspirations and reluctance to take on leadership roles. 'For many women, doing the job well is what matters most – being seen to do a good job is seldom regarded as important.' Therefore her advice to women relates in part to appearances, no doubt because she believes that women already are highly motivated about performance itself. She advises women 'firstly to up their energy levels by regular exercise, secondly to dress more like a leader, and thirdly to learn and use body language.'

Jean Denton agrees that women need to be more visible and active about self-promotion:

> I wouldn't have to tell men to keep moving and planning but it is necessary to tell women. Otherwise they become too comfortable. If you want to stay where you are, that's fine, but if you want to move up a corporate ladder, and want a new challenge, you will have to look ahead and tell people what you want.

Penny Hughes, in her 30s, very natural and self-confident, has succeeded by focusing on performance but has also been upfront when she thought she deserved promotion. Her approach to her career has been uncontrived but active. For both men and women, commitment above all to a job well-done is considered key to success and over time, with more role models, perhaps the special advice given to women by 'pioneers' will be less necessary.

23

Family and Personal Lives

Given the long hours and energy devoted to work, how have our business leaders balanced their personal and professional lives? Are their family lives as fulfilling and 'successful' as their working lives? Are there intergenerational differences and how have the women particularly juggled the demands of family (if any) and career. Can one both head up a large company and sustain close and happy relationships with a partner and children. What is the relationship between success at work and happiness at home and is it changing?

THE 'OLDER GENERATION'

Previous studies suggest that a supportive partner and family provide an important ballast to the lives of business leaders. This finding is not supported by our small sample of eighteen – eight marriages had failed and ten survived.

One of the few intergenerational differences tentatively discerned was that most of the younger generation of chief executives accorded a higher priority to their personal lives than most of the older generation.

Other than Steve Shirley, those of the 'older generation' with stable marriages, Graham Day, John Harvey-Jones, John Egan still speak poignantly about the sacrifices made, and putting work before family for most if not all of their careers. 'When the family's needs have conflicted with the needs of the job, other than providing for the family, the job wins. The family understands but I resented it' (Graham Day).

For much of John Harvey-Jones's career, he put career before family but at a certain point, although he continued to work long hours, his priorities changed.

> I will always need to believe that my work is worthwhile and of value, but now I know that there are many other things in my life which matter more. This feeling freed me to take risks and to stick to my belief in ways which I now realise actually made me more

likely to move ahead rather than the reverse. (Harvey-Jones, 1992, p. 305)

Both Graham Day and John Harvey-Jones diligently compartmentalise work and family lives, in an attempt to protect their valued private lives.

For Steve Shirley combining the demands of work and a mentally handicapped son at times had an impact on her own health and wellbeing.

Of the eight people who were divorced or separated, Allen Sheppard, Neville Bain, Neil Shaw, Gerry Robinson are remarried. Most, but not all, regard their divorce as failure, and as the result of excessive work and growing apart. Richard Giordano, recently divorced, speaks for his generation of CEOs.

> For people like me, work is a very, very jealous mistress. You try your best to have a private life and some succeed, some do not. It's not easy. Not only do wives suffer but children suffer. I have been lucky. I've got three grown-up, healthy, solid kids. No drug problems. But I know that they missed me and I wish that I had seen more of them over the years. I've got friends in business who have got kids with real problems, caused by the lethal combination of two ingredients – the inattention of parents and privilege. Professional priorities inevitably took priority in my life.

THE NEW GENERATION OF CEOs

Many of the younger generation did not evidence the same conflict and were more likely to acknowledge either that family came first or the importance and possibility of balance. Bill Castell, for instance, outlined his family details first on his curriculum vitae. He unambiguously puts his family first – his primary goal is happiness at home, although he acknowledges that he works long hours. 'I abuse the family because I am at work too much but if it's a choice between the family and work, then it is the family.'

Castell does believe that there is a generational difference in the value placed on work and the sacrifices his generation is willing to make. The older generation were in a 'survival' mode while his generation has the greater freedom of prosperity. This is supported by a survey of 12,000 men and women in 25 countries published by the

Harvard Business Review in 1991, which revealed that family life, education and the environment were the most important concerns of senior international managers. The typical senior manager respondent in the survey was male, in his early forties, married and bilingual.

For Penny Hughes, career emphatically does not come first. 'Life comes first but business is a fundamental part of life, and if there were an imbalance either way, I would correct it.' She works reasonable hours, never takes work home or works on weekends.

Gerry Robinson, although once divorced, fits into the pattern now of balanced personal and professional lives, arriving at work after 9 a.m. and almost always leaving before 6 p.m. He also likes to make sure that he takes 'plenty of Fridays off'.

Martin Taylor on the other hand acknowledges that he balances his personal and professional lives very badly and that his family suffers as a result, although he puts neither work nor family first. 'You render unto Caesar that which is Caesar's and leave the rest for God. One has to be sensible.'

Several of the successful marriages of the younger generation are 'interdependent' (Cox and Cooper, 1988, p. 67) with both parties having careers and supporting each other in their professional and personal lives.

WORKING WOMEN

Balancing career and family lives is of course a major issue for working women. Either women forgo children or both marriage and children, take career breaks or strive, often with great guilt and discomfort, to combine both. Our four women provide 'models' of different solutions.

Jean Denton is divorced, with no children, and has been able without conflict to devote herself to her work. Significantly she regrets divorcing her husband recognising in maturity that her marriage was better than most. Believing that 'team is best', she believes that her life could be better balanced if she were part of a team. She not only regrets her divorce but appreciates the financial freedom her marriage gave her and is philosophical about the give and take required of marriage.

Steve Shirley founded her own company in order flexibly to combine work and family. Her husband is endlessly supportive, and although she has worked punishingly long hours, she has also

created enough flexibility to spend time with her mentally handicapped son. This course was not without a toll, however, and at one
time she experienced a fully fledged nervous breakdown from the
stress of trying to combine both.

Penny Hughes, in her mid-thirties, is a good example of the
younger generation of manager, both male and female, who intend
to balance, without guilt, family and work. She told The Coca-Cola
Company when she joined that she intended to have children, and as
a new mother, has now chosen to leave the corporate mainstream for
a while to lead a more flexible 'portfolio' existence, including sitting
on the Board of The Body Shop. Observing her sisters and friends she
concludes that working mothers, full or part-time, can be just as
good, if not better, than those who stay at home. Although this
conclusion is not universally accepted, it represents a hopeful alternative and one pursued full-time, and without a career break, by Ann
Iverson.

Ann Iverson has two adult children and consciously and unambiguously puts them first in her priorities, with work second and
herself third 'which is why four of my marriages have failed'. Her
experience is particularly helpful to working women who struggle with
the question of conflicting priorities, guilt and consequent ambivalence about work. Her solution is to put her children first when they
need her and to give her work 100 per cent when she is there.

> Even though I have worked all my life, my children always come
> first. They come first in different ways at different times in their
> lives. If I have a very important meeting and they need me, I don't
> hesitate to cancel. If there is a school play, you *are* there. When
> they start growing up and studying and there are warning signals
> that something is wrong, you must be willing to give up work and
> time and to do something about it. I always made sure that I
> attended all school events, was there for all birthdays and whenever
> they were sick. Everyone at work can be replaced and you just
> can't bring back those times when you were needed by your
> children and not there.

For the working woman or man, the most successful strategy appears
to be:

> *to compartmentalise home and work, to be committed without*
> *reservation to work while there while having crystal clear priorities*
> *about when important personal demands will have priority.*

24

The Attributes of Leadership

What is so special about leaders? What sets them apart? How can you tell whether someone is a leader? Do you have what it takes? Can leadership be developed?

Search consultants are always being asked to find a 'leader' and it is conventional wisdom that contemporary conditions of unremitting change require leaders not managers.

But what are the attributes of leadership? Numerous empirical studies have been devoted to identifying the special qualities or characteristics of leaders. Different variables have been selected, evaluated and subjected to multivariate analysis, attempting to provide a scientific basis for a list of leadership characteristics. No study of leaders has yet produced a description of leadership qualities that is recognised as statistically significant.

What then are the views of our business leaders about the qualities of leadership, what do they look for in their high-flyers and do they believe that the chief executive in the year 2000 will be different from today? What does it take to reach the top in business?

If there was consensus, it was on the impossibility of defining a set of necessary and sufficient attributes that define leaders – all agreed that business leaders come in all shapes and sizes, with different styles, approaches, strengths and weaknesses. Several people were also swift to demystify the notion of business leadership, reinforcing that chief executives are not heroes, not perfect, but share the same all-too-human mixture of strengths and weaknesses as the rest of the population.

If no checklist is finally adequate, everyone none the less had a view about the relative importance of key qualities for 'true' leadership which not surprisingly resonated when business leaders identified the strengths they sought in the high-flyers within their companies. In summary these qualities were found to be vision, people skills, character and drive. Evidence of such qualities and leadership potential was sought in track record, the ability to operate effectively in teams, commitment to organisational objectives and independence/willingness to be counted.

LEADERSHIP QUALITIES

Vision

Whether described as 'long-term strategic thinking', vision, 'seeing the wood for the trees', 'the big picture outlook' or 'helicopter vision', almost all business leaders, supported by the leadership literature, give vision as the *sine qua non* of leadership attributes, exemplified by Jean Denton's pragmatic 'if you don't know where you're going, you have no hope of getting there'.

Most consider the goal, the purpose, the mission or vision in business necessarily to be a simple one. Gerry Robinson is swift to demystify vision as complicated:

> There is a tendency to think of a vision as something rather sophisticated and complex but actually most visions are terribly simple. 'I will rule the world' is the most classic and most simple of all visions, isn't it? You do have a vision as to what it is you are trying to do, at both a personal level and at a corporate level. It is important to be very clear, very repetitive, very simple about that. It is essential that people know what success is.

Neville Bain provides the classical expression of strategic vision making.

> The leader has got to have a clear vision that is capable of being enunciated in a simple way. At Coats Viyella we have a company mission statement and objectives which provide a statement of values and a framework. It is a bit like the rules of the game. You give your team freedom but there are some guiding principles they need to understand. It's not novel – just straight old standard business school principles applied to our business but it's had a big impact. Then the leader makes sure that he has got the right troops in the right jobs, gives them room to do their job within the constraints that he sets down, and helps them as team coach.

But where does the ability to think strategically come from? Is it independent from or related to intelligence? At least one business thinker, John Kotter, Harvard Business School professor, while also demystifying vision persuasively emphasises the importance of intelligence in its operation.

Too often, I fear, we fall into the romantic trap of believing that great vision comes from magic or divine grace. In the business world, it rarely (if ever) does. Great vision emerges when a powerful mind, working long and hard on massive amounts of information is able to see (or recognise in suggestions from others) interesting patterns and new possibilities. (Kotter, 1988, p. 29)

Does it in fact require a 'powerful mind' to successfully lead a complex business?

Although there was some ambivalence expressed on the need for high levels of intelligence, many people recognised it as important for leaders of large organisations, because of the enormous complexity of business. In Christopher Hogg's words:

Whatever else it is, business is an intellectual exercise. I could never understand how the impression arose that industry was a place for morons. I personally find it fantastically demanding on intellectual resources. You are dealing with an enormous range of variables. You are always trying to make decisions on inadequate information and against time. It means a constant process of selection of priorities.

On the other hand, Gerry Robinson, believing that business is essentially straightforward, does not share the view that high levels of intelligence are required of business leaders.

The danger of a high intellect is that it can veer into overintellectualising a business problem that is essentially very simple. People with lots of nous but average intelligence can be enormously successful in running large companies. You can learn very quickly what the ten key issues are in a company and unfortunately seven of them will be the same every time for every company!

As did Kotter, Kets de Vries (1989) in *Prisoners of Leadership* notes the relationship between creating the vision and the leader's ability to recognise patterns and relationships in disjointed events (p. 201). Leaders are seen as 'reducers' who are able to limit the stimuli impinging on them, handle multiple activities without discomfort and deal with complex, novel, interesting situations 'without impaired task performance, cognitive disorganisation or health problems' (p. 202). Gerry Robinson in examining a complex environment and articulating a simple vision is clearly a 'reducer', as is Penny Hughes, as she describes the ease with which she charts the right direction:

I have an uncanny feel for business which I find hard to share with or teach other people. It probably goes back to my training as a chemist and my maths. Without a calculator, or bit of paper I can work out the value of any decision almost to the last pound which really makes decision making easy. I think I have got a clear strategic brain and one that reaches the bottom line very quickly.

In the complex environment of today's multinationals, there seems little doubt that such 'reducing' requires a high level of a certain kind of intelligence – a good basic IQ.

Although creating a vision and direction for the company requires analysis, it also goes beyond analysis. For instance, Martin Taylor trusts his intuition more than his mind, believing that if his instincts do not support a conclusion it simply suggests that more information is required.

Reducing complexity and crystallising the vision is both the product of analysis and intuition and requires both the right and left brains. For this reason many who identified their Myers Briggs types were 'intuitives', seeing the possibilities, rather than 'sensing', most comfortable with facts and details.

If most agreed that intelligence was vital, many emphasized that it was clearly not sufficient. As often, people mentioned 'common sense' as critical.

Although intelligence is innate, to the extent that recognising patterns presupposes knowledge and understanding, creating a vision for a business also requires learning from the very experiences and approach outlined in Chapter 22.

People and communication skills

'People skills', an ability to communicate with and motivate people were recognised as fundamental to leadership.

Given that by definition a leader needs followers, the vision must be compellingly and clearly communicated to motivate people to action. Although the leadership literature speaks of 'charismatic' or inspirational communication, it is very clear from our sample, that not all business leaders are extraverts. In fact, many of the most successful are introverts.

It is clearly less eloquence than credibility that matters in motivating people. Thus no one spoke only of the need for communication skills. Jean Denton spoke of the ability to share the direction with people openly and honestly, Gerry Robinson of the need for consistency, people knowing where they stand, Martin Taylor of the ability to inspire trust. Martin Taylor himself enjoys above all the emotional and motivational aspect of management and describes his approach to management as 'feminine'.

Fundamental to motivating people is genuinely understanding, appreciating and empowering them. Penny Hughes believes that at the heart of her success is that she values people and creates an environment where they want to give of their best. Richard Giordano concurs: 'Having forged a vision and charted a course, the leader must create an environment where performance is valued, where people want to perform.'

Indeed, closely related to the ability to inspire trust were the next qualities identified by the majority as important to leadership.

Integrity/character

Perhaps the rather old-fashioned word, character, best epitomises a set of qualities that people judged to be fundamental to true leadership. These related not only to honesty and fairness but also to compassion, humility and being one's own person. Thus, above all else, Graham Day believes honesty to be integral to leadership. Martin Taylor looks for courage, generosity and imagination and Richard Giordano, Penny Hughes and Ann Iverson, fairness. Bill Castell values sound personal qualities and sincerity. Christopher Hogg emphasises the importance of putting the organisation first in order to win trust.

Not a single business leader supported the importance of understanding organisational politics or of cultivating image – getting to the top is, or should be, overwhelmingly about substance and performance. As Penny Hughes expresses: 'Tact and awareness are important, but the world is moving quickly enough for performance to be more important than politics.'

An integral part of earning the trust that is so vital to leadership is being one's own person and, as Gerry Robinson notes, there is a necessary loneliness to leadership. In this context, Professor of Business Administration at the University of Southern California, Warren Bennis speaks of the leaders 'mastering the context', refusing to be deployed by others (Bennis, 1989, pp. 36–7).

Thus Richard Giordano points out the need for both self-discipline and emotional stability to stay the course in leadership. Liam Strong

looks for 'strong-minded' people and understands that in an emotionally demanding role such as CEO, his emotional 'durability' is
necessary.

Along with self-mastery comes non-conformity, marching to one's
own drum. The ability to challenge and lack of conformity is
supported by Cox and Cooper (1988) who tested 26 managing
directors and found *all* to be 'innovators' not adaptors, according
to the Kirton test. They found that managing directors 'do not get to
their positions by following rules and accepting authority' but by
challenging the system, seeking new solutions which also 'challenges
the myth that the way to the top is to "toe the line" and not "make
waves"' (p. 141).

The common assumption about the narcissism and 'large egos' of
leaders was at odds with another frequently cited attribute of true
leadership, particularly by the 'older' generation – the requirement
for humility. For Neil Shaw, lack of arrogance is the key ingredient of
leadership.

Linked at least in part to humility and people skills was the
importance of courtesy and compassion in leadership. Graham
Day, having witnessed the power of implicit courtesy first-hand
from Buck Crump, the Chief Executive at Canadian Pacific, notes:

> Fear does not leadership equal. A friend of mine, Manfred Kets de
> Vries who teaches at INSEAD, used to teach at Harvard with
> Abraham Zaleznik. Zaleznik taught organisational behaviour and
> used to say 'we're woefully short of substance, humanity and
> morality and these are the attributes of leadership. It's not the
> gung-ho, follow-me, John Wayne kind of fix'.

Consistently, although few in the sample were conventionally religious, all expressed a well developed belief system or set of ethics that
provided both meaning to their lives and an ethical foundation for
their actions.

Many people showed a strong sense of duty and social responsibility and spoke particularly of their involvement in the community.
Bill Castell, Neil Shaw and Allen Sheppard were committed to the
developmental value of community involvement for their people.

Drive/ambition

Without exception, the business leaders described themselves as
ambitious and the need for exceptional commitment and drive was

explicitly recognised by most people. Richard Giordano spoke of dedication to winning, Archie Norman about 'driving energy', Iverson and Denton of a desire to come first, Charles Mackay about willpower and determination.

Many leaders attributed their own success simply to not giving up. The issue of motivation was dealt with at greater length under the chapter on motivation and decision-making. Again, it was reinforced that excessive personal ambition, that put self before organisation, was counterproductive as well as obvious.

Closely related to drive, hard work and long hours were accepted by most as necessary to business leadership, although as we have examined there was evidence that some members of the younger generation seek better balance between their professional and personal lives.

Other attributes

Vision, interpersonal skills, character and drive were the four attributes considered by the majority to be necessary for business leadership. No doubt other necessary attributes such as good health, energy and stamina were 'taken as read'. Indeed, physical abilities were rarely mentioned although Steve Shirley mentioned the importance of 'good genes, health record and high energy' and Christopher Hogg advises people to stay fit.

Above all, John Egan sees the ability 'to learn, to change and to motivate' as critical to leadership, reinforcing the already examined importance of an open and learning approach to experience. The business leaders also were optimists and enthusiasts, with the propensity, in the words of Ann Iverson and Christopher Hogg to 'see the glass as half full'.

SELECTING LEADERS AND HIGH FLYERS

Selecting the right management team is fundamental to successful business leadership and as examined, several people noted that they continued to make mistakes in this area, usually because they were over-optimistic about an individual's capabilities. As the hopeful evaluation of potential and taking calculated risks is critical in giving those with promise an opportunity to prove themselves, the best one can hope for is to reduce mistakes through understanding the attributes important to success. Although there was the expected correlation between the qualities they saw as necessary for leadership and those they sought in their management team, the emphasis was also different.

Track record

Above all, in selecting their high flyers, business leaders looked for experience and a track record of success. In identifying the attributes of leadership, track record had been taken very much for granted. Yet Kotter points out that demonstrated success might be the basis for continued success, because of the need for credibility and that proven performance and continued performance are vital in order to retain leadership.

> Attracting and maintaining the large network of resources necessary to accomplish a sound agenda demands enormous *credibility* which in turn usually requires (1) a very impressive track record and a good reputation (2) solid cooperative working relationships with lots of the relevant players in the industry or company or both and (3) the interpersonal capacity and integrity that are needed to develop credible relationships with a broad set of people fairly easily and quickly. (Kotter, 1988, p. 29)

As pointed out in *The Lessons of Experience*, the limitation of using successful track record alone is that this may not distinguish executives who later succeed from those who later derail. The authors suggest evaluating a cluster of skills/abilities in addition to examination of track record. (Including ability to set reasonable agenda, ability to handle diverse relationships, temperament to adjust to givens of managerial life, integrity, treatment of others, self-insight, ability to learn from experience.) (McCall, Lombardo and Morrison, 1988, p. 165)

Interpersonal skills and team orientation

Indeed, the ability to get along with others, specifically as a member of a team was identified as critical in promoting young managers.

Commitment and motivation

People who were not only highly motivated to succeed personally but more importantly who were committed to organisational objectives distinguished themselves. Neville Bain speaks of the need to be hungry for success, Steve Shirley of the importance of high energy, Liam Strong of people taking their work seriously, Archie Norman of people who are still fighting.

Independence

In their direct reports, business leaders looked for people who would tell them the truth, however unpalatable. Neville Bain sought 'irritants in the best sense of the word'; Archie Norman, people who are willing to put their head above the parapet and disagree with him; Ann Iverson and John Egan people who took responsibility and John Harvey-Jones those with originality of view.

People therefore sought the same strength of character in their subordinates as identified more generally for leadership but expressed this most fully as autonomy and willingness to be counted. Clearly these attributes are quite rare and of great value to chief executives who need the truth but are so often told what people believe they want to hear.

Other attributes

The majority of people valued experience and track record; inter-personal skills; commitment, particularly to the team; and independence above all in selecting their high flyers. In addition, in choosing members of their senior management team, many people recognised the importance of balancing individual strengths and approaches with several explicitly referring to Meredith Belbin's work on the composition of effective teams and the importance of including different personality types and perspectives. Christopher Hogg and Martin Taylor both seek people with strengths different from their own. Charles Mackay looks for a combination of 'producers and organisers' at Inchcape.

Graham Day in choosing future leaders looks for a 'good basic education as broad as possible, both qualitative and quantitative' .

LEADERSHIP IN THE YEAR 2000

As mentioned, in 1989 Korn/Ferry International in conjunction with Columbia University Graduate School of Business undertook a study of over 1500 top executives in twenty countries to gain an understanding of what they considered would be important to leadership in the year 2000. The study entitled *Reinventing the CEO* examined perceptions of what was required of leaders both at the time and in the year 2000 in terms of areas of expertise and personal characteristics. With this report in mind, and also the sort of changes envisaged by such business writers as Rosabeth Moss Kanter, Charles Handy, Tom Peters and John Harvey-Jones, I asked the business leaders in the study whether they thought that the attributes of leadership would be different in five or ten years.

Just as *Reinventing the CEO* concluded that the ideal CEO of the year 2000 'will not be able to meet the new demands by abandoning proven traits', many chief executives emphatically believed that the personal characteristics required of leadership would not change fundamentally, except perhaps to require more of the same. As Jean Denton expressed, 'where the good people are now is what will be required'.

The changes in personal characteristics are neatly encapsulated by Richard Giordano's view that successful managers will have to have both 'Type A' (hard-driving, individualistic, competitive) and 'Type B' (people-oriented, concerned with consensus, etc.) characteristics. John Harvey-Jones talks about the need for a more collaborative, creative and adaptive approach, Charles Mackay about a less autocratic consensus-orientation, Allen Sheppard about the importance of people-awareness, Jean Denton of motivational skills. Penny Hughes believes that future business leaders will need to be more fast-moving and flexible. Liam Strong considers not only that future business leaders will need to lead from 'among rather than on top' but also will have to hold their own with staff who are increasingly expert technically.

In terms of approach to business, several people mentioned the growing importance of being good corporate citizens and of community awareness. Consistently, in *Reinventing the CEO*, the need for ethics was deemed most important for future chief executives, followed by creativity, enthusiasm and open-mindedness.

Inescapably, then, business leaders will continue to require the same clarity of vision, derived from a powerful intellect reducing a complex reality to the critical essentials; the same credible communication and interpersonal skills to articulate the vision compellingly and motivate people to action; the same character, sincerity, generosity and self-mastery to inspire trust, withstand the necessary loneliness of leadership and not fall victim to the 'walk-on-water' syndrome; and the same high levels of motivation and physical energy to achieve the extraordinary.

These qualities, combined with a self-critical, open, flexible and life-long learning approach that draws on a track record of broad functional experience, early successful line management experience, international experience (increasingly) and the lessons to be learned from managing in diversity and adversity in fast-changing conditions will continue to be what it takes to reach the top in the new millennium.

Bibliography

Bateson, Mary Catherine (1990) *Composing a Life, Life as a Work in Progress: the Improvisations of Five Extraordinary Women* (New York: Plume).

Bennis, Warren (1989) *On Becoming a Leader* (London: Century Business).

Bolles, Richard Nelson (1993) *The 1993 What Colour Is Your Parachute? A Practical Manual for Jobhunters and Career Changers* (Berkeley, California: Ten Speed Press).

Briggs-Myers, Isabel and Myers, Peter B. (1980) *Gifts Differing* (Palo Alto, California: Consulting Psychologists Press).

Cadbury, Sir Adrian (1990) *The Company Chairman* (Cambridge: Director Books).

Calvert, Roy, Durkin, Brian, Grandi, Eugenio and Martin, Kevin (1990) *First Find your Hilltop* (London: Hutchinson Business Books).

Cox, Charles J. and Cooper, Cary L. (1988) *High Flyers: An Anatomy of Managerial Success* (Oxford: Basil Blackwell).

Forrest, Andrew and Tolfree, Patrick (1992) *Leaders: The Learning Curve of Achievement* (London: Industrial Society Press).

Gabarro, John J. (1987) *The Dynamics of Taking Charge* (Boston, Mass.: Harvard Business School Press).

Gardner, John W. (1986) *The Nature of Leadership: Introductory Considerations*, Leadership Papers, January 1986. Prepared for the Leadership Studies Program sponsored by the independent sector.

Garfield, Charles (1986) *Peak Performers: The New Heroes in Business* (London: Hutchinson Business).

Goldsmith, Walter and Ritchie, Berry (1987) *The New Elite: Britain's Top Executives* (London: Weidenfeld & Nicolson).

Golzen, Godfrey and Garner, Andrew (1992) *Smart Moves: Successful Strategies and Tactics for Career Management* (London: Penguin).

Guy, Vincent and Matlock, John (1991) *The New International Manager: An Action Guide for Cross-cultural Business* (London: Kogan Page).

Handy, Charles, Gordon, Colin, Gow, Ian and Randlesome, Colin (1988) *Making Managers* (London: Pitman Publishing).

Handy, Charles (1991a) *Inside Organisations: 21 ideas for Managers* (London: BBC Books).

Handy, Charles (1991b) *Gods of Management: The Changing Work of Organisations* (London: Business Books).

Handy, Charles (1991c) *The Age of Unreason* (London: Century Business).

Harvey-Jones, John (1989) *Making It Happen: Reflections on Leadership* (London: Fontana).

Harvey-Jones, John (1992) *Getting It Together: Memoirs of a Troubleshooter* (London: Mandarin Paperbacks).

Harvey-Jones, John (1993) *Managing to Survive: A Guide to Management through the 1990s* (London: William Heinemann).

Harvey-Jones, John (1994) *All Together Now* (London: William Heinemann).

Harvey-Jones, John with Anthea Masey (1990) *Troubleshooter* (London: BBC Books).

Herrmann, Ned (1990) *The Creative Brain* (North Carolina: Brain Books).

Jennings, Reg, Cox, Charles and Cooper, Cary, L. (1994) *Business Elites* (London: Routledge).

Keirsey, David and Marilyn Bates (1978) *Please Understand Me: Character and Temperament Types* (California: Prometheus).

Kets de Vries, Manfred F. R. (1989) *Prisoners of Leadership* (New York: John Wiley & Sons).

Korn, Lester (1988) *The Success Profile* (New York: Simon & Schuster).

Korn/Ferry Carré/Orban International (1994) *Boards of Directors Study 1994* (London: Korn/Ferry Carré/Orban International).

Korn/Ferry International and Columbia University Graduate School of Business (1989) 21st Century Report, *Reinventing the CEO*.

Kotter, John P. (1988) *The Leadership Factor* (New York: The Free Press).

Levinson, Daniel J. (1978) *The Seasons of a Man's Life* (New York: Knopf).

McCall, Morgan W. Jr. and Lombardo, Michael M. (1983) *Off the Track: Why and How Successful Executives Get Derailed* (Technical Report No. 21) (Greensboro, NY: Center for Creative Leadership).

McCall, Morgan W. Jr., Lombardo, Michael M. and Morrison, Ann M. (1988) *The Lessons of Experience* (New York: Lexington Books).

McCaulley, Mary H. (1981) *Jung's Theory of Psychological Types and the Myers-Briggs Type Indicator* (Gainesville, Florida: The Center for Applications of Psychological Type).

McCaulley, Mary H, (1988) 'The Myers-Briggs Type Indicator and Leadership', in *Measures of Leadership*, The Proceedings of a Conference on Psychological Measures and Leadership sponsored by the Center for Creative Leadership and the Psychological Corporation, 23 Oct.–26 Oct. 1988 (Gainesville, Florida: The Center for Applications of Psychological Type).

Moss Kanter, Rosabeth (1989) *When Giants Learn to Dance: Mastering the Challenges of Strategy, Management and Careers in the 1990s* (London: Unwin Books).

Moss Kanter, Rosabeth (1991) 'Transcending Business Boundaries: 12,000 World Managers View Change', *Harvard Business Review*, May–June 1991, pp. 151–64.

Nelson, Rebecca with Clutterbuck, David (1988) *Turnaround: How twenty well-known companies came back from the brink* (London: Mercury Books).

Parker, Hugh (1979) *Letters to a New Chairman* (London: The Director Publications).

Peters, Thomas (1987) *Thriving on Chaos* (New York: Knopf).

Robinson, Jeffery (1985) *The Risktakers: Portraits of Money, Ego and Power* (London: George Allen & Unwin).

Simcock, Corinne (1992) *A Head for Business: How Britain's Top Business Leaders continue to succeed* (London: Kogan Page).

Trapp, Roger (1993) *My Biggest Mistake* (Oxford: Butterworth, Heinemann).

Vaillant, George E. (1971) *Adaptation to Life* (Boston, Mass.: Little, Brown).

White, Barbara, Cox, Charles and Cooper, Cary (1992) *Women's Career Development: A Study of High Flyers* (Oxford: Blackwell Business).